AF324124

OPPORTUNITIES AND DEPRIVATION IN THE URBAN SOUTH

Cities and Society Series

Series Editor:
Chris Pickvance, Professor of Urban Studies, University of Kent, UK

Cities and Society is a series disseminating high quality new research and scholarship which contribute to a sociological understanding of the city. The series promotes scholarly engagement with contemporary issues such as urban access to public and private services; urban governance; urban conflict and protest; residential segregation and its effects; urban infrastructure; privacy, sociability and lifestyles; the city and space; and the sustainable city.

Opportunities and Deprivation in the Urban South
Poverty, Segregation and Social Networks in São Paulo

EDUARDO CESAR LEÃO MARQUES
University of São Paulo, Brazil and
Center for Metropolitan Studies (CEM), Brazil

ASHGATE

© Eduardo Cesar Leão Marques 2012

All rights reserved. No part of this publication may be reproduced, stored in a retrieval system or transmitted in any form or by any means, electronic, mechanical, photocopying, recording or otherwise without the prior permission of the publisher.

Eduardo Cesar Leão Marques has asserted his right under the Copyright, Designs and Patents Act, 1988, to be identified as the author of this work.

Published by
Ashgate Publishing Limited
Wey Court East
Union Road
Farnham
Surrey, GU9 7PT
England

Ashgate Publishing Company
Suite 420
101 Cherry Street
Burlington
VT 05401-4405
USA

www.ashgate.com

British Library Cataloguing in Publication Data
Marques, Eduardo Cesar.
  Opportunities and deprivation in the urban south : poverty,
  segregation and social networks in Sao Paulo.
  1. Sao Paulo (Brazil) – Social conditions. 2. Segregation –
  Brazil – Sao Paulo. 3. Poverty – Brazil – Sao Paolo.
  4. Equality – Brazil – Sao Paulo. 5. Social networks – Brazil – Sao Paulo.
  I. Title
  307.7'6'098161–dc23

Library of Congress Cataloging-in-Publication Data
Marques, Eduardo Cesar Leão.
  Opportunities and deprivation in the urban South : poverty, segregation
and social networks in Sco Paulo / by Eduardo Cesar Leão Marques.
    p. cm. — (Cities and society)
  Includes bibliographical references and index.
  ISBN 978-1-4094-4270-7 (hardback : alk. paper) — ISBN 978-1-4094-4271-4
(ebook) 1. Urban poor—Brazil—Sco Paulo. 2. Social networks—Brazil—Sco
Paulo. I. Title.
  HC190.P6M37 2012
  305.5'69098161—dc23

2012006251

ISBN 9781409442707 (hbk)
ISBN 9781409442714 (ebk)

Printed and bound in Great Britain by the
MPG Books Group, UK

Contents

'There is no such thing as society. There are individual men and women, and there are families.'

Margaret Thatcher, 1987.

'For too long, we have ignored the importance of social networks in the design of welfare policies because we have assumed that some combination of incentives and skills are sufficient to tackle the problem of social exclusion…

The only debate about the future of welfare that is worth having is one about how our system can become part of what sustains the network fabric of our society.'

Perri 6, 1997.

'Here it is each one together with its own'

(Aqui é cada um com o seu cada qual)

Interviewee of Jd. Elba, Sapopemb, a 2007.

List of Illustrations

Photographs

Photograph credits

Photographs 1 and 2: Lúcio Kowarick.
Photographs 3 and 4: Encarnación Moya.
Photographs 13 and 14: Raphael Soares
All others: Eduardo Marques.

Acknowledgements

This book is a reviewed and substantially enlarged version of my Livre-docente professorship thesis presented at the University of São Paulo in 2007. It is only fair, then, that I start by thanking the several important suggestions made by the Committee, composed by Maria Hermínia Tavares de Almeida, Brasílio Salum, Argelina Figueiredo, Celi Scalon and Naércio Menezes. Several of their comments were incorporated in the following phases of the research, which led me to enlarge the empirical dataset and include several other chapters.

This research is profoundly marked by the environment of the Centro de Estudos da Metrópole (Cem) – Centre for Metropolitan Studies. The motivation to explore networks and segregation together derived itself from previous studies developed collectively at the Center, especially *São Paulo: segregação, pobreza e desigualdades sociais* edited by me and Haroldo Torres in 2005. In this sense, this book brings the influences of several discussions I engaged in with researchers of the Center. I thank the colleagues that contributed to this research effort in a diffuse way.

It would be unthinkable to fail to register also an explicit acknowledgment to the Fundação de Amparo à Pesquisa do Estado de São Paulo (Fapesp) for financing the Center. In the case of Cem, more than financing specific research, Fapesp has made possible the articulation of findings through the years, thus enabling the construction of accumulated knowledge. Without this kind of financial support, research as this one would not be possible.

The English version of this book was made possible by the financial support of the Brazilian Council for Scientific and Technological Development (CNPq), which provided resources for translation via the INCT program. The difficult task of translating the manuscript was undertaken by David Rodgers, to whom I am also grateful. The idea of publishing a revised version of the research results, aimed at foreign audiences, began through conversations with Tim Butler, Patrick Le Galès and later Xavier de Souza Briggs. Their help and suggestions were essential for the project's success and I sincerely thank them for their encouragement and mobilization.

My most effusive thanks, however, go to the research team I had the pleasure of working with. The group included Renata Bichir, Miranda Zoppi, Thais Pavez, Igor Pantoja, Encá Moya and Rafael Soares. Their participation was decisive not only in our many conceptual, empirical and existential discussions, but also in their precious operational help in data collection and processing.

After having finished the Livre-docente professorship thesis, I returned to the field to collect new data and develop the qualitative part of the research, which resulted in a complete revision of the thesis and the inclusion of new chapters.

During this period, I had the generous and precise reading of Renata, Encá, Miranda and Val, who helped me remove ambiguities of the text and make it more accessible. This book would not be possible without the dedicated and lively work of that research team.

Finally, I thank Val for the happy though improbable daily combination of density and lightness.

Introduction

This book identifies sociability as being central to the understanding of urban poverty conditions. Although this statement may appear self-evident to the lay reader, for whom it would seem obvious that the daily lives of individuals influence their life conditions, the principal academic debates on the subject have been constructed in such a way as to end up pointing in other directions.

As such, a substantial part of what has been written on urban poverty, especially about Latin America and Brazil, has been polarized by two strong but disconnected sets of arguments. On the one hand, the field has been traditionally occupied by perspectives based on systemic or broad economic dynamics. In the 1970s, living conditions and poverty were derived directly from the specificity of our (peripheral) capitalism or from the dynamics of our labor markets, especially marked by unemployment and informality. More recently, neoliberalism and economic restructuring were brought to the forefront to explain social conditions and poverty, as well as urban precariousness and the appearance of squatters and shantytowns.

On the other hand, poverty was also associated by many authors to individual attributes and behaviors, at least since the conservative 'culture of poverty' debate. Within this same micro-level tradition, the field has more recently become dominated by a literature focused on individual attributes, decisions, strategies and behavior. In some cases, societal elements and processes have been incorporated, but as mere limiting factors in the individual's social insertion, such as in the ideas of neighborhood effects, role model or peer group effects. In all these cases social processes are understood as environmental elements that only influence those individual propensities and capacities already cited, and not as a locus of own dynamics that impact on social conditions.

This oscillation between 'holistic' and 'atomistic' understandings of poverty may perhaps be explained by the hegemony of a vision colored by the economic debate that focuses on economic processes, the existence of monetary income or at most, of individual assets within the boundaries of the discussions of human capital, and associates them with education, good health conditions, etc. According to this vision, the elements in question would be important in permitting the individual access to, or with better credentials to access, structures of opportunity similar to those thought of when only earnings are considered.

Probably the only exceptions worth mentioning are the contributions that mobilize broad sociological and political categories, such as vulnerability or citizenship to analyze Latin America. Although some of these works had shed light to important aspects of our societies, especially in the 1980s and 1990s, they do not explain the processes of poverty production or reproduction in themselves, nor the poor, but only interpret the consequences of the considered societal characteristics.

The topic's relevance is not only academic but also linked to social policy formulation and implementation. For a long time, policies aimed at combating poverty have departed from the idea that, in the absence of broad social changes, the important thing to do was to endow the individuals in poverty with strategic characteristics to supposedly lift them out of poverty and help them ascend socially. Albeit other dimensions have been incorporated over the course of time, an important part of the public initiatives continues in this vein.

Although I agree with the importance afforded to economic conditions and the labor market, as well as that given to the existence of attributes, credentials and individual behaviors, I nevertheless believe that societal midlevel elements associated with the relational patterns within which individuals are embedded have great importance in the understanding of poverty. They have been undervalued or treated as mere environmental elements in debates on the topic. In order to make advances in the understanding of poverty, a change of focus is necessary if we want to go beyond the atomistic paradigm and incorporate a truly relational ontology in the sense of Emirbayer (1997) and Tilly (2001). For this, we need to drag relationships to the center of the analysis, whilst still affording due consideration to attributes, as they dynamically influence each other on a continual basis. This book aims to show their relevance and to analyze how they operate in the production and reproduction of poverty.

In order to back up this point of view, I have based my results on research into the personal networks of individuals in seven situations of urban poverty in São Paulo selected on the basis of housing and segregation conditions. The study reconstitutes their attributes, the relational patterns in which they are inserted and investigates the conditioners of the networks, exploring their diversity. Since individuals access goods and services through these relational patterns, I investigate the consequences of different networks and sociability in terms of living conditions, as well as analyze their daily mobilization by the individuals. The results allow us to sustain the centrality of networks and of sociability for the reproduction of social inequalities and of urban poverty conditions in the city. Although referring to the city of São Paulo, the results bring important new elements to the discussions of the issue in other urban and metropolitan realities.

The most promising recent strategy to overcome the opposition between macro and micro-sociological analysis of poverty was developed by the urban sociology literature. The city-wide social precariousness multiplier effects were integrated into the analysis, mainly in terms of the cumulativity of negative processes, leading to some of the most important contributions of recent decades (Wilson 1987; Massey and Denton 1993). The spatial concentration of poverty and the separation between social groups caused by residential segregation were indicated as some of the most important elements in the chain of poverty and inequality reproduction, leading even to social exclusion according to a part of the debate (Levitas et al. 2007, Mustered and Murie 2002). Segregation was indicated as a major cause for the reduction of connections between social groups, as well as the diminishing of the sense of belonging that individuals have to collectivities (Wilson 1987; Jargowsky 1997; Mustered, Murie and Kesteloot 2006). Since then, several studies have highlighted the importance of segregation for poverty in Europe (Mingione 1996; Mustered, Murie and Kesteloot 2006), the US (Briggs 2005; Wacquant 2007) and Latin America (Auyero 1999; De La Rocha 2001).

The connection between space and poverty has also been incorporated by public policies since the 1980s, resulting in State actions operationally focused on the territory, such as the French 'Politique de la Ville' (Le Galès 1996; Bréville 2011). The introduction of these elements and the construction of policies orientated in this direction represented an advance, although not necessarily a solution (Lelévrier 2011; Le Galès 2005), especially because there is no identity between neighborhood and community (Blokland 2003). The presence of policies in this direction, however, is taking a long time to reach Latin America and Brazil (Torres 2005b and Marques and Torres 2005).

These negative effects of segregation may be counterbalanced or reinforced by various local factors, such as the role of the State (Wacquant 2008; Roberts 2005 and Marques and Torres 2005), broad societal institutions (Wu 2004), urban violence (Wacquant 2008), the family (Gonzalez de la Rocha 2001 and Wilson 1987), or by a combination of elements (Mustered, Murie and Kesteloot 2006, Mingione 2005, Andreotti 2006) all helping to explain differences among countries and cities. The presence of several patterns of social connections can also reduce the transformation of spatial isolation into social isolation. Social ties, in this sense, may help people bridge space or construct social cohesion through the bonding of identities (Briggs 2001), as well as provide several kinds of social support, associated with the neighborhood and the family (De La Rocha 2001), informal ties (Mingione 1994; Pamuk 2000) or communities (Small 2004).

In general terms, the question addresses the relations between social structure, geographic location and the relational social structure composed by the networks. More specifically, the question concerns the inequitable access of individuals to material goods derived from services, policies, labor markets or immaterial elements such as repertoires and ways of life. In this sense the networks could help to overcome geographical and social spaces and give individuals access to, or place them within, somewhat broader social circles. So, although with crossed signals, social networks and segregation mediate the accesses individuals have to the different structures of opportunities (Kaztman 1991), or to the different sources of welfare (Mustered and Murie 2002).

As such, networks must necessarily be incorporated into any model seeking to explain the reproduction of poverty if we mean to study it in a relational and multidimensional form in the sense afforded to the term by Mingione (1999) and Levitas et al. (2007). For this reason a substantial literature has cited the connection between networks and the realization of status throughout the life cycle (Lin 1999b) – the acquisition of individual characteristics that are constructors of social hierarchies, such as income, schooling, culture, etc. According to this conception various processes and attributes would depend on the existence of social capital composed of collectively produced and stored elements beyond the level of the individual, more precisely within their web of relationships (Perri 6 1997), including connections between social groups (Briggs 2005). For those authors who attempt to link social capital to networks, characteristics such as mutual trust and principles of citizenship (as from Putnam onwards) would be generated and produced by networks. This aspect has been highlighted by an important number of recent international diagnoses of the matter (Policy Research Initiative 2005a and 2005b, Cechi, Molina and Sabatini, s.d., Perri 6 1997, Levitas et al. 2007).

However, we should avoid relying on normative understandings of networks, as do the majority of the debates on social capital and on social exclusion. As will be seen in the first chapter, each network may produce negative or positive consequences (sometimes at the same time) and identical networks may be used differently by different individuals or by the same individual in diverse situations. Regardless of the importance of contributions relating urban living conditions and networks, such as Briggs (2005), Small (2009) and Blokland and Savage (2008), the focus and the proposal of this book – to systematically investigate the importance of networks on poverty comparatively among segregated situations – remains unexplored.

The literature about Latin America, however, had been preoccupied with other kinds of processes. The study of poverty has been marked, since the 1970's, by structural and systemic approaches informed by Marxism and by Dependence theory (Perlman 2008; Kowarick 2005 and Ward 2004). Since the 1990's different approaches have emerged, parallel to the discussion of the 'new poverty' developed in the Global North (Mingione 1996). Differently from abroad, however, the debate has been polarized by two different (and contradictory) developments. On one side, the field has been hegemonized locally by a literature focused on individual attributes and economic processes, with social dynamics understood solely as a set of constraints over individuals. At the same time, a tradition of other sociological studies has emerged, taking into account the multidimensionality of poverty and focusing on survival strategies, political participation, violence, residential segregation and the role of the State and of sociability, (Gonzalez de la Rocha 2001; Roberts 2005; Marques and Torres 2005; Ayuero 1999; Perlman 2008, Silva Telles and Cabannes, 2006, Kowarick 2009).

The analysis of the impact of social networks, however, remains unexplored by the literature about Latin America, in spite of the general citation of the associations between social networks and poverty. The truth is that we only start to learn how they really work beyond their metaphorical reference. In the same way, we can only intuit, from fragile empirical bases, their influence on the process of poverty reproduction, even if Latin America presents one of the highest presences of both urban poverty and social inequalities. This book aims at closing this gap by answering four associated questions on the topic:

- What are the networks of Brazil's metropolitan poor really like, and what conditions and influences them?
- What types of networks exist and how are they associated with distinct sociability patterns and with urban segregation?
- What consequences do these networks have for individuals and for poverty in general?

Considering that networks mediate the access individuals have to the various elements that constitute their welfare, this third question involves at least two sets of elements: the access to goods and services obtained in markets (in mercantile exchanges) and outside markets, both through social assistances from other individuals (in personalized exchanges) and from organizations and the State, since even in face of the universalistic logic of citizenship, the access to policies is mediated by social relationships.

However, networks are structures and as such they may lead to different results depending on their use by social agents. Consequently, our understanding of the causal elements associated with the above cited regularities will not be understood unless we incorporate the study of network mobilization by the individuals. This leads us to a fourth challenge, which is to understand:

- What are the mechanisms by which networks influence living conditions, poverty and social inequality through the daily lives of individuals?

The evidences presented in the following chapters indicate the existence of great heterogeneity in the networks of those individuals in situations of poverty. Their networks are, however, generally smaller, more local and less varied in terms of sociability than the networks of middle-class individuals. The results suggest that certain types of networks of those individuals in poverty are empirically associated with better life conditions, employment and income. This serves to demonstrate the relevance of the sociability of individuals for the definition, in a broad sense, of their social situations, and of poverty in particular. On the other hand, observation of the mobilization of the networks by individuals suggests that important regularities, associated with social mechanisms, are hidden behind the phenomenon's heterogeneity. As we will see, these mechanisms explain a great part of the heterogeneity of networks, as well as mediate the individual's access to opportunities and everyday assistance. They therefore contribute decisively to the production (and reproduction) of urban poverty.

Before properly getting into the topic however, it is important to establish a few methodological standpoints. The present work analyzes the main conditioners of personal networks in low income locales, as well as exploring their structure and variation, further down the line investigating their consequences. All this involves complex multicausality associated with the articulation of various processes and conditioners. The result is strongly influenced by the combination and order of the existing processes. For this reason the research was developed via detailed, intentionally chosen case studies, carried out in areas of concentrated poverty that evinced different segregational conditions, on a citywide scale (macro-segregation). The aim was not to statistically represent the dwelling places of the city's poor to later expand the sample and determine the types of networks of those living in poverty within São Paulo, but rather to cover the variability found within situations of urban poverty by means of a logic of case studies. This point will be expanded upon in the second chapter, as will the other methodological approaches adopted.

In technical research terms, the objectives of the investigation led to my using both qualitative and quantitative techniques, involving network analysis, geoprocessing, statistical tools, such as regression, and exploratory techniques such as factorial and cluster, as well as the carrying out of in-depth interviews. This is an important element as the utilization alone of a broad set of methods made for the understanding of the nature of the phenomena being studied (Wilson 2002 and Small, at press).

Another aspect of the fundamental method, which needs explaining, is that the research analyzes personal networks, and not community networks, or individual's egocentered networks. Community networks may be spatially or thematically constituted, and are the relational environments that surround individuals within a given context, occurrence or process, such as throughout a social mobilization, within an organization created to deliver a given public policy, in the interaction between organizations, or in the familial or economic relationships amongst patriarchal families, to proffer just a few examples. The present study analyzes networks that differ from these, looking at the networks of individuals and considering their sociability as the topic or theme upon which the interview questions are to be based. On the other hand the networks considered are not limited to the egocentric networks of individuals (or egonets), that take into consideration only information as to the individual's primary contacts and the ties between same of them[1]. Unlike the greater part of the international literature I consider that an important portion of the sociability that influences poverty and living conditions occurs at greater distances from the ego than its immediate surroundings[2], this being the reason for picking here the networks of the individuals entirely, without placing prior limits on their size.[3] This decision worked out well as the networks

---

1   Primary tie here is a technical denomination and refers to the direct ego ties. In other chapters I explore the primary bonds in a sociological sense.

2   Or, technically, at just a step from the ego.

3   For operational research reasons a limit was placed on the number of rounds of interviews, which theoretically placed limits on the size of the networks chosen. However, in the case of those individuals in situations of poverty, the name generator reached the edges of the networks before this, and, as such, we may consider the networks constructed as corresponding approximately to representations of the total networks of the interviewees. Chapter 2 presents the method in detail.

found in the research varied in size from five to 148 nodes, that is to say the method itself caught the variability of the phenomenon.

The decision to center attention on personal networks was based on the assumption that, it is through these (either in isolation or nested within other networks) that individuals obtain access to the diverse elements involved in their social reproduction and which contribute towards their well-being. This delimiting however, possesses mere analytical sense, given that these networks represent methodological snippets of broader societal relational contexts in which all individuals and entities are involved. In spite of making methodological use of individual networks, the research nevertheless considers a strongly relational social ontology. The elements involved in this starting point are discussed in detail in the first chapter.

The research information, on the other hand, was derived from interviews with the actual egos of the networks. The data are of a cognitive type – they pass through the individual's understanding and perception of their own networks (Marsden 2005). This method may appear initially problematic as we run the risk of being led astray by the participant given the differences in understanding of their own networks. It is true that significant differences were observed during the interviews in relation to the individual interviewee's understanding of his or her network. I nonetheless consider that this did not introduce bias into the analysis, but rather represents part of the observed phenomenon's own dynamic. Individuals mobilize the relations (and the relational patterns) as they understand them, and if they understand them differently, tend to use them differently in their daily lives. In truth, if we adopted a non-substantialist conception of the networks, we would arrive at the conclusion that the networks are exactly as the individuals in question take them to be, and not structures hidden somewhere whose 'real' configuration is to be discovered by the method. As such, considering that the way individuals understand their networks is what defines and orientates their everyday social use, what we obtain from the method, based on cognitive data, is what is really important for the reproduction of the social conditions of the individual.

With this methodological framework in place, we can now succinctly describe the research. The study chose the personal networks of 209 individuals in situations of poverty, and 30 individuals of the middle class, the latter so as to set up a basis for comparison. To explore the effects of spatial segregation on personal networks I chose locales, all quite distinct from each other from an urban insertion standpoint, taking as a starting point previous studies on the spatial distribution of social groups in São Paulo. Approximately 30 personal networks were chosen in each locale studied, apart from the middle class control group, without specifying dwelling place. In truth, if we had controlled the residential location of the middle class we would have found a pattern concentrated in the expanded center of the metropolis, although their networks fan out over a wide territory and include virtually nobody in their immediate physical vicinity, in a pattern similar to that which Wellman (2001) has denominated as personal communities, as we shall see in Chapter 1. This pattern is very distinct from that found amongst individuals in situations of poverty, which in itself indicates enormous differences in relational patterns and the ways in which those relations might be utilized.

The choice of locales studied resulted from an intentional sample of the locations of individuals in situations of poverty in the city from the standpoints of distance from center, the degrees of consolidation of the areas in question, housing patterns and levels of State intervention. Within the locales studied the most centralized locations included city center slum tenements. The most segregated and distant locations included a 'favela' on the peri-urban fringe of the metropolitan region, between the municipalities of Taboão da Serra and São Paulo – Vila Nova Esperança -, a large scale housing project on the fringe of municipal São Paulo's urban Eastern Zone – Cidade Tiradentes – and a fairly peripheral area of the Southern Zone, the so-called 'fundão' of Jardim Ângela. Apart from the above mentioned, social networks were also researched in two very large 'favelas' located fairly close to the expanded center – Paraisópolis, the object of innumerable previous studies, contiguous to Morumbi, a very high income neighborhood, and Vila Nova Jaguaré, bordering on middle and upper class neighborhoods and near the University of São Paulo. A third small 'favela', near to the municipal center of Guarulhos, and within an industrial district – Favela Guinle – completed the set of locales studied. The interviews were carried out on weekdays and weekends between September 2006 and August of 2007.

A semi-open questionnaire and a name generator were used in all of the locales where interviews took place. The choice of interviewees in each field was purely random and took place whilst traversing the chosen locales. Individuals were approached in public spaces and at the entrances to their houses on both weekdays and weekends. In some cases entrance to the locales studied was mediated by participants of previous pieces of research or members of local associative movements.[4] Throughout the work in each field, the sample of interviewees was controlled by certain basic social attributes such as gender, age, migratory and occupational status, and dwelling place within the locale being studied. This control had uppermost in mind the guaranteeing of a reasonable correspondence to the average characteristics of the local population and the avoidance of bias. As we shall see, the comparison between the interviewees' characteristics and that of the population studied suggests that this aim was achieved with no little success.

Middle class was defined in a broad sense, mixing income and professional criteria and included the liberal professions, civil servants, persons involved in intellectual activities and owners of commercial establishments. The delimiting of the group had no other conceptual or methodological concerns, given that the

---

4   I would like to thank my colleagues Encá Moya, João Marcos de Almeida Lopes, Teresinha Gonzaga, Letizia Vitale, Gabriel Feltran and Henri Gerveseau who, at various times helped with contacts for interviews. In the case of Favela Guinle, Rafael Soares carried out the interviews in their entirety for his Masters dissertation. Rafael subsequently made this raw data available to me for use in the present work for which I am heartily grateful.

objective of the interviews with the individuals so classified was simply to set up a level of comparison for the analysis of those individuals living in poverty. The information derived from the middle class networks was just used as a parameter and never in more fundamental or conclusive analyses.

The sets of information thus generated were subsequently run through social network analysis tools resulting in 239 personal networks. I then explored several characteristics of the networks of individuals living in poverty, trying to access their principal conditioners and the processes that influenced their formation and dynamic, and how this differed from the middle class networks. The processes of creation and maintenance of ties, the dynamics of homophilia[5], and the social conditioners of network construction and maintenance were all studied. The networks differed in certain key attributes and specific variables, amongst which were gender, life cycle, and migratory and occupational status. As a general rule, relationships between individuals of different social and income groups were found to be practically non-existent. This is, perhaps, one of the most important characteristics of the role of these networks in the perpetuation of poverty and social inequality. The problem itself does not, of course, originate in the networks but just represents a relational facet of the Brazilian social structure.

With the statistical analyses already carried out, I chose a set of personal networks with which to undertake the qualitative part of the research. Criteria for choosing the cases combined types of network found, the fields studied and the personal characteristics of the interviewees. In all, qualitative interviews were carried out with twenty individuals, between the end of January and the beginning of May 2008. The interviews explored the networks' transformations since the first interviews, done one year before. The interviews dealt with, amongst other things, how the networks are used by the individuals in their daily lives, such as in migration, the obtaining of work, how they may help in health related matters, with child care, with accommodation, in the acquisition of various types of loans as well as in providing access to emotional support and public policies. This information enabled me to understand the dynamic of relational patterns and their mobilization by individuals. The patterns and the recurrences observed led me to delimit social mechanisms responsible both for the networks' constitution and transformation, and for their mobilization by individuals in their practices.

The structure of the work follows the four questions previously presented. In the first chapter I perform a succinct review of the literature relating to poverty, segregation and social networks, highlighting those elements most important to the arguments of the research. However, more than just exhaustively following the debates, the chapter's objective is to formulate the conceptual bridges necessary for the articulation of various elements of this research, given that it is located at an intersection point between the debates on poverty, networks and segregation.

---

5 Homophilus relations are those holding between persons of the same attribute. The following chapters will explore this important dimension, which associates the production of relationships to attributes.

Given the relative newness of the topic, a number of research instruments were developed, or adapted, to facilitate the carrying out of field research and the obtaining of information. The second chapter presents the principal instruments of research that were applied, as well as putting the reader in the picture as to the general characteristics of the metropolitan space of São Paulo, its poverties and the locales studied.

The third chapter starts with an analysis of the collected data, exploring the attributes of individuals and of their networks. It is the first exercise in approaching the problem, and addresses the first question, outlined at the beginning of this introduction – what are the networks of individuals in situations of poverty like and what conditions them? I start the analysis with a characterization of the interviewees, their networks and their sociability, then immediately move on to investigate the associations between social attributes and relational patterns. Although the exercise is essentially descriptive, some important results do emerge. When we compare these with the middle class networks, we discover that the networks of those in poverty tend to be smaller, more local and less cohesive and possess a less varied sociability. In spite of this, within the living in situations of poverty group, the variation found is considerable, and some networks were found with rich and dynamic relational characteristics and sociability. The networks also evinced intense variability where basic social attributes such as sex, age, income, schooling and migratory patterns were concerned. More segregated locales, on the other hand, have networks evincing little difference in size and cohesion, although they do house less local networks, in average terms, contrary to what one would intuitively anticipate, suggesting that some networks at least have successfully integrated some spatially segregated individuals. Taken together, the information indicates the heterogeneity of the networks of poor individuals and the existence of non-direct and considerably complex associations between networks and social attributes.

The question posed initially therefore, unfolds in the investigation into the networks' patterns of variation, so as to explore their heterogeneity. The fourth chapter develops this analysis, delimiting the types of network and sociability present, with the objective of answering the second question – what types of networks exist and how are these associated with distinct sociability patterns? The data suggest the existence of different (and very regular) network types depending on the size, structure, urban insertion and sociability contained within them.

The fifth and sixth chapters analyze the consequences of the networks for the living standards of individuals, in particular for the presence of situations of poverty and social precariousness, attempting to answer the third of the questions that guide this work – What consequences do these networks have for individuals and for poverty in general?

The fifth chapter investigates the effects of the networks on access to markets. Using the previous types of networks, together with socio-economic variables classically considered as central to the characterization of poverty, I quantitively analyze the consequences of networks to the access of goods and services.

Then, the investigation explores the main conditioners of those individuals with employment, those who have employment with some degree of protection, and those in situations of social precariousness, as well as their respective per capita income. The results suggest the central position occupied by the networks and sociability in the definition of each of the above mentioned elements, demonstrating the necessity of their integration into both studies of the topic and into those polices geared towards the combating of poverty and the promotion of well-being.

Nevertheless, as I consider poverty multi-dimensionally, the analysis would not be complete if I did not take into account the elements that generate or mitigate situations of social privation, but are obtained outside markets through personalized exchanges not subject to the usual mercantile logic. The sixth chapter explores this aspect, analyzing the effects of the networks upon access to goods and services mobilized on an everyday basis by individuals outside (or partially outside) markets. Using the information garnered from the qualitative part of the research, I discuss how relational patterns influence the mobilization of those goods and services that make for the solution of such daily problems as child care, care of the elderly, the obtaining of small loans, tools, food and appliances, or emotional support, and how these all contribute towards the mitigation of poverty.

The seventh chapter addresses the last question – In what way do the networks influence living conditions, poverty and social inequality through the daily lifes of individuals? –, discussing the transformations undergone by the networks and the relational mechanisms present in the studied situations. These substantially explain not only the great differences between the networks of individuals, but also their differentiated mobilization in the solving of everyday problems, thereby generating unequal access to help and relational opportunities. Whilst this difference is merely analytic, and in practice the processes are often concomitant, in the first case the networks are impacted by the mechanisms, while in the latter access to opportunities is mediated by mechanisms that involve networks. The results confirm what was discussed in earlier chapters, namely the central role played by sociability in determining conditions of life. Quite apart from this, it also allowed us to pass from the correlations to the mechanisms, specifying in what way the networks matter and helping us understand their specific role in the reproduction of conditions of life and poverty.

Finally I sum up the presented results and briefly discuss the consequences for public policy of the patterns found. The set of results allows us to affirm the relevance of sociability to the explanation of situations of poverty. It also throws light on the differentiated effects of diverse relational contexts in the individual's access to structures that affect life conditions and poverty.

Chapter 1

Constructing Conceptual Bridges between Poverty, Segregation and Networks

I take poverty to be a multidimensional phenomenon produced by a range of social processes linked to the participation of individuals in social and economic processes through their life trajectories. In these trajectories, they access opportunity structures depending on attributes and qualifications, but also construct strategies, practices and events in the context of their everyday sociability. Access to these structures is mediated, among other things, by the location of individuals in urban space and by the social networks in which they are included, through the operation of specific but diverse and interconnected social mechanisms. Consequently, their social situation is influenced by their social networks and the degree of segregation of their place of residence. The aim of the present chapter is to construct this approach conceptually on the basis of the relevant literatures. It is not my intention to review the debates, some of them already sufficiently well-known, but to define my point of view about urban poverty and its relationships with urban segregation and social networks.

The chapter is divided into three sections. It begins with a general discussion on the issue of urban poverty and its connections to the production of space. The chapter's second section presents the literature on social networks and its social ontology, as well as the academic analyses of personal networks. In the chapter's final section I discuss the association between the three highlighted elements – urban poverty, segregation and social networks.

1. Urban poverty and segregation

Poverty has been one of the phenomena most heavily analyzed by the sociological and economic literature over recent decades. The large majority of the studies, however, have focused on economic processes and on income. In the case of Latin America, economic aspects and labor markets were central on the existing explanations at least since the 1950s, when modernization paradigm dominated development studies (Frank et al. 1969). This continued to be the case in the subsequent critique built by dependence theory, arguing against the existence of convergence in development, but sustaining the centrality of the different forms of participation on the international division of labor to explain development inequalities (Cardoso and Faleto 1973). Though nuanced, this direct association of poverty with economic processes marks various studies until today, especially in Latin America.

For some authors, the continuing emphasis on income is connected to their relevance (Rocha 2003) but is also associated with the problems faced in incorporating other information (Boltvinik 1998, Iceland 2006), despite recent efforts to develop more complex forms of measurement (Levitas et al. 2007). Establishing a single standardized unit of measure that can be easily calculated is an important step in the development of comparative studies, which is why studies using income distribution and so-called poverty lines are so widespread (Rocha 2003 and Hoffman 2000), including intense discussions over the absolute and relative dimensions of poverty (Boltvinik 1998, Iceland 2006).

A wide range of authors have introduced other variables into analyses of poverty, reflecting an emerging consensus that living conditions are actually strongly affected by a wide range of elements. However, this incorporation does not necessarily go so far as to alter the individualistic or atomistic ontology attributed to the phenomenon by the economic literature, treating social processes as quasi-economic processes. In an analytic style now predominant in the Brazilian debate, social attributes are employed as assets in determining monetary income (Barros, Henriques and Mendonça 2000 and Neri 2000). Neri (2000) lists these assets as physical capital (access to housing, owning durable goods), human capital (education, professional experience) and social capital (participation in associations, political activities and access to information). Poverty is presumed to be caused by an absence of assets in Moser (1998)´s terms and the geographical areas where poverty is most heavily concentrated are taken to be marked by what Wacquant (1996:149) critically refers to as the 'trope of disorganization.'

Undoubtedly assets are extremely important and owning or lacking them influences various processes relating to the reproduction of poverty, especially in terms of the qualifications presented at the labor market, generating monetary income. But several processes that strongly influence living conditions happen at broader scales than the individuals. And to incorporate theses scales only including more variables is not enough. Seen from this viewpoint, although the incorporation of other individual attributes may appear to add complexity to the models – as in the case of school education – they remain based on the idea that poverty is produced by the individual's incapacity to obtain income in an atomized form within the market.

Alternatively, if we wish to understand how the phenomenon is produced in all its complexity, we need to start out from the idea that welfare in contemporary market societies is produced (and reproduced) by markets, but also by at least two other spheres: the State and the community/family/sociability (Esping-Andersen 2000, Mingione 2005). These are associated with different forms of integration – market relations, redistribution and solidarity (Musterd and Murie 2002) – or linked to three distinct opportunity structures in a narrower economic sense (Kaztman 1999, Kaztman and Retamoso 2005).

The State undeniably provides a wide range of policies and services that, though varying considerably between countries, 'decommodify' a significant portion of the labor sector in contemporary capitalist societies (Esping-Andersen 2000). State intervention means that urban poverty is heavily influenced by the range of policies provided by the State in different situations, as shown by the comparison between the US and European situations (Wacquant 2008 and 2001, Kazepov 2005), and between European countries (Mustered and Murie 2002, Mingione 2005). In Brazil, the recognition of rights and the access to welfare policies were historically associated with insertion in the labor market (Santos 1979), not leading exactly to a decommodification in Esping-Andersen's sense (2000), while also attaining only a portion of the country's population (Draibe 1989a and 1989b). Since the 1980s, however, with the return to democracy and with the participation of both popular movements and reformist technical communities, the Brazilian social protection system has been altered and extended towards more universal coverage (Arretche 2000 and 2002). Though large problems in coverage and quality persist, especially among the poorest sectors, access to social policies is essential to providing some level of welfare for part of the population living in poverty.

The third source of welfare is society-based and associated with the provision of social support. This may come from family processes (Gonzalez de la Rocha 2001), social networks (Small 2004), social contacts and support networks (Andreotti 2006), or elements linked to both neighborhoods, identity tied collectivities and formal associations (Mingione 1994, Silva Telles and Cabannes 2006). The importance of this source of welfare is reported to be high both in countries of the global North (Small 2004; Mustered, Murie and Kesteloot 2006), especially in Southern Europe (Mingione 2005, Andreotti 2006) and in the global South (Gonzalez de la Rocha 2001; Silva Telles and Cabannes 2006), but considering the relative fragility of the other two sources in Southern countries, its centrality for the living strategies of the poor are supposedly higher in relative terms.

Welfare is produced by a dynamic combination of these three spheres, while poverty is characterized as lack of welfare – whether in terms of quantity or quality. In this sense, social vulnerability arises in part from the absence of assets, producing what Moser (1998) calls asset vulnerability (including tangible and intangible assets, such as family relations and social capital). But poverty might also be caused by insufficient access to these spheres, since individual strategies, but also several mid-range structures such as institutions, space and social networks, might help or difficult the access individuals and groups have, hindering the use of poverty resources, to adopt Gonzalez de la Rocha's terminology (2001). In other words, vulnerability can be caused by deficiencies in opportunity structures (Kaztman and Retamoso 2005) but also by the difficulties encountered by individuals in accessing them (Briggs 2001).

In line with a growing literature, therefore, I take poverty to be a multi-dimensional phenomenon (Mingione 1996, Levitas et al. 2007, Mustered and Murie 2002, Andreotti 2006) influenced by various processes, including the supra-individual and the extra-economic. The definition of these elements depends on the cultural frameworks and levels of justice accepted by any given society (Sen 2000) and instituted through State policies (Paugam 2005), which set minimum standards of welfare that receive wide social recognition. Multi-dimensional comprehensions of poverty allow us to include within our framework individuals who, though managing to survive above the bare minimum, lack access to the most important benefits of modern urban societies. This also accounts for the fact that events such as illnesses, aging and unemployment can transform vulnerability into social deprivation. Here by vulnerable I refer to a condition of susceptibility in the face of contingencies and/or crises, increasing the likelihood that such individuals will experience deprivation, in the strict sense of the term, sometime in the future. In fact, it is probable that these individuals will shift between situations bordering on deprivation over time[1]. The meaning of these contingencies and the responses to them tends to vary substantially according to the different welfare institutions, cultural contexts and reciprocity arrangements present (Mustered and Murie 2002, Esping-Andersen 2000, Andreotti 2006, Mingione 1994).

Rather than assuming the existence of a single form of poverty, we can therefore postulate various forms, each associated with distinct social attributes linked to age structure, family composition and insertion in the labor market. Therefore, poverty is not only multidimensional, but also highly heterogeneous. The spatial distribution of these diverse forms of poverty further accentuates the complexity of the phenomenon, since the insertion of these groups in urban space can alternately facilitate or hinder people's access to goods, services and opportunities. Another source of diversity lies in the fact that social deprivation tends to accumulate in particular regions, though never in complete or perfectly homogeneous form, as Bichir, Torres and Ferreira (2005) have shown in the case of São Paulo. Consequently, certain regions concentrate vulnerability more intensely than others with a series of negative consequences for their inhabitants (Wilson 1987, Massey and Denton 1993).

Spatial concentration of poverty and segregation

It is precisely spatial elements that are emphasized in the more sociological analyses of urban poverty. Concentration in space is perhaps the aspect of poverty most widely emphasized by the literature. The negative effects of spatial concentration on situations of social deprivation become even more pronounced when the latter is accompanied by social segregation in space, understood as the separation of social groups into relatively homogeneous and spatially distant areas within the city boundaries (Marques and Torres 2005). In this case, 'families have to cope

---

1   Ruth Levitas and colleagues (The multi-dimensional analysis of social exclusion. Bristol: Department of Sociology and School for Social Policy 2007) differentiate these events into risk factors – associated with underlying social dimensions such as aging, precarious insertion in the labor market and causal triggers – events that explain deprivation in causal terms, such as illness, job losses or the breakup of the family.

not only with their own poverty, but also with the social isolation and economic deprivation of the hundreds, if not thousands of other families who live near them' (Jargowsky 1997:1).

The most important reference here is undoubtedly the classic work by Wilson (1987). As is widely known, the author developed his ideas in a highly polarized intellectual environment in theoretical and political terms by the clash between conservative culturalists, who argued for the existence of cultures of poverty and tended to blame the poor for their situation, and structuralists who argued for the importance of processes of economic reorganization in the rise of poverty in the major US cities. Wilson's own explanation took into account both macro-social dynamics and the everyday lifes of residents of the so-called black ghettos, deconstructing the idea of a culture of poverty, as well as the central importance attributed to racism as an explanation for the increase in poverty and social problems. The author demonstrated that the worsening of poverty in central areas of the United States was the combined result of economic transformations that increased unemployment and reduced incomes among the poorest with a rise in the spatial concentration of poverty and the social uniformity of the so-called black ghettos.

Although race is not a central dimension of causality in Wilson's work, it is central to Massey and Denton's explanation (1993) where the authors associate the poverty spiral with racial prejudice. For Wilson (1987) the increase in the segregation of disadvantaged social groups was produced by the migration of more affluent families (principally the black middle class) to better regions, leaving behind only the portions of the 'community' in worse social conditions and reducing the mixture of (black) social groups. The findings obtained by Jargowsky (1997) on segregation in major US cities confirm Wilson's hypothesis (1987), though Jargowsky and Yang (2006) suggest that the concentration of urban poverty in the USA has declined over recent years. Although the central argument of these works contains a very strong relational dimension, the authors make no use of network analysis, an approach later pursued by authors such as Briggs (2001).

Wacquant (2002 2008), on the other hand, extends Wilson's arguments further in claiming that the new forms of urban poverty no longer arise from the absence of development but precisely from the economic dynamism of contemporary capitalism in its most advanced versions, associated with a new phenomenon in large cities all over the world: the hyperghetto. The latter is produced, Wacquant argues, in a process associated with the increase in inequalities and dualization of the labor market, the shrinkage of the Welfare State, the increase in the concentration of poverty and the association of its territorial spaces with stigmas linked in particular to violence, confronted by the State policies based on the logic of penalization. These spaces are characterized by their disconnection from the dynamism of the wider economy, by territorial fixation and stigmatization, associated with the dissolution of place, understood as the loss of a territory in which the population feels safe and with which it identifies (Wacquant 2007,

Auyero 1999, Auyero and Swistun 2009), by the loss of grassroots support groups present in the previous ghetto, and by symbolic and social fragmentation in a context of deproletarianization. Each of these dimensions reinforces the isolation and political subordination of the groups resident in these areas.

Although studies of São Paulo have accentuated the importance of territorial stigma, as well as strategies of penalizing poverty, most of the evidence refutes the idea of polarization. Despite the high levels of poverty and vulnerability affecting the large Brazilian cities, the State's presence in providing welfare has increased since redemocratization. This means that in Brazil penalization has been concomitant with the growing recognition of rights, the expansion of the importance of civic associations, the media and the judiciary, leading to complex, and sometimes contradictory, outcomes.

Even in the US, the use of the term ghetto is metaphoric, since it remains a polemical issue whether black and latino neighborhoods in today's large US cities represent ghettos (Massey and Denton 1993, Marcuse 1996, Jargowsky 1997, Briggs 2001, and Wacquant 1996 and 2008). Nonetheless most authors agree that the levels of segregation found in these urban areas, although high, lack the well-defined physical limits or above all the legal mechanisms required to sustain the existence of ghettos per se, except in a metaphorical sense. In analyses of the major European cities, the literature is almost unanimous in rejecting any use of the term ghetto, though several authors emphasize the widespread presence of poverty situations in less or more segregated forms, in cities like Paris, Stuttgart, London, Hamburg, Brussels, Berlin and Milan (Mingione 1994, Kazepov 2005, Musterd and Murie 2002). Likewise the absence of legal mechanisms in Brazilian cities has lead authors to reject the concept of ghetto to describe the country's urban peripheries, even though we can observe very high levels of separation that remain resilient over time (Bichir, Torres and Ferreira 2005, Torres 2005c and Marques, Bichir and Scalon 2010).

In this sense, the ghetto situation of complete spatial isolation represents a culminating point in a continuous of varying forms of residential segregation (Grafmeyer 1996). In cases where isolation is voluntary, typically associated with the exclusionist strategies of social groups that resort to self-segregation, the process is described as the formation of a citadel (Marcuse 1997a). In both cases physical or institutional barriers need to be overcome in order to leave (the ghetto) or to enter (the citadel) and very frequently legal rules exist that limit circulation and access (Marcuse 1997a and 1997b). From the social viewpoint, however, these are completely distinct phenomena (Wacquant 2001 and 1996, Fainstein, Gordon and Harloe 1992, Mingione 1996, Davis 1993 and Massey and Denton 1993).

This conceptual distinction is important because over recent years these self-segregation processes have created wealthy citadels or fortified enclaves within the urban fabric of innumerable cities across the world, especially in the Americas (Davis 1992, Sabatini 2001, Salcedo and Torres 2004, Duren 2006) and including in São Paulo (Caldeira 2000 and Salgado 2000). According to some authors, this has led to a fragmentation of urban citizenship (Alsayyad and Roy 2006). In the case of the São Paulo metropolis, the phenomenon is widely visible in political and symbolic terms (Caldeira 2000). But although the extent of these occupations is significant in the western zone of the metropolis, as will be seen in the next chapter, the scale of the phenomenon is not so high, relatively speaking, when compared to the middle class population located in the city's *Centro Expandido* (Expanded Center), at least as of the year 2000 (Marques e Torres 2005)

Considering the scale of cities such as the largest Latin American metropolis, with São Paulo as a major case, as we will in the second chapter, segregation should be taken as a continuous phenomenon incorporating physical distances. This incorporation can introduce difficulties in terms of the strategies used to measure the phenomenon quantitatively,[2] yet I argue that it is essential to consider this factor for conceptual reasons. In the absence of physical or institutional barriers (like those present in a ghetto), the separation of social groups into socially homogenous spaces only makes sense if there are difficulties in establishing frequent contact between them. Distances therefore give rise to more continuous patterns of the phenomenon than those captured by the above-mentioned concepts of ghettos, citadels and enclaves. In the case of the large Brazilian cities, marked by the high level of segregation in sprawling peripheries, the question has been at the center of debate since the 1970s (Bonduki and Rolnik 1982, Kowarick 1979) and remains today a core element in the reproduction of social vulnerability (Kowarick 2009).

In more technical terms, segregation can be analyzed by measuring the levels of separation and homogeneity existing between social groups (as in Sabatini et al. 2001, Sabatini 2004, Torres 2005c and Preteceille 2003), or the concentration and predominance of these groups (Jargowsky 1997 and Preteceille 2006) focusing on a specific social characteristic (occupation, income, education, race, etc.). These studies have sometimes led to the generation of sets of measures, the most important of which is the Dissimilarity Index (DI), used for São Paulo by Torres (2005) and Torres and Bichir (2009) and calculated for innumerous cities in the United States by John Logan.[3] Other studies used spatial statistics to investigate the phenomenon, both at the scale of the city and to explore spatial concentration around specific points, such as Bichir (2006) did to analyze São Paulo. The question involves a number of analytic problems since the scale used to analyze segregation significantly alters the results obtained (Sabatini et al.

---

2   The indices most frequently used to quantify segregation fail to take distance into account as a central dimension, as in the case of the Dissimilarity Index (DI), which ignores space completely. The global Moran Index (I), on the other hand, includes distance as a factor only in order to establish the patterns of contiguity, which makes the concomitant analysis of Local Moral maps (LISA) indispensable to understand both macro and micro segregation.

3   The Dissimilarity Index measures the proportion of a given population that would have to be moved between spatial units in order for the incidence of a given attribute to attain the city average in all locations. For a large number of applications to US cities, see Internet: http://mumford.albany.edu/census/data.html.

2001 and Bichir 2006). In fact this problem is not simply technical, given that segregation can occur differently at different scales, ranging from the city as a whole (macro segregation), or within separate neighborhoods and locals (micro segregation). Consequently the measuring instruments and methodology have to be chosen appropriately (Sabatini et al. 2001, Bichir 2006 and Torres 2005c). When segregation is cited over the course of this book, I refer to macro-segregation, or segregation at the scale of the city as a whole. At this scale, the issue of distance between social groups cited above is implicitly incorporated.

Other works attempt to delimit and typify urban poverty spatially, taking into account the multi-dimensionality of the phenomenon discussed earlier. These are based on methodological choices that emphasize the details and complexity of the patterns, including in spatial terms. In the case of São Paulo, the combination of statistical analysis with geographic information techniques over recent years has enabled the development of studies like Cem (2004), for example, which produced typologies of situations of vulnerability in highly disaggregated spatial units based on a series of social indicators. This typology indicated the existence of different forms of poverty and vulnerabilities according to family structure and life-cycle, and not just income and schooling. The spatial distribution of these types suggested the presence of an intense social diversity in these spaces, including the peripheries, as I shall discuss in the next chapter. Similar results have been obtained for analyses on the distribution of social structure in space by Marques, Scalon and Oliveira (2009) and Marques, Bichir and Scalon (2010). These works were the basis for the selection of the sites studied in the following chapters.

This heterogeneity is explained partially by the association between segregation and inequalities in access found frequently in our cities.[4] These two elements are connected in both directions. On one hand, segregated groups have different kinds and levels of access to the opportunities and facilities found in the city, with negative social consequences, both in European cities (Pinçon-Charlot et al. 1986), US cities (Massey and Denton 1993, Morenoff 2003 and Briggs 2001) and Latin American cities (Kaztman and Retamoso 2005, Sabatini et. al. 2001b, Torres, Ferreira and Gomes 2005, Gomes and Armitrano 2005 and Bichir 2006). On the other hand, differences in access also contribute to segregation through the structure of land prices, especially in cities marked by scarcity of amenities (as in the Latin American cases) or by the built environment degradation of certain areas (as in the large US cities).

Hence it is not just segregation that specifies unequal access, but also (and simultaneously) inequality of access that specifies and reproduces segregation.

---

4 The literature on stratification differentiates inequalities in results from inequalities in opportunities. Inequalities in the access to policies represent inequalities in opportunity, since they mediate the acquisition of schooling, good health, etc. On the other hand, they have a direct impact on inequalities in results via living conditions. Since it is not my intention to discuss social inequalities in general in this book, I do not highlight this distinction constantly and return to it only in Chapter 7.

However when one problem is eliminated, the other may persist, such as in the cities where the universalization of access to goods and services provided by the State failed to reduce segregation substantially. So although segregation and inequalities in access continually influence each other, they relate to distinct processes and should be separated conceptually.

This viewpoint is not unanimous in Brazilian and Latin American discussions where the empirical association of the phenomena means that a sizeable part of the literature treats them in undifferentiated form. In the Brazilian literature on the theme, it is impossible to find a unified position on the problem: instead, the concept of segregation is used to designate separation between distinct social groups and inequalities in access to public policies. In Lago (2002) and Maricato (2003), for example, segregation refers to both phenomena simultaneously, while in Vetter (1981), Smolka (1983), Ribeiro (2002), Caldeira (2000) and Villaça (1998), segregation acquires the meaning of separation and social homogeneity.

For greater conceptual precision and analytic capacity, I take segregation to refer to the separation and spatial isolation of social groups in areas that are relatively homogeneous internally in terms of each group's social makeup. Over the course of this book, segregation is therefore taken as a phenomenon distinct from poverty and the existence of social inequalities in the city's space, though associated with these in diverse ways.

While segregation appears as a central dimension in the literature on urban poverty, spatial contiguity is emphasized by another set of authors through the notion of 'neighborhood effects' (Durlauf 2001, Morenoff 2003, Sampson and Morenoff 1997, Sampson and Randenbush 1997, Case and Katz 1991). These refer to the existence of empirical regularities between neighboring units in relation to a given variable or process, such as a possible physical contiguity in levels of teenage pregnancy.

The similarity between the general argument of this literature and the ecological approach is considerable and is sometimes defended explicitly (Osterling 2007), although the processes of causality postulated are not necessarily the same (Sampson and Morenoff 1997). Although this literature has produced important contributions on the association between variables and processes in the study of poverty (Case and Katz 1991 and Sampson and Morenoff 1997), it presents serious conceptual limitations that restrict the reach of its findings and advances (Small and Newman 2001).

These limitations derive from the fact that the existence of empirical regularities between spatially contiguous units in relation to a determined variable tells us little or nothing about the social processes that explain these regularities. Authors like Yinger (2001), for example, identify the cause of poverty in residential discrimination, which can lead to certain location preferences among disadvantaged groups (Ross 2001). This reasoning may appear reasonable at first sight, but a more detailed analysis shows that while discrimination can indeed lead to segregation and isolation, the latter are the potential causal mechanisms behind poverty. In fact by raising an empirical association to the level of a concept, this literature contributes to a certain fetishism that hides the causes and confuses the processes under analysis. It involves precisely what Mahoney (2001) critically refers to as correlation analysis. Although there is nothing intrinsically wrong with this kind of analysis, they fail to tell us anything meaningful about the causes for the observed regularities. The focus of the analysis should be on determining the singular processes and the causal mechanisms associated with the phenomena surrounding poverty (Durlauf 2001).

Seeking precisely to describe the mechanisms associated with the reproduction of poverty, another set of authors has stressed the importance of various socialization processes (Small and Newman 2001). The first such mechanism involves 'role model effects,' which describe the impact on individual behavior caused by positive and negative role models among the people close to any given person (Durlauf 2001). Another form of understanding the influence of the group is to consider 'peer group effects.' These concern the influence on individual activities of small closed groups with strong identities and materially and symbolically marked collective behaviors.

Although in both cases the idea was initially applied to young people, it has a potentially much broader relevance encompassing all social groups. Peer group studies usually present difficulties in separating the effects of group influence from the effects of group selection, given that individuals more inclined to certain types of behavior tend to come together and connect, as I shall discuss later when we turn to the question of homophily (McPherson et al. 2001).[5] Some authors have developed methods for delimiting peer groups through social networks, including large-scale instances (Moody 2001), but the question of causality remains a problem that can only be resolved through the precise theoretical formulation of the processes involved.

In any event, although taking into account peer group and neighborhood effects introduces collective elements into the analysis, these are understood merely as environmental influences on individual behavior, failing to break with the individualist and atomist ontology of poverty. Overcoming this vision presumes a shift of emphasis to focusing on the social dimensions of poverty, highlighting sociability and social relations rather than individual attributes and behavior.

b. Social capital and integration

Perhaps the most important and wide-ranging effort to incorporate social dynamics in studies of the theme is the notion of social capital. As is widely known, the founding texts of this approach can be traced to Coleman (1988), Bourdieu (1986) and Putnam (1996). The concept meant very different things for each of these authors, what marks the discussions until today. Coleman (1988) developed the concept as part of an attempt to integrate elements of the social structure in the conceptual framework of rational action in order to explain school context and in

---

5　　Homophilic relations are those between people with the same attributes.

particular school dropout. Social capital in this sense involves supra-individual dimensions associated with expectations, social norms and obtaining information that influence individual behavior.

Bourdieu used the concept as part of his explanatory model of the economy of symbolic goods, which led to the development of a theory of relations between social positions and cultural dispositions (Bourdieu 1986 and 2007a, Pereira 2005). In this theory, individuals accumulate various types of capital that can be exchanged among themselves – economic, social, cultural and symbolic. For Bourdieu, therefore, social capital amounts to 'the aggregate of the actual or potential resources which are linked to possession of a durable network of more or less institutionalized relationships of mutual acquaintance and recognition – or in other words, to membership in a group – which provides each of its members with the backing of the collectively-owned capital, a 'credential' which entitles them to credit, in the various senses of the word' (Bourdieu 1986: 251). It therefore comprises a middle level sociological category, albeit of wide application, able to be used to describe and explain both specific behavior and societal characteristics.

Putnam, in turn, explained the differences in development between regions of Italy on the basis of differences in civic values and behavior, measured in a long-term study using survey data. The author argues that these differences are explained historically and therefore comprise a general category to be used in a macro-sociological sense. Later the author used the concept to suggest that the loss of dynamism of democracy in the US in the second half of the 20th century derived from the declining presence of a type of associative life governing civic behavior and social capital (Putnam 1995).

Based on these founding approaches, various authors argued for using the concept to define a wide range of elements, what lead to a certain imprecision on the debates. These elements are located at individual, collective and societal level, including trust and associativism at the level of society to interpersonal trust and patterns of connection between individuals, passing through civic behavior, trust in the local school and the neighborhood in general, and so on. These elements were seen to derive from the structure and content of certain social relations that 'combine attitudes of trust with conducts of reciprocity and cooperation' (Durston 2003:147). The beneficial effects of these characteristics are seen to vary widely and have impacts on everything from the quality of democracy to economic development, including better or worse implementation of public policies. This tradition converges on the importance of three elements – norms/values, reciprocal trust/civic behavior and social networks. In economic terms, these characteristics of societies contribute to reducing the costs of transition in the sense highlighted by the literature on the new institutional economy (North 1990).

Although the literature on social capital is both wide-ranging and diverse (Durston 2003, Briggs 2005), here our interest lies in discussing the contributions that help us gain a better understanding of the subject matter of this book, using the concept to describe collective elements that affect living conditions in city regions and in poor districts in particular (Cechi et al. 2008, Rao and Woolcock 2001,

Fontes and Eischner 2004, Pavez 2006, Briggs 2003, Sampson and Raudenbush 1997). These are presumed to be caused by sociability in communities, their associative life, but also by State policies, especially those focused on specific areas, such as those intended to combat so-called 'area poverty' (Power 1996). It is worth adding that for some authors the relation between social capital and neighborhood has clearly environmental or even ecological dimensions (Osterling 2007), but for other authors social capital is not just influenced by public policies, it can also be actively produced by them (Policy Research Initiative 2005a and b, Peri 6 1997).

The literature on the theme sets out from the existence of an intense association between district (or neighborhood) and patterns of connection between individuals, even if sometimes implicitly. For some authors, networks (and the resources that can be mobilized through them) are one of the aspects of social capital. Networks impact on three sets of elements: individual strategies, the construction of cohesion within social contexts – bonding social capital – and the insertion of these contexts in wider social communities – bridging social capital (Lin 1999a, 1999b and Briggs 2003). Many authors argue that access to these types of social capital can help to overcome situations of poverty (Briggs 2001 and 2005 and Policy Research Initiative 2006). But in what way do networks produce social capital?

The first obligatory reference on the theme is the work of Nan Lin (1999a and b) on the place of networks in status attainment, understood as 'a process by which individuals mobilize and invest resources for returns in socioeconomic standings' (Lin 1999b:467). These resources are personal and social, the latter being specified as elements accessible through the direct and indirect links of their networks of relations. The author argues that: a) social resources affect the results of instrumental actions in search of status; b) social resources are affected by the positions occupied by individuals in the resource structures; c) social resources tend to be more influenced by weak links than strong links (Lin 1999b:470). The attainment of status over the life-cycle[6] therefore involves both access to social capital, understood as the set of resources accessed by a given individual through his or hers origin and networks (education, initial and family status and initial relational resources), and his or hers mobilization, which is influenced by the use of networks (structure and force of bonds and the status of contacts).

---

6   In studies of stratification, the idea of the life-cycle looks to capture the phases of status attainment: origin (family structure, networks, economic capital and culture of origin), internalization (health and socialization of values), formalization (obtaining educational qualifications and skills), autonomization of status (work market and marital choice) and realization of status (position in the socio-occupational structure and wealth). The dynamic element of the process is inter-generational mobility. See Nelson do Valle Silva, 'Prefácio,' In: Ribeiro, C. *Estrutura de classes e mobilidade social no Brasil*. São Paulo, Edusc/Anpocs 2007 and Carlos Ribeiro, *Estrutura de classes e mobilidade social no Brasil*. São Paulo, Edusc/Anpocs 2007.

Ronald Burt, on the other hand, focused on the topic of economic networks, studying competition (Burt 1992) and generating innovation (Burt 2004). Certain network structures create advantages for determined positions occupied by some economic agents whose ego-centered networks are marked by low redundancy, creating what the author dubbed structural holes. Close to these, the author argues, profits are higher (Burt 1992) and new ideas tend to be created, producing innovation (Burt 2004). In both cases the presence of structural holes is seen to increase the control exerted by a given ego over his or hers network, generating social capital, which can also have effects on other social situations. Later in the book I shall test the effects of these structures in the networks of individuals in a situation of poverty.

Adopting a different approach, Briggs also makes use of the idea of social capital as a network, but specifically explores the relation between poverty, social networks and segregation in the city. For him, the relation between social capital, inequalities and poverty can be understood with three emphases (Briggs 2001 and 2005). The first focal point is on Lin's individual support and status attainment (1999a), based on the improvement of individual attributes through what can be obtained via network contacts. Usually studies of this type focus on personal networks or small groups, the majority concentrating on the search for jobs and occupations (status attainment), as well as the search for care, trust and companionship (social support) (Briggs 2005). The second focal point analyzes the capacities of communities and their collective effectiveness in exercising social control, as in Sampson and Raudenbush (1997), discussion of organization and trust at community level or in small areas. The third focal point is the only one concentrated on the macro level, investigating civic and economic performance at national or regional level, in Putnam's sense (1996). As cited earlier, in this case the themes are generalized trust and participation in associations, but in the case of this specific literature they involve the study of societal networks.

Working in the first of these lines of analysis, Briggs (2003) investigates the bridge-producing ties between socially different individuals. The author emphasizes the existence of a dense fabric of ties between individuals with equal attributes as an important source of social cohesion, but distinguishes these 'bonding ties' from those that produce bridges between people with distinct characteristics, dubbed 'bridging ties.' Developing an argument presented earlier in Briggs (2001), the author underlines the importance of the former for individuals to 'get by' in their everyday activities and situations, but highlights the latter as the key to improving individuals' life situations, enabling them to become socially mobile or 'get ahead.' Using information on social networks in diverse locations in the USA, the author explores the main conditioning factors of the 'racial bridging ties.' The research indicates that the existence of inter-racial ties varies between social groups as a function of associative practices and sociability. Residential segregation tends to increase the homogeneity of the patterns of ties between individuals, in part because preferences are spatially organized, as well as representing a barrier to contact and opportunities (Briggs 2005).

Thus one of the central issues seems to concern the presence of ties between poor people and socially different individuals, something which seems to be hindered by segregation. The question takes us to the classic discussion on the tendency of individuals with similar characteristics to relate among themselves, or in the words of Robert Burns 'birds of a same feather flock together' (Burns apud McPherson et al. 2001:417). The literature has examined this question through the concept of homophily – the evidence that individuals tend to build and maintain contacts more frequently with individuals with similar social attributes (McPherson et al. 2001).

While homophily is produced and maintained by intrinsic dimensions of sociability – practices, tastes, language, and so on – it tends to be reinforced by space and segregation. As segregation groups socially similar individuals, homophily is provoked primarily by a numerical effect related to the greater availability of similar individuals to construct contacts, a process the literature denominates 'baseline homophily.' However this effect is supplemented by at least another two, linked to individual preferences (Ortiz, Hoyos and López 2004) and to the behavior of organizations and institutions (Tilly 2000 and 2005) that in various forms lead to the construction and reconstruction of homophilic relations, choosing and maintaining relations between equals more easily. The question is not related, therefore, merely to the different constitution of ties, but also to the different tendency to maintain ties. Since most of the literature on the theme deals with the United States and since the main social division in the country involves race (Massey and Denton 1993), the latter is the focal topic of most of the studies (Briggs 2005). However the question also imposes itself in relation to gender, migratory origin, religious creeds, ethnicity, income and geographic location (McPherson et al. 2001). Homophily, the authors claim, is reproduced by geographical and organizational effects, cognitive processes and the selective breaking of ties (McPherson et al. 2001). As we shall see in the following chapters, homophily is a central dimension present in the analyzed networks, producing important consequences for the relational patterns of individuals and for their living conditions. However, the patterns are highly complex and do not allow us to affirm mechanical relations between networks, attributes and space. We shall also see that difficulties in maintaining ties go a long way to explaining the differences between networks of middle class individuals and those living in poverty.

In summary, the literature suggests that social isolation combines with spatial isolation and the harmful effects of concentration to produce poverty by making access to opportunities (Briggs 2001) much more difficult along with the accumulation of social capital (Cechi et al. 2008, Rao and Woolcock 2001, Fontes and Eischner 2004, Briggs 2003, Sampson and Raudenbush 1997, Osterling 2007). Following this premise, a generation of policies for combating poverty set out from the idea that mass public initiatives could help to reduce it. This would be achieved through spatially concentrated policies or by moving residences and families spatially and taking pro-active measures against segregation. The design and the implementation of these policies have already been analyzed by a series of studies, showing contradictory results (Curley 2008; Briggs, Popkin and Goering 2010). In cases where large inequalities in access to policies persist and where the quality of services available in regions far from the urban centers is very different, as occurs in the large Latin America and Brazilian cities, this kind of initiative could generate extremely positive social effects (Torres 2005b).

Nonetheless, in many cases these policies presume that changes in space will actively generate social capital by altering the relational patterns between individuals in the neighborhoods and communities (Cechi et al. 2008, Rao and Woolcock 2001, Policy Research Initiative 2005a and b, Peri 6 1997). A growing international literature has pointed to the failure of this aspect of public policies, or at least the attainment of results quite different from those intended (Greenbaum at al. 2008, Curley 2008 and 2009, Briggs, Popkin and Goering 1010). Various questions seem to be involved here. The first is the observation that contiguity in space does not correspond to a feeling of community (Blokland 2003) or to patterns of connection between individuals and social groups (Blokland and Savage 2005). Moreover these policies ignore or minimize the strong effects that mechanisms of homophily have on conserving the separation of the relational patterns of distinct groups of individuals. In the absence of much better knowledge concerning the inter-relations between attributes, networks and space, not to mention the complete lack of knowledge concerning the effects of policies on these networks, the production of policies can only generate socially and politically naive initiatives. This naivety becomes patent when the literature reports that even when families are moved from high concentration neighborhoods to mixed areas by social mixture policies, their social networks do not tend to increase in size or diversity, but on the contrary shrink (Greenbaum at al. 2008). In other cases, the networks transform in unintended ways (Curley 2008 and 2009), although moves to more segregated areas tend to lead to relational impoverishment as predicted by the literature (Soares 2009).

I believe that only the full incorporation of a relational ontology of poverty can help to solve our blind spots concerning the theme and produce more realistic and dynamic representations of the phenomenon. Poverty situations are dynamic and multi-dimensional states of deprivation, measurable through diverse attributes, which have been constructed over life trajectories and are reconstructed on a daily basis in practices of sociability and survival strategies. While this involves individual attributes and decisions, it also depends on supra-individual and relational processes that cannot be captured by environmental representations or by broad categories like social capital. The relational contexts in which individuals are inserted should be analyzed with the best formulation available to us: social networks. But we gain little advantage from normative descriptions of these networks like those contained in aprioristic uses of the ideas of bridging and bonding, since relations and networks produce both at the same time. Additionally, the same ties can enable a variety of uses in distinct situations, for different individuals, or for the same people at distinct moments. All these elements are socially and spatially specific, as well as full of the conflicts intrinsic to human action and relations. So, networks must be incorporated, but not only to allow the quantitative analysis of their structures. It is essential to incorporate also the consideration of the different uses people make with these structures, what will be achieved only with the additional use of qualitative analytical tools.

I turn now to a more detailed look at social networks.

2. Social and personal networks

The concern of the social sciences with the effects of patterns of connections between individuals is long-established. However systematic analysis of these patterns, based on detailed empirical studies, dates from the first decades of the 20th century, especially the pioneering works of Jacob Moreno on what he called 'psychological geography' and later 'sociometry' (Freeman 2004:39). In the more specific field of the social sciences, the systematic study of relations in specific social contexts was introduced by anthropology and by studies of organizations from the 1930s onwards, reaching sociology and political science only in the 1970s and 80s (Scott 1992 and Freeman 2004).

a. Social networks

From the 1970s onwards an international research program developed focusing on the intermediate level and concentrating in particular on the analysis of the relational patterns of individuals and entities surrounding social situations (Knoke 1990 and Johnson 1994). These relational patterns were present in almost all the dimensions, making it very difficult to study social phenomena without considering these patterns, as in the field of economic sociology, for example (Granovetter 2000).

The central theoretical grounding for the analysis of social networks is that the basic units of social phenomena are social relations rather than individual attributes. In this sense the social world is ontologically constituted by relational patterns of various types and intensities in continual transformation. Even the ontology of social subjects depends on their insertion in situations and relations (Emirbayer 1997). The incorporation of social networks therefore allows the construction of an *a posteriori* structuralism, deduced from empirical analysis (Tilly 1992b), in contrast to the kinds of structuralism induced by various earlier theories.

In the earliest theoretical formulations of the problem, attributes and relations were conceived as almost mutually exclusive analytic emphases (Emirbayer 1997). Today the two elements are examined in association, since entities with shared attributes have a greater probability of establishing relations due to the presence of mechanisms associated with homophily (Kadushin 2004, McPherson et al. 2001). At the same time, relations help to construct attributes of various types, frequently making it difficult to establish a single causal direction (McPherson et al. 2001).

On the other hand, the characteristics of the social setting where ties are build influences the types of networks people construct (Small 2009).

Networks may be considered solely in metaphoric form (as in the case of works that use networks in descriptive and discursive terms), normatively (as per business administration studies that aim to improve networks) or methodologically for the investigation of specific social situations through the analysis of the social connections present in them, as in the case of this study. In the case of phenomena with low-complexity relational patterns, the use of metaphors is, in most cases, the most profitable mode of analysis. However the most important advance occurs with the use of networks as an investigative method, shedding light on social situations in which relational patterns display such a high degree of complexity that they could not be analyzed satisfactorily through narratives that explore networks metaphorically.

In terms of research, network analysis attempts to use graphic and mathematical representations to reproduce the varied relational contexts in which social actors are embedded. In these kinds of analysis, persons, groups, organizations and entities are represented as nodes (points) and relations as various kinds of connections (lines). These ties may be material or immaterial, can present multiple contents and are usually conceived to be in continual transformation.

In very general terms, the incorporation of networks transforms the way in which we represent social structure in our studies. For studies of social stratification, from those inspired by Marxism to contemporary works based on more or less complex occupational classifications, comprehending social structure involves the analysis and correlation of the attributes of individuals, forming groups (Santos 2005) or groups in space (Preteceille 2006, Preteceille and Cardoso 2008, Marques, Bichir and Scalon 2010). In fact there is a certain disconnection between this form of comprehending the structuring of society and studies focused on processes, actions and relations.[7]

For authors such as Bian et al. (2005), achieving a better understanding of social structure involves the integration of studies of attributes and relations, incorporating social relations (and networks) in studies of stratification. This certainly does not mean abandoning attributes since, as we have seen, so-called

---

7   The problem naturally appears in more expressive form in theoretical fields that look to interpret structure and action conjointly. For most Marxist authors, for example, the question is resolved almost by definition, given that both positions in the structure and political action are specified by the relative positions in class relations. In the case of studies inspired by Pierre Bourdieu, on the other hand, the problem is formulated theoretically as an association between positions and dispositions apprehended through the concept of habitus. The latter is comprehended through the modal characteristics of the population, which leaves open the question of what mechanisms are involved in its introjection by individuals (see Pierre Bourdieu, *Distinção: crítica social do julgamento*, São Paulo: Edusp 2008; for a similar but more recent study outside of France, see Virgílio Pereira, *Classes e culturas de classe das famílias portuenses*, Porto: Ed. Afrontamento 2005).

homophilic effects increase the probability of relations developing between people with shared attributes. The objective, therefore, resides in integrating these two dimensions, superimposing the stratification by attributes with a second structure constructed and reconstructed by social networks. Pursuing this approach, the study of networks allows us to incorporate elements associated with the sociability of individuals occurring in what Bourdieu (2007b) denominates the social microcosm – the family, neighborhood, workplace, etc. – into the study of the social macrocosm represented by social structure itself. Evidently the two structures are interconnected and influence each other continually, rendering the question highly complex in methodological terms.

At a more concrete level, the study of social networks relates directly to the patterns of sociability found in a given context. This dimension was already present in the classic works of Simmel (1972 [1908]) who argued that modern sociability was based on a large number of secondary connections varying considerably in content, weak in intensity and no longer necessarily organized in territorial form. The epithet of these patterns of connection was found in the life of the modern metropolis, which provided individuals with considerable freedom of circulation and social choice, in contrast to the patterns typical of the rural world and small towns (Simmel 1973 [1902]). The process of constructing modernity therefore had a direct impact on the patterns of relations between individuals, constituting what Wirth (1972 [1938]) called 'urbanism as a way of life.'

Recently, Wellman (2001) revisited these arguments in the attempt to characterize sociability at the start of the 21st century, arguing that the new technologies of communication and transportation have reduced the presence of localism[8], and intensified the importance of social relations in overcoming the physical barriers of neighborhood and communities. For Wellman, the recent decline of the community based on localization has led researchers to the mistaken belief in the end of the community in general with consequent impacts on solidarity, democracy or even society as a whole. Countering this assumption, the author argues that communities have not recently disappeared, but simply transformed.

However, if we turn to Simmel's classic interpretations and recent works such as those by Blokland (2003) and Blokland and Savage (2008), we are led to believe that there never was any identity between community and neighborhood in modern societies, although the neighborhood as a context for forming and maintaining ties and sociability may have declined even further over recent years in some social contexts. Studies of contexts of poverty, on the other hand, have shown that the neighborhood can still be a fundamental element in the construction of sociability (Verbrugge 1983 apud McPherson et al. 2001:430). As we shall see later, the results from São Paulo point exactly in this direction, suggesting that different

---

8   Localism is the proportionally high presence of people from the individual's own area in his or her network. Technically, this is a type of homophily based on the area of residence.

social groups are subject to different conditions in terms of this aspect, although for the poor the neighborhood remains very important.

In the specific case of studies of urban poverty, both relations and attributes are absolutely fundamental, including those associated with space. Picking up on some of the points made in the previous section, we can formulate the question as follows. Individuals' access to the structures of opportunities that lead to social conditions in general, and situations of poverty in particular, are mediated by the relational patterns these individuals have with other individuals and with various kinds of organization. This includes the access to people from the three sources of social welfare – markets, the State and the family/community –in a similar form to the effect of segregation on poverty.

However the separation of network effects and segregation effects is merely analytical, and in the concrete social world space and networks act simultaneously and interconnectedly. Thus given that individuals are located in space (a property of networks called *propinquity*), network connections also function as links between more or less segregated spaces. In this sense, networks with higher relative proportions of people not living in the same residential locality as ego tend to integrate individuals more intensely with different contexts (though not necessarily less socially homophilic).

The relation between networks and space, therefore, involves two distinct characteristics: segregation and localism. As we have seen, segregation concerns the spatial concentration of certain social groups in relatively homogeneous spaces separated from other groups. I argue that one of the important properties of relational patterns is the proportion of nodes in a given personal network who inhabit the same locality as ego. I refer to this property as localism. Although it is related to segregation, it concerns a distinct dimension. While localism is a property of each network, segregation is a property of the space inhabited by individuals. In fact localism is a type of homophily relating to sharing the attribute of residential locality between the individuals present in a given relation. In many empirical cases these elements seem to be associated, but since they involve distinct socio-spatial processes, they can vary separately. Hence we frequently encounter segregated areas in our cities with networks possessing high levels of localism (with few outsiders) marked by a high level of social homophily. This is the situation we would expect to find more commonly. As we shall see in the following chapters, though, in these same segregated areas we can also find networks with less localism and a higher level of urban insertion. The different combinations of these characteristics has important effects on the social condition of individuals.

Networks can also play a key role in mediating access to State policies and services with important effects on welfare. Generally speaking, the relation between networks and policies involves two distinct forms of interaction. The first is related to the impact State policies might have over networks. As we have already discussed, networks have recently been cited as one of the elements that could be impacted by State actions, as in the case of policies designed to promote social capital (Levitas et al. 2007, Policy Research Initiative 2005a and Perri 6 1997). International experiences have shown that various fundamental elements were not taken into account by such policies, in particular because of the adoption of a normative and instrumental view of relational patterns (Blokland and Savage 2008), especially considering our level of knowledge of the phenomenon.

Secondly, networks can mediate the delivery of State policies. For a long time the literature on public policies considered that the logic of universalization meant the existence of a kind of depersonalized automatism in policy implementation and delivery. At least since Lipsky (1980), however, we know that very often policy delivery involves a complex and continuous process of translation, creating discretionality. The incorporation of networks in policy design can help improve implementation, making public initiatives more capable of achieving their goals (Trotter 1999), such as in the inclusion of non-governmental associations in the policy for combating AIDS in Brazil, for example. Networks may also help customize policies to local aspects, including cultural elements, as in the recruitment of community agents in healthcare policies, also in Brazil (Lotta 2006 and 2010). This mediation, however, also involves traditional clientelist relations, as well as the daily circulation of information on policies among citizens and with local organizations. In all these cases, relations and networks mediate the implementation and delivery of policies. This is especially true when policies are not universal, but also happens at moments of intense increase in policy delivery and when information on policies is not widely available.

In fact, the large Brazilian metropolises are good examples of this at the moment. Recent data analyzed by Figueiredo, Torres and Bichir (2005) on the city of São Paulo suggests that access to State initiatives occurs in direct form with a very low level of political mediation, even among the poorest sectors, contradicting perceptions of politics arguing that clientelism is central to the distribution of State benefits in Brazil. On the other hand, studies like those by Lotta (2010) and Kuschnir (2000) demonstrate the existence of various kinds of social mediations on policy delivery. As we shall see in chapter 6, the study of networks allows us to qualify the idea of mediation itself, leading to a more complex understanding of clientelism and the role played by networks in the implementation of policies, confirming both the absence of political mediation and the presence of diverse social mediations. Even in the case of the universalization of policies, therefore, social relations and networks can facilitate or block access to public policies, influencing the amount of welfare provided by the State.

In terms of method, there are basically two forms of investigating patterns of connection: through the so-called whole networks, studying entire networks or parts of specific social contexts, or through personal networks, which include each individual's contacts of sociability.

The first line of analysis covers a vast number of studies, spanning from analyses of the internal dynamics of state agencies and their policies (Laumann and Knoke 1987 and Marques 2000 and 2003) to the interactions of organizations in lobby structures (Heinz et. al. 1997) or in estuary management committees (Schneider et. al. 2003). In addition specific thematically or physically delimited communities may be studied, such as friendship networks within the financial elite (Kadushin 1995) or the role of networks of musicians in the construction of musical styles (Kirschbaum 2006). Finally, analyzing political and social dynamics in a wider sense, studies may focus on fields of political and social action as distinct as the consolidation of a political party at national level (Hedstrom et al. 2000), sexual relations among teenagers (Bearman et al. 2004) or political mobilizations of students and young people (Mische 2007).

Another form of approaching the question, though, involves investigating individual networks. Strictly speaking, individual networks are a particular case of a network in a specific social context when we take a given individual's sociability as the context at hand. Although social networks always represent artificial extracts of a wider relational context, in the case of individual networks the degree of artificiality in the (necessary) analytic exercise of 'cutting' them from wider contexts is greater. Nevertheless, also in this case the considered ontology is entirely relational and the 'extracts' are merely analytic devices used to enable the investigation.

When we turn to just the individual's direct relations and the potential relations between these primary contacts – that is, just the direct and unmediated relations one step from ego at most – we are working with the so-called ego-centered networks. Most of the existing studies of individual networks work with this type of network, especially since these networks can be reproduced on the basis of survey data. The US General Social Survey, for example, includes data that allows us to discuss ego-centered networks of individuals (Bearman and Parigi 2004, Beggs 1996 and Moore 1990). Although this analytic strategy is important, especially by allowing representative studies of large populations, it limits the sociability of individuals to primary contacts.

A second strategy for analyzing individual networks is to study personal networks. These are constructed without any prior delimitation of the extent of the network, focusing on ego's relations and the connections between those related indirectly to the person irrespective of distance, keeping ego's sociability constantly in mind. Focusing on these personal networks avoids the problems caused by the *a priori* limitation of connections made by ego-centered networks (Lonkila 2010), although the strategy presents limitations in terms of producing studies with large numbers of cases representative of populations. This book makes use of this analytic strategy, researching personal networks understood as relational contexts that individuals recognize as their own but which may or may not be linked directly to them.

But how are these personal networks constructed and what constructs them? Degenne (2009) helps us to comprehend this point by specifying the content of relations. His work sets out from the distinction between interaction – 'a basic exchange, short-lasting and representing a single unit of action' – and relation – 'a set of interactions between the same people for a period of time.' The author identifies four types of interactions, according to: the rules governing their regulation (whether pre-defined or negotiated); whether the roles are pre-defined or not (such as doctor/patient; father/son); whether or not they occur within organizations; and whether they depend on the contexts of the relation or are autonomous (like friendship and love). In the latter case, individuals know each other so well that the uncertainties involved in the interaction tend to be reduced. This interaction is the most personalized and transitory in terms of the constitution of a relation. For the author, the length of time and frequency of the interactions leads them in the direction of relations.

The framework developed by Grossetti (2009) based on panel research with French youths complements the anterior. The author argues that only a small proportion of the connections derive from social relations properly speaking, the rest deriving from collectives or organizational environments (family, work, etc.), as well as prior relations and common interests/activities, on the basis of which some construct autonomy. A collective is formed when people become aware of the structures of communication occurring within it and begin to map boundaries of belonging. Operating within the collectives are the basic processes of embedding and decoupling, as well as the use of mediation resources (material, cognitive or immaterial). The former means an increased dependency on belonging to the collective while the latter implies autonomization in relation to the former, leading to the constitution of relations in Degenne's sense (2009).

Since this book investigates the effect of various types of ties in determining living conditions, I consider both interactions and relations in Degenne's sense (2009). As we shall observe, though, especially in the final chapters, the differences between them, as well as effects similar to what Grossetti (2009) calls decoupling, appear to be fundamental. This is so because interactions and relations specify the levels of trust present in the relations and influence the kinds of help that can flow dynamically through the networks of individuals living in poverty. This dimension combines with the earlier critiques of the individualistic comprehension of poverty and of the classification of networks into bridging/bonding or strong and weak, since depending on the regulation of relations and mediations present, the same connections may convey very distinct elements.

But how do personal networks work? Now that we have established the main conceptual elements involved in the study of networks, in the section that follows I discuss how personal networks can help us comprehend the findings presented in the subsequent chapters.

b. Personal networks

The literature on personal networks is not as vast or as consolidated as the one on whole networks. In this rapid overview of the literature, I focus on works that contribute to our understanding of two themes: the social characteristics and conditioning factors of personal networks, and the promotion of social integration and support through networks.

Firstly, what are personal networks like and what processes influence them? To date, the only Brazilian study published on personal networks discusses this question. Fontes and Eichner (2004) analyzed the ego-centered networks in a low-income community of Recife, assessing their contribution towards the construction of social capital. The authors identified a high level of homophily in the ego-centered networks, in terms of sex, age and schooling, especially among older individuals with higher levels of education. The study indicated that most ties involved people from the community, the most present being neighbors and relatives. Finally, the authors assess the effects of tie strength on resource mobilization and social support, considered as forms of social capital. As we shall see, these results are partially confirmed by the networks of São Paulo.

The general characteristics of personal networks are also the theme of Fischer and Shavit (1995). The authors compared networks of people inhabiting California in the 1970s with individuals who live in Israel, in the beginning of the 1980s. The results suggest quite similar network characteristics, although with denser and longer-lasting networks in Israel. The relative presence of the family also tended to be larger in Israel. Grosseti (2007) compared the Californian networks studied by Fisher with networks in France, replicating the same methodology. Although the networks tended to be similar, the French results suggested an association between network characteristics and level of schooling. The São Paulo results also point out to stable differences between networks considering social group, defined by income of schooling.

The differences between networks of urban and non-urban contexts in the USA were explored by Beggs (1986), who constructed ego-centered networks based on information from the 1985 General Social Survey. The findings suggest that social networks outside cities tend to be smaller and denser, are based on older ties and more frequently based on kinship and neighborhood. Given the smaller size of non-urban networks, the author encountered a tendency for multiple roles, but, contrary to what was expected, the non-urban networks did not present more homogeneous contents than the urban networks. The latter result may be due to the inclusive nature of the definition of urban used.

The potential existence of gender divisions in personal networks in the USA was analyzed by Moore (1990), using the same information as Beggs (1986). The findings suggested that women's networks were generally more strongly based on families and men's on work colleagues. However, when the data was controlled by insertion in the labor market and by age, the differences shrank considerably, although the women's networks still contained more individuals from the family. As we shall see in the following chapters, differences between the networks of men and women exist, although the findings suggest differences to those reported by Moore.

Family ties also appeared as central in Bastani (2007)'s work on middle-class personal networks in Tehran. The author shows similar personal networks by gender in terms of size and presence of family ties, but not in gender composition. More educated people tended to present larger networks, but the presence of kin tended to be high in all networks. Bastani explained this finding mobilizing cultural elements of the Iranian society, but also sustaining that the social and political environment of post-revolutionary Iran turned the family sphere as the most important meeting place for sociability.

The contribution of social support networks in coping with situations of poverty and inequality is also analyzed by Andreotti (2006) based on qualitative data, comparing three different socially excluded groups – single mothers with minor children, long-term unemployed males and foreign immigrants. People receive resources from the labor market, social networks, public services, nonprofit services and the local space. The group that presents the worse situations is the unemployed males, who tend to receive low amounts of resources form almost all these sources. Single mothers are the ones in better conditions and also the ones who get the most from social support networks, especially from kin.

The origins of the ties in individual networks are explored by Grossetti (2005 and 2009) based on survey research conducted in Toulouse (France). The author focuses his analysis on what he calls social circles, defined as including organization, group, family or context (where mutual recognition occurs). The research looked to access the degree to which social ties originate in circles and shared concerns or are constructed through other relations. In general around a third of the ties originated in the family and almost two-thirds were acquired in circles. The proportion of ties obtained through a network tended to be higher for people with higher levels of schooling, in contrast to the educational, work and associative ties, which were more frequent for individuals with lower levels of schooling. In relation to life-cycle, the findings showed a wide predominance of family ties in childhood, followed by an explosion of sociability ties (networks) and studying and later a relative rise in the importance of work, especially for individuals with higher levels of schooling.

Bidart and Lavenu (2005), on the other hand, have explored the temporal dynamic of personal networks. The authors analyzed the impact of events on the networks in the transition from adolescence to adult life, based on a panel with young people at three different moments in Normandy (France). The results indicated the specific effects of certain events in terms of reducing or expanding the networks. In general, they contributed to their expansion: remaining at school or going to college; obtaining a long desired job and leaving the parents' home or separating. Networks tend to be reduced, on the other hand, when: the person concludes studies, begins to work or emigrates; a stable emotional relationship begins (marriage in particular) and the person devotes him or herself to family life and the home (birth of children, for example). Changing the pattern of sociability can contribute to increasing or reducing networks. The main motives for maintaining ties are affective (family, etc), followed by possessing friends in common.

The authors claim that networks of individuals with lower income depend more strongly on contexts and reduce earlier due to the earlier occurrence in the life cycle of network reducing elements. Although the authors sometimes confuse an event that affects the network with the result on sociability of the event in question (for example, dedicating oneself to the family), their work indicates some important elements to be tested in later studies.

Bidart (2009) later returns to the theme, arguing that the stronger and more intimate the relation, the freer it is from contexts, in a form compatible with what Grossetti (2009) calls decoupling. The same effect is produced by duration, and older and more stable relations tend to depend less on contexts.

These findings are echoed in the trajectories and narratives presented in Chapter 6 on the effect of events on personal networks, and touch on some of the mechanisms that explain network dynamics, as we shall see later.

However, how do these relational patterns integrate individuals in the wider contexts surrounding them? A second set of works focuses on the relation between personal networks and cohesion/integration and social support. Campbell and Lee (1992) explore the theme in the US context, assessing the extent to which the characteristics of the individuals and their time availability affect their social integration. The authors interviewed people living in different districts of Nashville (USA), collecting information on acquaintances in the neighborhood and the topics discussed with them. The results suggest that more integrated people – women, older and married people, those with higher incomes – have more extensive networks within the neighborhood. By contrast less integrated people, especially those with lower income and schooling, tend to have more frequent and longer lasting contacts, a result contrary to the authors' intuition.[9] The findings presented in the following chapters suggest that ties in distinct contexts cannot be analyzed in a dissociated form, and that the result obtained by the authors may be due to the existence of wider sources of sociability than the neighborhood for the most integrated individuals, as occurs in São Paulo, especially for the middle class.

The same theme has been explored by Ignácio Jariego in various works, most of them specifically discussing patterns of social integration and support among immigrants, but with broader analytic consequences. Jariego (2002) studies personal support networks among immigrants of Morrocan, Filipino and Sengalese origin in Marbella (Spain). Classifying networks according to socio-economic and relational variables, the author delimited five types of personal networks: small networks of compatriots with friendship and family; specialized ethnic networks with a predominance of friends; ethnic networks with a predominance of relatives; mixed networks with a predominance of friends and mixed networks of family regrouping integrated with the receiving community. Next, the author analyzed the

---

9   Similar results in terms of the relation between networks and integration were obtained by José Molina and Alba Gil, 'Reciprocidad hoy: la rede de las unidades domésticas y serviços públicos de dos colectivos de Vic (Barcelona).' In: Porras, J. and Espinoza, V. *Redes: enfoque y aplicaiones del análisis de redes sociales (ARS)*. Santiago do Chile: Universidad Bolivariana 2005, on networks of elderly people and immigrant families in a small town in Catalonia. The small number of cases (eleven), however, prevents us from drawing any general lessons from the work.

relation between networks and the presence of psychological problems, showing that these were more frequent in relational contexts with lower levels of integration and support.

The relation between integration and networks was again explored in Jariego (2003) on networks of immigrants who took part in job training courses in Spain. The author developed a typology of networks for immigrants who had been in the country for less than ten years, based on the size and composition of the networks and on attributes of the individuals, especially homophily and the presence of Spaniards in the networks. The investigation was complemented by a detailed look at networks of Peruvian and Morrocan women. The author encountered six types of networks, spanning from what he calls 'minimal' networks with less than three individuals (predominantly homophilic with little integration) to the 'wide networks of family regrouping integrated with the local community' (already present in the previous study) with between twelve and fifteen individuals, typical of single male youths. As we shall see, São Paulo's networks are significantly larger, on average, than those reported in this study. These differences arise from the fact that networks of sociability are usually larger than personal support networks. Nonetheless the study identified networks of sociability in São Paulo of comparable size to Jariego's minimal support networks. Apparently in situations of high social isolation, personal networks of sociability shrink down to minimal support networks.

Jariego's findings are useful in terms of thinking about the relation between integration and networks since migration represents a process of adaptation to a new cultural, social and relational environment. The networks of immigrants of various origins differ according to their composition (relatives, compatriots and Spaniards), their structure (density and format), the multiplicity of determined members of the network and its size. After migration, the individuals seem to experience considerable difficulty in maintaining the ties with their networks of origin with strong effects on their relational patterns, which become smaller and more concentrated on the family. During their subsequent integration, new ties are built and time may lead to a relaxation of the original characteristics of the networks, leading to their increase, as well as a higher proportion of non-compatriots. However, this occurs in a heterogenic form and among the diverse groups of different origins we encounter different support networks. The role of the networks in providing instrumental and psychological support also varies significantly.

The results obtained in São Paulo display a considerable similarity with these, although the adaptation involved in Brazilian inter-regional migration is less intense or problematic than that of African migrants in Spain. However, the mechanisms involved are basically the same, as shown in the study by Dujisin and Jariego (2005) on personal networks of students who regularly move between Alcalá and Seville to study in the latter city. In general terms, the article assessed the effects of metropolitan life on the networks of individuals at the moment of gaining their personal independence. The emphasis, therefore, was on analyzing the transformations of the networks of non-local people with greater or lesser social integration, following the example of the studies of immigrants. In this case, though, both the networks of origin and of destination maintained themselves active together, though separated by the territory.

The idea that different networks integrate individuals in different forms is also explored by Blockland (2003). The author carried out detailed qualitative research in a district of Rotterdam, Holland, and although she did not develop network analysis in methodological terms, she obtained very interesting results from the viewpoint of this research.[10] Following the clues left by Ulf Hannerz (1983) in a classic work on urban anthropology, Blockland delimits four types of personal networks: specialized, integrated, encapsulated and isolated. Although these types are constructed in the individual trajectories, they are influenced by gender and by life-cycle phase, among other attributes.

The specialized or segregated networks are based on various clusters (or groupings/layers of sociability) with different individuals and are usually linked to a variety of themes (for example: one for playing, another for going out at night, and so on). These are described as typical of individuals who the author classifies as 'modern city dwellers,' or cosmopolitans. These individuals perform constant translations between languages, linked to specialized networks constructed over the course of personal trajectories that provide them with many different attributes. They circulate between these spheres but do not belong to them, which allows them to wander between them. The integrated networks are networks that, although not closed, present groupings that encourage regular encounters. These tend to be the networks of the majority of the individuals, situated between the specialized and encapsulated networks. In general the thematic distance between the existing spheres is not particularly large (or else they would become specialized). Encapsulates networks are similar to peer groups – dense and closed networks with few members and frequent contacts. The spheres of sociability linked to these networks are marked by a strong ritualistic and sometimes initiatory character. And finally isolated networks are very small and low-density, typical of isolated and solitary individuals, being particularly common among the elderly.

Although the following chapters do not attempt to match Blokland's classification, the dialogues between her types of network and the networks of sociability I encountered in São Paulo are evident. Even in contexts of poverty, we found individuals with very small networks, highly specialized relational patterns or very diverse sociability. Since people's access to opportunity structures is mediated by networks, the types of networks have a substantial influence on individual living conditions.

This same kind of result is obtained in Dominguez's ethnographic study (2004) of the relational contexts of low-income immigrant women in Boston. The results

---

10   The findings described in the work represent just an intermediate and methodological step in the work of the author, in fact interested in problematizing the relations between community and neighborhood.

suggest the huge importance of socially diverse networks that include bridges for those individuals located in other parts of the social structure, not just in terms of opportunities, but also in terms of their access to repertoires and information. The mere existence of bonds, however, does not appear to guarantee the effectiveness of the bridges, which depend on other elements such as attributes of ego and the bridging individuals. On the other hand the author shows that patriarchal family structures contribute decisively to blocking contacts and mobility. Although I was unable to explore this dimension in much depth, some of the interviews conducted in São Paulo also brought to light the relational problems affecting individuals, usually women, but also young men who live in patriarchal family structures.

The importance of heterogeneity and social bridges is also explored by Ferrand (2002), although in this case these are geographically defined in urban French communities. The author emphasizes the importance of studying what he calls the duality found on local relational systems: the presence of internal and external relations (local and non-local). His empirical concern is linked to the study of healthcare systems, especially the advice and support networks related to the issue in France. Both the conceptual model and the empirical material are linked to local communities, although the connection of the latter is understood to result from the personal connection of their components. For the author, therefore, the typical composition of micro-structures tells us about the meso-structures that connect the communities to wider social contexts. The author argues that personal networks can be classified according to their patterns of internal and external ties, generating four possibilities for the overlap between high/low and local/outside. The author analyzes the networks found in two communities, identifying six types of networks depending on the presence of local and non-local ties. The two communities present very different average compositions, the first characterized by intense internal and external connections and the second by scarce internal and external connections. These results display parallels with the findings presented in the following chapters.

Lonkila (2010) explores the importance of organizations in social support through networks, comparing personal networks in Russia and Finland. The results suggest the much larger centrality of ties with co-workers in Russia than in Finland. This finding is interpreted by the author as part of the legacy of socialist past, in line with the results presented by Ruan et al (1997) about social support among workers in China. The same kind of results was obtained by Lee, Ruan and Lai (2005) comparing ego-centered networks in Beijing and Hong Kong, although in their case the importance of kin appeared as a major characteristic of the networks.

3. Poverty, Segregation and Networks

But how are all these elements associated and how do they influence living conditions and urban poverty? I set out from the hypothesis that space and networks are structures that incorporate (or include) potential causal mechanisms for situations of poverty. These mechanisms mediate individuals' access to diverse opportunity structures and elements that affect their welfare.

By mechanism I am not referring to something concrete ontologically present in the networks or space, but to their place in our explanations, in the sense given to the concept by Tilly (2001 and 2005), Mahoney (2001) and Elster (1998). In this sense, mechanisms are regularities observed in social dynamics that, in the face of certain situations, lead to determined outcomes or cause specific processes. Constructing a mechanism-based explanation is intended to avoid simple correlations between processes, in the sense given to the term by Mahoney (2001).[11]

Tilly (2001) argues for the existence of three types of mechanisms: environmental, cognitive and relational. In the first case, we have elements that are connected to the contexts in which social life unfolds. Among these I include institutions, highlighted by the neo-institutionalist literature, and space, highlighted by urban and regional studies. Cognitive mechanisms are related to the perceptions and mental states of individuals and social groups, encompassing the various explanations derived from rational choice theory and their apparent violations, such as adaptative preferences and wishful thinking. Most of the elements classified by Elster (1998) as mechanisms can be included in this category. Finally, we have the so-called relational mechanisms, which make explanatory use of the relations between individuals, groups and organizations, as well as the overall patterns formed by these sets of relations, shaping social relations.[12]

Based on this conceptual framework of explanations, I argue that networks and segregation contain relational and environmental mechanisms (respectively) that mediate access and have a decisive influence on living conditions. As we have seen, numerous works have shown the importance of social segregation in space in producing and reproducing situations of poverty. Social networks, on the other

---

11   This point is developed in more detail by Eduardo Marques, "Leis gerais, explicações e mecanismos – para onde vão nossas análises?" in *Revista Brasileira de Ciências Sociais*, Vol 22, No 64, June 2007, from where I take the discussion presented here.

12   It is worth adding that Tilly's classification, in my opinion, sometimes confuses the ambition of the explanations (present in the three first) with the localization of the causal element (present in the mechanisms), since it is possible to argue that a given mechanism is so important that it represents the grounds for a general law. Consequently, explanations by mechanisms, though situated at mid-range levels, can aim for a high degree of generalization.

hand, by inserting individuals in diverse social contexts in differentiated form, also include mechanisms that might integrate (or not) individuals.

Given the variability of individual trajectories, it is to be expected that these processes affect people in very diverse ways, generating complexity in the cases and a high level of heterogeneity among individuals. Hence, the analytic strategy adopted here attempts to explore precisely this heterogeneity and to extract its consequences for living conditions.

In the cases of networks and segregation alike, access to opportunities depends on the functioning of the mechanisms present in these mid-range relational and environmental structures (in the sense defined by Tilly 2001). These mechanisms involve regularities associated with combination of attributes and processes, which function as causal 'triggers,' leading to situations of poverty and reproducing them. A better understanding of the effects of these mid-range social structures is the aim of this book.

Chapter 2
The Spaces and Poverties of São Paulo

This chapter presents the São Paulo metropolis and the localities studied, as well as the main procedures and tools adopted in the research. To help situate the reader, the first section briefly describes the São Paulo metropolitan region, focusing in particular on its urban structure, peripheries and segregation patterns. The second analyzes the recent dynamics of poverty and inequalities in the access to services and policies. The third section discusses the choice and localization of the studied fields, followed by the systemization of the methodological procedures employed. In the fifth section, I describe the study and in the last section compare the different locations researched based on indicators.

1. The São Paulo metropolis and its spaces

São Paulo is Brazil's largest city in in terms of population and one of the biggest in the world if we include its metropolitan region.[1] The region accounts for a substantial portion of the country's industrial production and services – in 2005 it concentrated 12.5 per cent of Brazil's GDP – although this concentration has declined over recent decades and, based on current trends, will continue to do so.

In spatial terms, the city is marked by an intense process of segregation. Although this dates from at least the beginning of the 20th century (Toledo 2004, Langenbuch 1971, Caldeira 2000), the current metropolitan configuration took shape in the period of rapid demographic growth and intense migration from rural to urban areas from the 1950s to the 1970s (Martine 1995). During this period, large waves of poor migrants arrived in the country's large urban centers in a process also experienced by other countries of Latin America (Gilbert 1996) and the Global South (Gilbert and Gugler 1992). The vast majority of this migrant population settled in peripheral urban regions lacking adequate public facilities and services, inhabiting self-built dwellings on patches of invaded land or areas bought from private developers who never actually completed the division of the lots (Kowarick 1979, Camargo 1976). Consequently, urban poverty in São Paulo (and in Brazil) was associated from the 1970s onwards with peripheries and their production.

These processes have been subject to intense scrutiny. The origin of this analytic tradition can be traced back to the debates on urban marginality and its critique by Latin American sociology, space being understood here as one of

---

1   See: http://esa.un.org/unup/index.asp?panel=2.

the structures associated with the processes responsible for reproducing Brazil's peripheral capitalism (Maricato 1977, Bonduki and Rolnik 1982). According to the analytic framework developed by this literature, poverty and space were to be explained conjointly through macro-interpretations that deployed systemic economic elements. The topic was studied in the 1980s by anthropological analyses that looked to incorporate the periphery's view of itself and the rest of the city (Durham 1988). During the same period, urban lots, neighborhoods and favelas were studied by numerous monographs analyzing housing production processes (Chinelli 1980, Santos 1985, Santos 1985, among others), as well as the 'new actors who entered on stage,' to use Sader's (1988) apt expression for the period's new urban social movements (Santos 1981 and 1982; Nunes 1986 and Jacobi 1989). At a different analytic level, studies like Santos and Bronstein (1978), Brasileiro (1976), Taschner (1990) and others shed light on general patterns of segregation in cities like São Paulo and Rio de Janeiro.

More recently the study of territorial structures and segregation in São Paulo has been updated with detailed empirical analyses using socio-economic data and techniques not available at the start of the debates (Villaça 1998, Bógus and Taschner 1999, Marques and Torres 2005). Measurements of city segregation have confirmed earlier qualitative analyses, revealing segregation levels by income (Torres 2005) and social classes (Marques, Bichir and Scalon 2010, Preteceille and Cardoso 2008) that are comparable to US cities (Jargowsky 1997) and much higher than the levels found in both European cities (Preteceille 2006; Maloutas 2007) and Asian cities (Yip 2008).

Existing analyses concur that São Paulo's territorial configuration is broadly radial and concentric with most amenities and wealthier social groups located in the center and the poorer groups in the peripheries (Marques and Torres 2005, Bógus and Taschner 1999, Preteceille and Cardoso 2008). This structure is present in a number of Brazil's metropolises (Villaça 1999) and has proven extremely stable (Marques, Bichir and Scalon 2010, Carvalho et al. 2004). The distribution can be observed in Map 1 below, which shows the distribution of the International Socio-Economic Index of Occupational Status (ISEI) calculated for the studied areas of São Paulo's metropolitan region for 2000. The ISEI is a status index widely used by the literature on social stratification (Ganzeboom, De Graaf and Treiman 1992) and measures the job attributes that convert an individual's education into income. In a scale construction for São Paulo, Scalon (2006) ranked occupations according to the indirect influence of education on income, taking into account the variables of education, occupation, age and income. The index ranges from zero to 100 with better social situations associated with higher values.

As can be seen, the distribution is indeed broadly radial and concentric, at least at an aggregate scale, with a reasonably large center – the so-called expanded center – which concentrates the wealthier social groups, surrounded by areas with worse social situations. Nevertheless, even at this scale and in relation to a complex indicator, various sub-centers can be observed outside the expanded center, especially in the West and Southeast of the region.

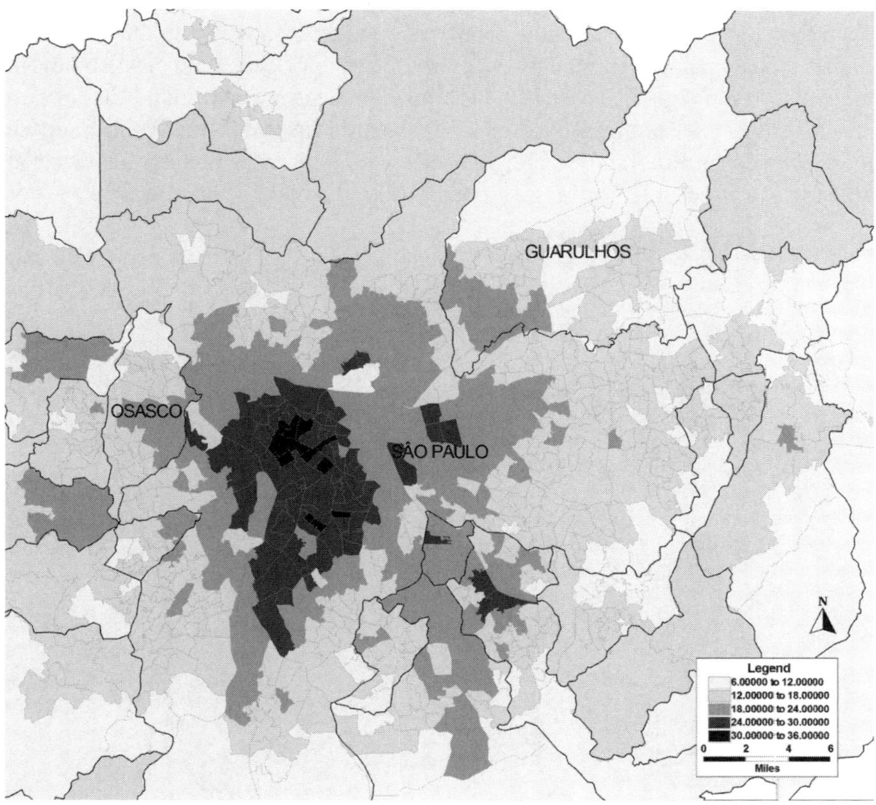

Map 1   Distribution of the International Socio-Economic Index of Occupational Status (ISEI), survey areas of the census, SPMR 2000. Source: Marques, Bichir and Scalon 2010.

Indeed a more detailed analysis suggests that this distribution overlaps with other important and wide-ranging dynamics. I highlight just two of the latter, involving social groups located at opposite ends of the social structure. The first concerns the existence within peripheral areas of wealthier groups with higher schooling and better insertion in the social structure. Most of these live in fortified enclaves or 'cities of walls,' to use Caldeira's apt expression (2000), prominent features not only in São Paulo, but also in numerous other large cities around the world, especially in the Americas (Marcuse 1997, Caldeira 2001, Salcedo and Torres 2004). Map 2 below illustrates the presence of these nuclei in the Western portion of the metropolis, showing the distribution of average per capita income of household head by census tract, which reveals a much more detailed territorial disintegration than in the previous map.[2] As we can see, along with the traditional higher income nucleus formed by the expanded center (located on the map next to the name of the city of São Paulo), high income areas are also found to the West and Northwest in the municipalities of Santana do Parnaíba and Cotia. Many of these patches correspond to wealthy closed condominiums, which are also visible, albeit in lower densities, in Map 1 to the West of the metropolitan region.

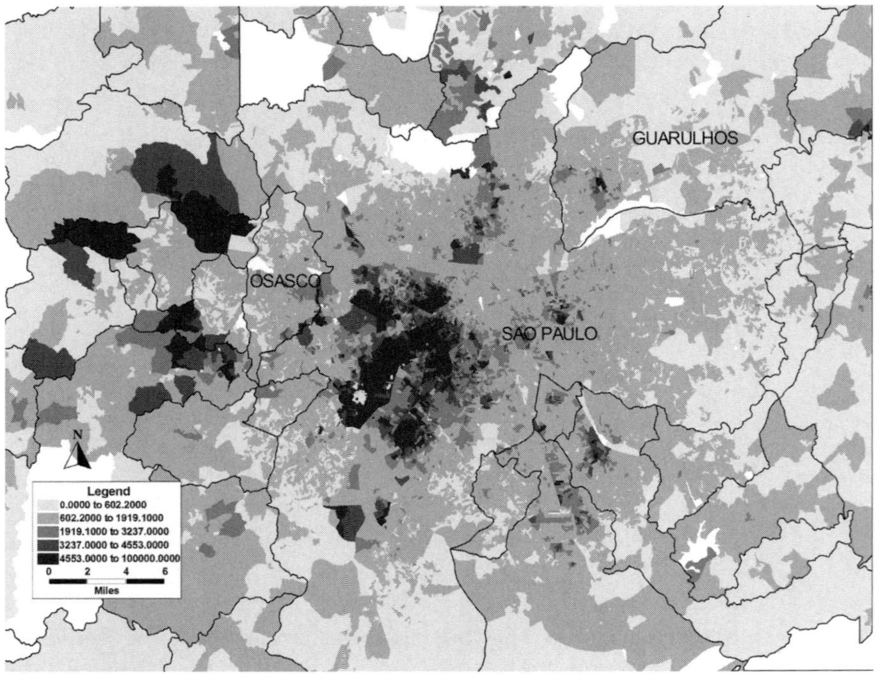

Map 2   **Distribution of average per capita income of household heads, census tracts, SPMR 2000. Source: Center of Metropolitan Studies and IBGE 2000.**

Note: At the time of the reference study, the minimum wage was R$ 151.

At the same time we can note the higher social diversity of peripheral spaces and other areas inhabited by low-income populations, matching the results of other studies (Marques and Torres 2005, Saraiva and Marques 2005, Taschner 2002 and Valladares and Preteceille 2000). As can be seen, the urban fabric reveals a mosaic-

---

2   The change in scale is central to understanding the diversity of social structure in space. However since the existing data does not enable disaggregation of the occupational data used in Map 1, income data must be used to get a sense of the degree of heterogeneity involved.

like pattern when analyzed in closer detail. This diversity has been generated by improvements in the average living conditions of the vast majority of spaces, albeit combined with the maintenance of highly vulnerable areas, though these are more localized than previously (Cem/SAS 2004, Bichir, Torres and Ferreira 2005 and Torres and Marques 2001). This growing diversity runs counter to the description of poverty and its spaces predominant in the international literature, which tends to consider the phenomenon in a homogenizing form (Gilbert and Gugler 1992, Davis 2006). On this point, it seems to be essential to consider peripheries (Vetter 1981) and favelas (Valladares and Preteceille 2000) in the plural when speaking about contemporary territories of urban poverty in Brazilian metropolises.

2. Poverty and the access to public services in Brazil and São Paulo

But how can we characterize the dynamic of poverty and inequalities in access to policies in Brazil and São Paulo over the recent period? Since we shall be discussing the poor section of the urban population in the rest of this book, it is important to situate the recent dynamics of the living conditions framing the situation under study.

The last fifteen years in Brazil have seen a reduction in poverty and extreme poverty as measured by income, albeit with some significant variations (Rocha 2001). The data suggests a pronounced fall in the proportion of poor people immediately following the economic stabilization achieved by the Plano Real,[3] dropping to 33.8 per cent of the population in 1995, followed by stable levels until 2003. Thereafter the proportion of poor and extremely poor people began to fall again, reducing to 23.6 per cent in 2007 (Rocha 2006b). Metropolitan poverty, however, rose significantly between 1995 and 2003, increasing from 21.9 per cent to 28.7 per cent (Rocha 2006a). At the epicenter of this dynamic was São Paulo, which experienced the sharpest rise in poor people between the mid-1990s and the first years of the new century, increasing from 14.1 per cent of the population in 1995 to 24.2 per cent in 2003. At the same time, unemployment and informality in the job market rose considerably and average wages declined, all due to the restructuring of the economy in the 1990s.[4]

From 2003 onwards, however, the proportion of poor and extremely poor people again began to decrease significantly – falling from 24.2 per cent in 2003 to 15.7 per cent in 2008.[5] Considering a slightly different poverty line, Soares (2010)

---

3 After a long period of very high inflation with some bursts of hyperinflation and several failed macroeconomic plans, the Real Plan managed to stabilize the economy in 1994.

4 Stabilization of the Brazilian economy was accompanied by a substantial opening up to foreign investment and trade, leading to intense economic restructuring in the 1990s.

5 Despite these changes, studies such as Ribas and Machado ("Distinguishing chronic poverty from transient poverty in Brazil: developing a model for pseudo-panel data." Brasilia, International Poverty Centre 2007. See: http://www.undp-povertycentre.

found an even lower poverty rate in 2009 – 13.7 per cent, despite the effects of the international crisis.[6] Unsurprisingly, the economy had returned to growth and formal jobs, while wages and average income had increased. Income inequalities showed the same steady downward trend from a Gini Coefficient of 0.592 in 2002 to 0.538 in 2009 (Soares 2010).

However during periods of rising poverty and declining poverty alike, social indicators improved continuously and apparently paradoxically as economic conditions became worse. The question displays similarities to the issues debated in the 1980s, considered by many the 'lost decade.' The problem raised then was explaining how a period marked by bouts of recession and uncertain economic growth (Fiori and Kornis 1994) could register such pronounced improvements in the social indicators (Guimarães and Tavares 1994 and Tavares and Monteiro 1994). For some authors this apparent paradox was caused by progress at the political level after the return to democracy and the presence of powerful social movements. For others, the inertia of the military regime's policies at least partially explained the advances (Faria 1992, Silva 1992). In general, though, the debate revealed the limitations of using explanatory models that derive social conditions directly from economic dynamics.

The 1990s followed a similar pattern, albeit with its own nuances. Democratic freedoms had already been experienced for some time, and most of the public policy systems inherited from the military regime had been substantially reformed (Arretche 2000 and 2001). On the other hand, the changes affecting the job market were much more intense than in the 1980s, driven by the macro-economic adjustments and currency stabilization programs implemented in the second half of the decade. As a result, unemployment levels increased and job protection became much more fragile (Hoffmann and Mendonça 2003 and Guimarães 2009a), leading to an expansion of the employment services sector (Guimarães 2009b). Finally, average wages tended to fall, making the shifts in the job market extremely dramatic and negative in relation to practically all indicators (Hoffmann and Mendonça 2003 and Baltar 2002). All these processes tended to have a stronger impact on the country's most important economic centers, in particular São Paulo. On the other hand, when the Brazilian economy started to expand once more from 2003 onwards, the process was again more intense in the most dynamic centers, now restructured. It is worth highlighting that studies such as Marques, Bichir and Scalon (2010) suggest that despite these intense negative transformations, São Paulo's social structure remained practically constant between 1991 and 2000.

From the viewpoint of access to services, though, studies have shown a very large increase in the coverage provided, moving towards the universalization

---

org) suggest that the vast majority (73 per cent) of relative urban poverty between 1995 and 2003 remained chronic with the same individuals still living in this condition.

6   Soares, S. "Pnad 2009 - Primeiras análises: distribuição de renda entre 1995 e 2009." Comunicado Ipea, 63 2010. See:http://www.ipea.gov.br/portal/images/stories/PDFs/comunicado/101005_comunicadoipea63.pdf.

of basic public services, despite the maintenance of pronounced inequalities, especially in terms of quality (Torres, Bichir and Pavez 2006). Similar findings were obtained by Figueiredo, Torres and Bichir (2006) who, using data on access among the poorest 40 per cent of the municipality of São Paulo, also observed increased access to policies and services even among this sector.

Another important set of changes with a major impact on poverty in the region have been the demographic transformations under way over recent decades. The intense processes of migration from rural to urban areas that were once a dominant feature of Brazil's population dynamic from the 1940s to the 70s have tended to decelerate sharply in the years since (Martine 1995), leading to fairly low rates of demographic growth in the large cities, including São Paulo, over the last few decades (Baeninger 2011). The intra-urban dynamic, however, indicates a more complex process at work. The São Paulo metropolitan region showed negative growth in central areas as early as the 1980s and more intensely in the 1990s (Perillo and Perdigão 1998 and Januzzi and Januzzi 2002), but simultaneously extremely high rates in very peripheral areas located in the urban outskirts (Torres 2005a). Another new phenomenon over recent decades has been the resurgence of international migration to São Paulo, with immigrants now arriving from Latin American countries (Lazo 2003). Birth rates, on the other hand, continue the downward trend recorded over recent decades (Seade 2000 and Berquó and Cavenaghi 2006), making the age structure significantly older and less youthful (Seade 2000). In parallel, family configurations have become much more diverse (Seade 1995 and Baeninger 2011) with somewhat contradictory effects on social vulnerability.

To complete this panoramic overview of social conditions in São Paulo, it would be impossible not to highlight the issue of urban violence. This is the area exhibiting the biggest decline in social conditions in São Paulo, as in Brazil's other large cities. Violence has become an omnipresent dimension of people's life experiences in peripheral urban spaces, for some authors comprising one of the key elements mediating the relations between residents of these areas and the rest of the city, as well as their relationship to politics (Feltran 2008 2009a and 2009b). For others, the boundaries between the legal, informal and illegal now have to be reformulated (Silva Telles and Cabannes 2006). In the last few years some indicators relating to violence have also improved, although it is probably too early for us to affirm any consistent trend. However the phenomenon has become increasingly complex and multifaceted, even reconfiguring the limits placed on the State in terms of its control of parts of the metropolitan territory, now disputed with agents and organizations from the criminal world (Miraglia 2011). As a result, strategies that penalize the poorest sectors of the population and stigmatize their spaces are increasingly commonplace, in the sense attributed by Wacquant (2001 2007 and 2008). It is worth adding, though, that the coincidence of these strategies with the process of consolidating democracy and asserting rights has lent particular hues to the phenomenon in Brazil. Hence, although police violence is overwhelmingly present, a close reading of the accounts contained in works such as Feltran (2008) and Kowarick (2009) suggest that this coexists and vies for space with rights recognition processes, making the phenomenon an open field of conflicts with competing vectors and non-uniform results.

Although summarizing the complex social scenario in São Paulo is a far from easy task, the dynamic of living conditions has clearly altered substantially over recent decades due to the intense transformations in the work space, in migration patterns and intra-urban dynamics and in the roles played by the State, family and market in ensuring the well-being of individuals. These processes combine to diversify situations of urban poverty, as well as rendering their spaces in the metropolis more complex in terms of segregation, access to services and housing conditions. The outcomes of these processes sometimes point in incoherent directions, but in various aspects they contradict the homogenizing representations of urban poverty dominant in the international literature on São Paulo and other cities of the Global South and still found in debates at national level. The fields chosen for study in the following chapters look to capture this heterogeneity.

3. Research strategies

In order to explore this heterogeneity and analyze the effects of spatial segregation and personal networks in conjunction, locations with fairly distinct forms of urban insertion were selected for the network survey. On the other hand, the localization of the middle class individuals interviewed was not controlled and almost all of them were found dispersed across the expanded center.

In terms of research design, locations were chosen so as to explore the configuration of elements, as well as their ordering and combination, rather than be representative of the general population at a statistical level (Ragin 1987, Tilly 1992a and Skocpol 1984). Thus although the networks surveyed represent a sample of the population living in poverty in São Paulo (from which there is no significant bias, as we shall see at the end of this chapter), this sample is not intended to be statistically representative of the population as a whole. Consequently sample expansion techniques are not used to determine, for instance, how many thousands of people in the city possess networks of a particular type. Neither is there any intention to cover all the urban situations, although the choice of study locations has attempted to represent broadly the types of segregation and housing solutions associated with urban poverty in São Paulo.

This research design aims to capture what Ragin (1987) calls the 'multiple conjunctural causation' typical of the social world, in which experiments can seldom be constructed, causes almost never act in isolation and the effects of such causes are always context dependent, even potentially reversing their direction. In fact, given the specificity of the phenomenon, I believe that this is the only analytic approach to allow a clear understanding of both poor people and poverty itself, following Mingione's differentiation (1996). The capacity to generalize results in this type of design, on the other hand, is a product of the saturation of the combinations of explanations in the cases (Ragin 1987 and Tilly 1992a), which is why the choice of cases takes into account the different existing situations in terms of segregation, access to services and housing conditions.

Approximately thirty personal networks were surveyed in each study location and in the middle class control group. The research sites were chosen from areas with high concentrations of poverty previously mapped by studies using geoprocessing and statistical analysis of socioeconomic data from demographic censuses (Cem 2004 Bichir, Torres and Ferreira 2005, Saraiva and Marques 2005, Marques and Torres 2005).

Map 3 below illustrates the location of these areas. In order to show the pattern of spatial occupation and the degree of segregation of the fields, the map highlights in gray the areas with a population density of over 35 inhabitants per hectare, using as units of analysis the census tracts of the 2000 Census.[7]

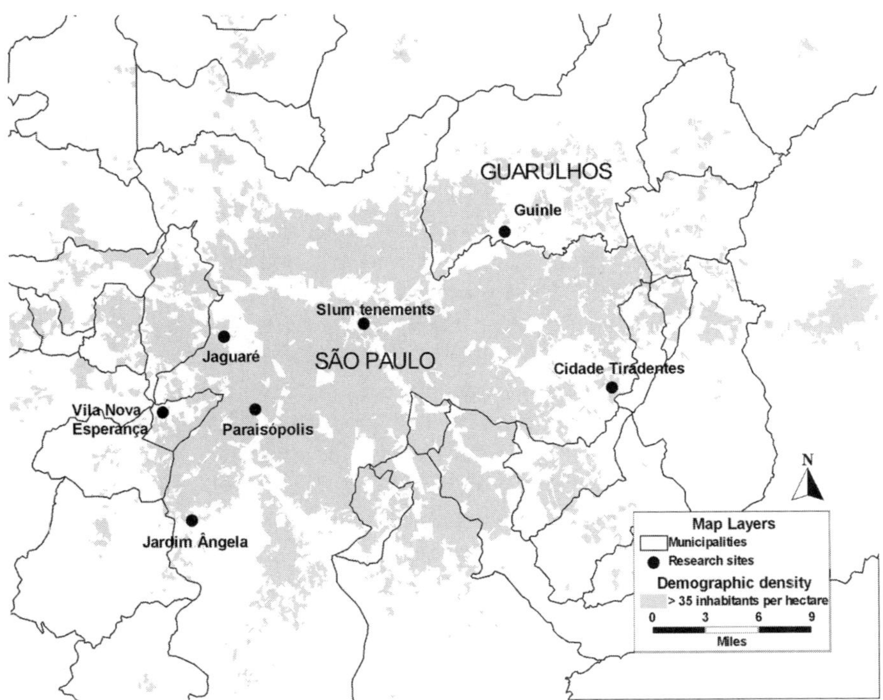

Map 3   **São Paulo Metropolitan Region (research sites indicated). Source: Author, based on cartographic databases of Center for Metropolitan Studies 2007.**

---

7   This density is fairly low and merely aims to eliminate the spaces with very sparse levels of occupation. To give an idea, the density corresponds to a 100m x 100m square occupied by less than 35 people.

As we can see, although the region encompasses a wide geographic area containing 39 municipalities, the territory cover by a relatively dense and continuous urban fabric is smaller, although still vast. Lower density areas within the more central continuous dense area correspond to parks or large institutional areas, as well as the valleys of the Tietê river (running east-west) and the Pinheiros (south-north). The map also indicates the names of some municipalities to help orientate the reader. As the graphic scale shows, the distances involved are substantial and the distribution of the research sites covers several different types of macrosegregation.

The study examines individuals' perceptions of their networks using cognitive-type data (Marsden 2005). As explained earlier, these representations give access to relational structures in the form mobilized by the individuals concerned. However this creates a difficulty concerning the duration and the persistence of ties. The research focuses on each individual's network at the present moment, even though the contacts may have been constructed for some time and others may even be latent or 'asleep.' Here too the perception of individuals concerning their ties is crucial and, as along as the individual believes that this tie can be activated, he or she can be cited as participating in the network. As we shall see later, when I returned to the interviewees a year after the first meetings some of them opted to include or remove some nodes from their networks, indicating that important individuals had not been cited in the first interview because they had fallen out, moved away from the neighborhood or lost contact momentarily, for example. In this sense, ties can remain latent for a certain period of time without being excluded from the network. Their reactivation depends on the time lapsed, the intensity of the relation and, in part, the type of connection involved – family ties last almost the person's entire life, while strong bonds of friendship last less when latent, though more than casual acquaintances. Methodologically, though, we can only gain access to the ties cited by the interviewee, influenced by cognitive elements that form their perceptions at that given moment.[8]

To enable a detailed analysis of sociability, I asked the interviewees to classify the individuals in their networks according to the spheres in which social encounters take place. By sphere I mean a region of sociability generally organized around some process of specialization (functional, practice-based, cultural, idea-based, etc.). These spheres are a product of the specialization of social activities in a broad sense, including circles of interest (discussion circles and those centered on specific practices), circles of sociability and conviviality (groups of friends) and specific institutions (like the family). In concrete terms, the spheres include certain sets of individuals and organizations, the relations established between each other (of various types and in constant transformation), as well as particular identities, sets of signs and discursive patterns in the acceptation given by Mische and White (1998) and White (1995). In this sense, spheres bear a similarity to the

---

8   Given our research questions and the length of the interviews, I opted not to look for data related to strength or frequency in the quantitative analysis. These elements are discussed in Chapters 6 and 7 based on the information obtained in the qualitative interviews.

network domains of the latter authors, although they aim to describe more specific, structured and long-lasting contexts. Perhaps we could say then that spheres, in the sense defined here, include the more stable versions of the *netdoms* described by Mische (2007). In some cases spheres may overlap through the existence of individuals who take part in more than one sphere of sociability simultaneously.

The delimitation of spheres does not correspond directly to the type of ties involved, nor to their strength, but relates instead to the social spaces recognized by individuals in their activities and sociability. A neighborhood sphere, for example, does not include all the neighbors, nor necessarily only neighbors. It includes all those individuals who interviewees took to be found together within a space of their sociability that they themselves defined as a neighborhood. This is, therefore, the neighborhood as a cognitively understood social space that does not necessarily correspond to a neighborhood in the sense of a measurable physical distance as in Wellman (2001).

Spheres are also distinguished from the entry contexts of the nodes in the network, information that was also included as an attribute to be surveyed during the interviews. The context tells us how a given node entered into ego's sociability, as researched by Grossetti (2005):by chance, in the neighborhood, after being presented by someone, or within the family, for example. This information attempts to capture the ways through which individuals acquire nodes and expand their networks.

The data was obtained in two rounds of interviews directly at the sites, conducted both on weekdays and at weekends. The first round focused on quantitative information and the second on qualitative data and included interviewees selected from the first round. The main technical procedures involved in the data collection are described in detail in the methodological appendix at the end of this book.

4. Research locations

This section provides an overview of the studied locations in order to situate the reader in terms of their main characteristics. At the same time, the section exemplifies the diversity of urban situations present in São Paulo, both in terms of segregation and in what concerns housing conditions.

a. Central city tenements

The tenements where interviews were conducted are located in the center of the city of São Paulo. They occupy large 19th century houses typically in poor physical conditions and poorly adapted to functioning as collective housing units. Each family occupies just a single room, and each tenement typically houses from ten to 20 families, some located below street level in basements not originally intended to be inhabited. Bathrooms, kitchens and laundry rooms are all collective.
Privacy is something entirely absent and conflicts are frequent between family members and neighbors. The overall environmental and health conditions are

Photograph 1   Corridor, Central city tenements. Credit: Lúcio Kowarick, 2008.

probably the worst among the chosen research sites, especially in the basements where it is very common to encounter rooms with no windows, very low ceilings and regularly subject to flooding. In terms of access to jobs and facilities, however, the location is much more favorable than in the majority of the favelas and irregular settlements. As a result some interviewees had been living in tenements for decades, even paying rents of up to 1.5 minimum salaries per month for a room (with no bathroom or kitchen).

Photograph 2   Collective laundry and bathroom, Central city tenements. Credit: Lúcio Kowarick, 2008.

b. Vila Nova Jaguaré

Vila Nova Jaguaré is a favela of around 10,900 people (in 2000)[9] located in the expanded center of the metropolis. It has been occupied since the 1950s when the neighborhood corresponded to an industrial area. Today the region is composed mainly of middle and upper class neighborhoods, although the direct vicinity of Jaguaré still contains a number of warehouses. By bus it is possible to reach the center of São Paulo in one hour and ten minutes during off-peak hours, according to information provided by the Municipality of São Paulo.[10]

---

9   This section uses demographic data from the 2000 IBGE Census.

10   See: http://200.99.150.164/PlanOperWeb/ The official information almost certainly underestimates the journey time: however I have decided to include this data for all research locations so that the reader can obtain some sense of the relative distances involved.

Photograph 3   Consolidaded área, Vila Nova Jaguaré. Credit: Encarnación Moya, 2008.

Photograph 4　　Shacks, Vila Nova Jaguaré. Credit: Encarnación Moya, 2008.

Jaguaré occupies a small hill next to the valley of the Pinheiros River, the location of a major highway forming part of the primary metropolitan ring road. A large favela, it is served by a system of streets, some of them of official width. The area shows considerable internal diversity: the higher areas have better housing and infrastructures and concentrate most of the local commerce and public facilities, while the lower areas possess very poor living and environmental conditions. The regions next to the highway exhibit the worse situations, frequently subject to flooding and possessing extremely poor housing conditions, typified by narrow winding alleys in which sewage flows in the open air between wooden shacks and where rats and other disease-transmitting vectors are a constant presence. The municipality has recently been carrying out urban improvement projects in this area. The interviewees live in both the best and the worst areas.

c. Paraisópolis

Paraisópolis (meaning Paradise City) is one of the largest favelas in São Paulo with a population of approximately 34,000 inhabitants in 2000. It is the only large-scale favela located on private land (Bueno 2000) and adjoins one of the richest neighborhoods in the city, Morumbi. Because of this location, Paraisópolis receives several social projects from both the public sector and from business

Photograph 5 Consolidated area, Paraisópolis. Credit: Eduardo Marques, 2007.

Photograph 6   High slope area, Paraisópolis. Credit: Eduardo Marques, 2007.

philanthropy,[11] while its inhabitants have particular access to low qualification service jobs (Almeida e D'Andrea 2005). Due in part to these projects, the favela has an impressive network of local organizations, although political participation is low, around the average for the city's low income population (Gurza Lavalle and Castello 2004). The distance from the favela to the center of São Paulo by bus is one hour during off-peak hours (taking two buses), according to official data.

The favela began to be occupied in the 1930, through invasions of a private development, resulting in a quite regular street layout and relatively easy internal access for cars, buses and trucks. Paraisópolis occupies a large and heterogeneous area with conditions ranging from areas which present very good quality housing, low population density, service infrastructures, commerce and easy accessibility to much poorer and more vulnerable regions located on very steep slopes or by the side of ditches that become small rivers during the rainy season. These differences are expressed in the large disparity in property values. According to Baltrusis (2005), while houses in the best areas of the favela were sold for as much as R$ 11,500 (around US$ 5,000), the average price in the most vulnerable regions was

---

11   See for example: http://www.einstein.br/voluntariado/, http://www.portoseguro. org.br/comunidade.asp, and http://www.terra.com.br/istoedinheiro/314/empresasdobem.

Photograph 7   Consolidated area, Vila Nova Esperança. Credit: Eduardo Marques, 2007.

R$ 4,900 (US$ 2,100), while a wooden shack located almost in a creek cost just R$ 100 (US$ 45).

The interviews included people who live in both the best and the worst areas.

d. Vila Nova Esperança

Vila Nova Esperança is a small favela – home to just around 1,000 inhabitants in 2000 – situated on the Western outskirts of the metropolis, in a peri-urban area situated on a small hill. The area is quite isolated and located about 1.5 kilometers from the nearest bus stop. The inhabitants use the public services and the commercial facilities of the neighboring low middle-class region. Not counting the time needed to reach the bus stop and wait for the bus, it takes two hours (using three different buses) to reach the city center of the city, again according to official figures.

According to the interviewees, the occupation began some ten years ago, mainly with families who paid rent in the surrounding neighborhood. Today most of the favela is composed of good quality concrete houses, although an area of expansion (basically invading the surrounding forest) is made up of wooden shacks and lacks even basic infrastructure. The whole favela faces serious problems with electricity provision, relying on illegal hookups to the grid which are continually removed

Photograph 8   Expansion area, Vila Nova Esperança. Credit: Eduardo Marques, 2007.

by the electricity company and reconnected by the residents. The favela lacks any community organization whatsoever.

e. Housing projects in Cidade Tiradentes

Two things impress the new visitor to Cidade Tiradentes: its size and its distance from the center of São Paulo. Tiradentes is a complex of housing projects built between 1975 and 1997 by the municipal government[12]. In 2000 these constructions were home to around 160,000 people, plus 30,000 inhabitants in the 19 favelas located within and between the housing projects, as well as in tenements inside them.[13]

The complex is located in the far Eastern part of the metropolis, where the Municipal Housing Company, Cohab, basically transformed rural land into urban fabric. In many ways it is the most paradigmatic example of the housing policies implemented by the military government and continued ever since: the production

---

12   See Kazuo, Nakano. "Quatro COHABs da zona leste de São Paulo: território, poder e segregação. São Paulo: Fau/Usp," MSc dissertation 2002 and information on the websites of the Municipality of São Paulo and Cohab-SP.

13   See Internet: http://www.centrodametropole.org.br/t_transf_bases.html and Internet: http://portal.prefeitura.sp.gov.br/secretarias/habitacao/departamentos/habi/0001.

**Photograph 9   General view of part of the complex, Cidade Tirandentes.
Credit: Eduardo Marques, 2007.**

of large-scale housing projects of new units for financed sale located in the extreme peripheries of Brazilian cities.[14] Until the end of the 1990s, the region had almost no public facilities, but under the most recent local administrations Tiradentes received a substantial set of investments. Today the region has 75 elementary schools 18 high schools, ten primary healthcare units and one general hospital. In 2002 Tiradentes became a sub-municipality, with some autonomy in relation to delivery of services. But although the problems of service provisions have been reduced, the lack of jobs continues to be a major issue for the area's inhabitants, who usually work in the center of São Paulo. The distance to the city center is 32 kilometers, reachable by a two-hour bus trip (using three different buses) during off-peak hours, according to official data.

---

14   See Ermínia Maricato, *Política habitacional no regime militar* (Rio de Janeiro: Paz e Terra 1987) on the national policies of the military regime and Eduardo Marques and Camila Saraiva, "As políticas de habitação social, a segregação e as desigualdades sociais na cidade," (in Marques, E. and Torres, H. eds. *São Paulo: segregação, pobreza e desigualdades sociais*. São Paulo, Editora SENAC 2005) on recent housing policies in São Paulo.

Photograph 10   Housing project, Cidade Tirandentes. Credit: Eduardo Marques, 2007.

f. Jardim Ângela

Jardim Ângela is the most representative of the studied sites in terms of its mixture of highly segregated favelas and irregular settlements, typical of the peripheries of large Brazilian metropolises. According to the municipal authorities, it takes one hour and 45 minutes to reach the center of São Paulo from the region (on three different buses) during off-peak hours. The studied area includes both a favela and an irregular settlement.

Settlement of the area began in 1990 with the subdivision of a large plot into small parcels of land, sold by a private developer with the promise that legal approval would be obtained. After a while, though, the developer disappeared without completing the infrastructures necessary for approval by the local authorities, resulting in irregular land tenure, not to mention poor physical conditions. After years of mobilization by local inhabitants, the settlement received several infrastructural works and at the time of the interviews it was in the process of being legalized by the municipal government. The area's history is very similar to many others described since the 1970s (Kowarick 1979) but compressed into a shorter period of time. While the settlements started under the military regime received urban infrastructures some 25 or 30 years after the occupation, the more recent settlements have tended to be completed with a 10-year time span.

Photograph 11   Favela, Jardim Ângela. Credit: Eduardo Marques, 2007.

Photograph 12   Irregular settlement, Jardim Ângela. Credit: Eduardo Marques, 2007.

The favela began at the same time as the settlement and is located in below it at the bottom of a valley, next to a large creek. The houses tend to be of good quality, mainly because the worst ones were recently demolished by the municipal government to enable canalization of the creek and urban improvements to the favela. Although the new construction provided essential urban infrastructures, a substantial part of the remaining houses are now at a lower level than the streets and experience serious humidity problems.

g. *Guinle*[15]

Guinle is a small favela located within an industrial district of Guarulhos Municipality, very close to major highways connecting São Paulo to Rio de Janeiro and Belo Horizonte. The interesting characteristic of this site is precisely the high presence of low paid jobs within walking distance of the complex's industries, despite its high level of macrosegregation. The center of Guarulhos can be reached in a half hour bus ride, though it takes one hour and 30 minutes on three separate buses to travel to the center of São Paulo during off-peak hours.

Photograph 13   General view, Guinle. Credit: Rafael Soares, 2007.

---

15   At this site, the interviews were conducted by Rafael Soares alone as part of his MSc dissertation ("Estado, segregação e desigualdade: Um estudo sobre o impacto das políticas de habitação a partir das redes sociais da favela Guinle, Guarulhos." São Paulo: Dcp/Usp, MSc dissertation in political science 2009). My thanks to the researcher for making his raw data available for the present analysis.

In 2007 and 2008, the municipality transferred Guinle's population to a highly segregated housing project, a process analyzed by Soares (2009). By this time Guinle had around 5,000 households.

Photograph 14   House, Guinle Credit: Rafael Soares, 2007.

5. Comparing research sites

This section provides a comparative overview of the conditions of the residential locations occupied by the individuals included in the study, based on social indicators that map the diversity of conditions encountered.[16] The table below presents this information.

---

16   Information was taken from the IBGE 2000 Population Census produced by a Geographic Information System based on the census tracts for the areas where the interviewees live. The data was generated by Renata Gonçalves, who I thank for her help. The average data corresponds to seven tracts (Jaguaré), one tract (Cortiços), one tract (Vila Nova Esperança), seven tracts (Paraisópolis), fifteen tracts (Tiradentes), twelve tracts (Ângela) and two tracts (Guinle) respectively. The data does not correspond, therefore, to the populations of the areas studied (as in the case of the information cited in the previous sections of this chapter), nor to the interviewees (as in the case of the information cited in the following chapters).

Table 1 Selected indicators for the residential locations of interviewees 2000.

Local	Type of locale	% of people from 0 to nine years	% of people from ten to 19 years	% of people 60 years and over	% with public water supply	% with public sewage	% with garbage collection services	average years of study of household head	% illiterate	% household head without income or income equal to or lower than three minimum wages	% of female household heads
Cortiços	Slum tenements	16.5	13.6	4.3	99.5	99.5	100.0	5.9	6.4	42.6	24.0
Nova Jaguaré	favela	24.1	21.6	3.4	99.7	(*)	(*)	4.1	8.1	78.3	28.0
Paraisópolis	favela	25.4	20.6	1.9	99.8	38.3	65.8	4.0	9.8	74.1	22.2
Vila Nova Esperança	favela	26.5	18.9	2.2	65.2	66.1	80.3	5.1	5.8	58.1	16.1
Cidade Tiradentes	Housing projects	19.4	22.1	3.7	99.8	99.5	99.9	6.5	4.0	52.9	32.3
Jardim Ângela	Favela and irregular settlement	22.9	19.8	2.8	98.5	45.5	76.1	5.6	6.1	58.3	18.6
Guinle	favela	27.2	21.8	3.1	100.0	94.8	100.0	4.2	12.0	79.4	17.9

*Sour*ce: 2000 Population Census, IBGE.

Note (*): These variables showed a large discrepancy and were not considered.

As we can see, the youngest age structure is found in the four favelas and the oldest in Cidade Tiradentes and in the slum areas of the central zone. As was to be expected, the worst infrastructural conditions are found in the most recently occupied favela – Vila Nova Esperança – followed by the other favelas. The better urban conditions are found in Tiradentes and Guinle. The overall schooling level is very low, but varies between the worst levels in Guinle, Jaguaré and

Paraisópolis and the best in the slum areas and, in particular, Cidade Tiradentes. By way of comparison, the average schooling of household heads in the São Paulo metropolitan region as a whole in 2000 was approximately 7.5 years. Consequently all the studied areas have worse schooling levels.

The relative presence of household heads also varies considerably, with the best situations being encountered in the slums and Cidade Tiradentes and the worst in the favelas of Paraisópolis, Jaguaré and Guinle. Again to provide a benchmark for comparison, the presence of household heads in the favelas located within the São Paulo municipal region in 2000 was estimated by Saraiva and Marques (2005) at 73.2 per cent. Hence three favelas show a situation very close to (and slightly worse than) the average for the favelas in their municipalities. Although extremely segregated, Vila Nova Esperança has a much better level than the average with 58.3 per cent.[17] Finally the number of female household heads varies between the ratio encountered in Cidade Tiradentes and Jaguaré of around one third of families and the ratio observed in Guinle and Vila Nova Esperança of a fifth of families.

General speaking, therefore, the population with better social and urban conditions is found in the housing complexes of Cidade Tiradentes, followed by the slum tenements and Vila Nova Esperança. Among the locations included in the study, the population with the worst conditions is Guinle followed by Jaguaré and Paraisópolis. Here it is worth emphasizing that Vila Nova Esperança shows average conditions among the field sites, despite the area's urban localization being much more segregated. This illustrates the fact that the relationship between segregation and poverty is complex and prevents any direct inferences from being made. On the other hand, as we shall see, the networks of Vila Nova Esperança tend to be less local than those of other favelas, despite its high level of segregation.

---

17   Camila Saraiva and Eduardo Marques, "A condição social dos habitantes de Favelas." In: Marques, E. and Torres, H. (eds.). *São Paulo: segregação, pobreza urbana e desigualdades sociais.* São Paulo: Senac, p.143-167 2005) also produced a classification of the favelas according to their average conditions, resulting in five groups. The income of the three favelas in this study would place Vila Nova Esperança among the favelas with better conditions, but would place Paraisópolis and Jaguaré in the second best group and Guinle in the second worst group.

Chapter 3

What are the Networks of Metropolitan Poor Really Like?

This chapter presents the main features of the personal networks under study and analytically explores their regularities, considering social attributes. The topic is relevant to the descriptions contained in the following chapters, since it comprises an exploratory analysis of the association between attributes and relational patterns. As we saw in the first chapter, these two sets of elements influence each other mutually. But since in this chapter I analyze only associations, our focus remains for now on the analysis of correlations (Mahoney 2001), while the effects of the networks will be analyzed in the following chapters, and their mechanisms and transformations in Chapter 7.

The chapter begins with a presentation of the interviewees, firstly those individuals living in poverty, followed by the group selected from the middle class. The second section defines the network indicators utilized and discusses the overall features of the analyzed networks. We will see that attributes and networks alike reinforce the pattern of diversity within poverty highlighted earlier. Next, in the third section, I discuss the main associations between networks and socio-demographic attributes.

1. Profile of the interviewees

Two hundred and nine individuals were interviewed, comprising approximately 57 per cent women and 43 per cent men, distributed in a roughly even pattern in the field sites. The average age of the interviewees is 36 years and varies very little between the areas, though the ages range from the age of 12 to 77. The average schooling of the interviewees was low – 6.1 years of study, but varied substantially between 4.7 years in the central slums and 8.7 years in Cidade Tiradentes. The average monthly family per capita income of the interviewees was R$ 271 (around US$ 160), but varied between R$ 12 (with 48 cases of incomes equal to or lower than R$ 100) and R$ 1,600 (four cases of incomes equal to or higher than R$ 1,000). The average family income was R$ 1,125 (around US$ 660).[1]

---

1   It is worth noticing that I assumed family income to be the income of all the individuals in a household, since social situations and poverty in particular, are produced within families and not just through individual dynamics. Likewise, personal networks generate forms of access that can be used not only by individuals but also by members

Most of the interviewees were migrants – 70 per cent, although this proportion varied between 86 per cent in Jardim Ângela and just 33 per cent in Cidade Tiradentes. Among migrants, most (71 per cent) had arrived in São Paulo more than ten years ago and just 16 per cent had arrived during the last five years. The most recent migrants tend to live in the slum tenements and in Vila Nova Esperança, a recently occupied favela, where around 24 per cent of migrants arrived five years ago or sooner. Conversely, the most well-established localities are Jaguaré and Cidade Tiradentes where 83 and 80 per cent, respectively, of the migrant interviewees had arrived in São Paulo ten years ago or longer. Overall this migratory data is in keeping with the slowdown in migration to São Paulo's metropolitan region over recent decades (Januzzi and Januzzi 2002), even in districts occupied by the poorest sections of the population in the more central areas. On the other hand the high presence of migrants in one of the most peripheral favelas – Vila Nova Esperança - confirms analyses such as Torres (2005), which suggest continued growth through recent migration in localized spots in the so-called urban outskirts.

Considering marital status, 56 per cent of the interviewees had partners at the time of the interview, a proportion that varied considerably between 70 per cent in Jaguaré and 43 per cent in Cidade Tiradentes. Among those in stable conjugal relations, 34 per cent had lived for less than ten years with their partner and 19 per cent for less than five years, indicating a significant proportion of recent relationships. Approximately a third of people with partners (31 per cent) were first presented to the latter by other individuals (through networks), while 28 per cent met their future partners locally 12 per cent in leisure activities and just 8 per cent via the family. The vast majority of couples met in São Paulo, while just 30 per cent met their partner in the area from where they originally migrated, indicating that even for most migrants, nuclear families were formed in the São Paulo metropolis.

In terms of religious belief, 63 per cent of interviewees identify themselves as Catholic 24 per cent as Evangelical and 12 per cent as non-religious. The largest proportion of Catholics was in Jaguaré (87 per cent) and of Evangelicals in Cidade Tiradentes (40 per cent). When church attendance is analyzed, however, 43 per cent frequented services at least once a fortnight and 43 per cent very rarely or never. Comparing the religions, attendance among Evangelicals was much higher (69 per cent go to temples more than once a fortnight) than Catholics (just 34 per cent). However, even among those identifying themselves as Evangelical 17 per cent claimed that they never or very rarely went to church.

In terms of dwellings, 66 per cent of interviewees lived in a brick house, while 13 per cent lived in an apartment, 9 per cent in a room without a bathroom, 7 per cent in a shack made from salvaged material and 5 per cent in a room with a bathroom. At least partially, this distribution results from the deliberate choice

---

of their closest circles, especially the family. Hence, in strictly technical terms, the family income discussed here actually refers to household income.

of the field sites. Household density was relatively low – 3.8 inhabitants per household – and varied little, between 3.2 in Guinle and 4.3 in Ângela and Vila Nova Esperança.

The participation of the interviewees in the labor market was very precarious: 21 per cent were self-employed (a percentage rising to 40 per cent in Vila Nova Esperança) and 8 per cent were employed without a signed work card, against only 16 per cent employed with a signed work card (rising to 33 per cent in the Guinle favela).[2] Overall 12 per cent of interviewees were unemployed, but these figures ranged from 3 per cent in Vila Nova Esperança (not coincidentally where dependence on self-employment was higher) to 21 per cent in Ângela. Overall the group of interviewees also included housewives, students and pensioners.

Among those in employment at the time of the interview, no less than 66 per cent had obtained their current job via a network of contacts, compared to 3 per cent through an advert and 2 per cent via a job agency, confirming data obtained by Guimarães (2009b) for the city as a whole. Around 48 per cent of those employed worked in the community, showing the importance of the local economies. However the better quality jobs were situated outside the community and 87 per cent of those with a signed work card worked externally. By contrast, 61 per cent of those employed without a signed work card (excluding domestic workers) worked locally. The incomes earned by those working inside and outside the local home area did not vary significantly and the length of the interviewees' current jobs was fairly evenly distributed with 29 per cent of individuals in their current job for less than a year and 35 per cent in the current job for five years or more.

Taking into account the dimensions of social vulnerability discussed in Chapter 1, I developed a set of indicators capable of identifying the incidence of social precariousness. The indicators attempt to capture situations with the potential to become more vulnerable quickly, although they may be situated outside a condition of poverty in the strict sense. Four situations of precariousness were considered associated with work, income, housing and family, as well as a combined dimension of social precariousness. The first two dimensions almost need no explanation as sources of vulnerability, since they are respectively associated with the stability and level of monetary resources available for accessing goods and services provided by markets. The third dimension, linked to housing conditions, looks to incorporate the effects of the local area of residence on vulnerability, such as the absence of sanitary conditions, population density and building construction quality needed to provide minimal conditions of health, intimacy and well-being for individuals. Likewise the dimension of family precariousness looks to detect

---

2   In Brazil, a set of important social policies such as unemployment benefit, pensions and work-related accident benefits depend on the employer signing the employee's work card. This guarantee also ensures access to rights such as compensation for dismissal and annual paid leave. Although various degrees of informal work exist with distinct characteristics, jobs with work cards correspond to formal employment.

the presence of family configurations that generate instability in an individual's income and survival conditions. This is the case of configurations with a single adult provider responsible for minors (generally a woman), a situation in which the advent of unemployment or illness can lead a relatively prosperous family to poverty in a very short time span. Strictly speaking, the levels of precariousness of all the individuals included in this book tend to be intense, but these indicators attempt to differentiate the most extreme situations of deprivation from less intense configurations.

The most common precariousness condition was related to the labor market. I considered as precarious concerning the following conditions: unemployment, living off casual jobs or being employed without a signed work card. This condition affected 60 per cent of those connected to the labor market and was encountered at a higher level in the slum tenements (78 per cent). The locations containing individuals with less job precariousness are Guinle and Ângela with 55 per cent and 48 per cent, respectively. The participation of men in the labor market tended to be precarious more often (51 per cent compared to 40 per cent of women).

Next I considered an income situation precarious when the average family per capita income was equal to or less than R$ 120.[3] Overall around 29 per cent of interviewees had precarious income with the proportion varying between 50 per cent and 33 per cent in Guinle and Vila Nova Esperança, respectively, and 17 per cent in Cidade Tiradentes. Women were more likely to be subject to this condition.

In terms of housing, I defined precariousness as living in a wooden shack or a room without a bathroom. This situation was present in 16 per cent of the sample and is obviously more frequent in the slum tenements given the definition of the indicator itself (66 per cent of the interviewees from the slums were classed as living in this condition).

Fourthly, to highlight the presence of vulnerable family configurations, an indicator of family precariousness was applied when the family nucleus was composed of a single adult with children under the age of 12. Among interviewees as a whole 12 per cent were in this situation, ranging from higher levels in Cidade Tiradentes and Guinle (20 per cent) to almost completely absence in Jaguaré and Ângela (3 per cent). Only women corresponded to family heads living in this situation.

Finally when individuals presented two or more of the above four precariousness conditions, I classified their social situation as precarious in general. This condition affected 30 per cent of the sample, ranging from 59 per cent in the slum tenements to just 17 per cent in Cidade Tiradentes. This condition affects women (40 per cent) more than men (22 per cent).

---

3   This amount matches the income level used at the time of the research by the Bolsa Família CCT Program for poor families with children or teenagers under the age of fifteen. See Internet: http://www.mds.gov.br/bolsafamilia/o_programa_bolsa_familia/criterios-de-inclusao.

Obviously the characteristics of the middle class individuals included in the study were very different. Among those interviewed 57 per cent were women and 43 per cent men. Their average age was 41, varying between 24 and 79 years old. At the time of the research, 47 per cent had a stable partner. Among those with partners, around 17 per cent had been in the relationship for ten years or longer. Average schooling was 14 years and the average monthly family per capita income was R$ 2,250 (around US$ 1300).

Most people in this group were non migrants (73 per cent) and the large majority of migrants had lived in the city for over ten years (86 per cent). The average number of people in the household was also lower than among those individuals living in poverty – 2.3. Among the interviewees, 57 per cent declared themselves to be non-religious, 33 per cent Catholic, 7 per cent Spiritist and 3 per cent Evangelical. Just 13 per cent stated that they frequent church more than once a fortnight and only 10 per cent belong to some kind of association, indicating that even among this social group participation in associations is very low.

Among the employed, 43 per cent had been in their current job for more than five years. For the middle class interviewees as a whole, the most effective way of obtaining jobs was through network contacts, though this ratio – 50 per cent – was lower than that for individuals living in poverty. Another 14 per cent got their jobs through public entrance exams and 12 per cent through job adverts. Just 37 per cent of interviewees were employed with a signed work card, another 43 per cent were self-employed (in this case including self-employed professionals and freelance intellectual occupations), while 10 per cent were housewives, 7 per cent small property owners and around 3 per cent students.

2. Networks and sociability

A set of measures was created for each network. Network measures highlight characteristics of the relational patterns, enabling the analysis of positions and structures, as well as the comparisons between them. Given the aim of this book, the technical and operational details on producing the measures matter little: it is much more important for us to keep in mind their significance in terms of the social processes involved.[4] Eighteen measures were developed as indicators of size, cohesion, connectivity, group formation, relational activity, ego-centered

---

4   For an introduction to the measures and procedures used, see John Scott. *Social Network analysis*. Newbury Park, California: Sage Publications 1992. For more detailed technical information on specific measures, I refer the reader to Stanley Wasserman and Katherine Faust. *Social Network Analysis: Methods and Applications*. Cambridge: Cambridge University Press 1994; Robert Hanneman and Mark Riddle. *Introduction to social network methods*. Riverside, CA: University of California, Riverside 2005 and Stephen Borgatti, Martin Everett and Linton Freeman. *Ucinet for Windows: Software for Social Network Analysis*. Harvard, MA: Analytic Technologies 2002.

network structure, variability in sociability and localism.[5] Several of these were highly correlated among themselves and an analysis of these patterns of association indicated that the most important dimensions of the networks were: their size (measured by the number of nodes), variability in sociability (measured by the number of different spheres) and localism (measured by the proportion of individuals who live in the same area of residence).[6]

The measures indicated that the networks of individuals living in poverty have an average of 53 nodes, varying between 40 nodes in Paraisópolis and 60 nodes in Cidade Tiradentes. In the sample as a whole, however, the networks ranged between four and 179 nodes. The number of ties followed the same pattern with a total average of 107, but varying from 78 ties in Paraisópolis to 159 in Guinle (with a total amplitude ranging between seven and 449).[7]

Within migrants' networks, the presence of persons from the same Brazilian region (migration homophily) was 8 per cent, while average gender homophily (the proportion of men in men's networks and women in women's networks) reached 62 per cent. The presence of people from the same place of residence - localism - was 63 per cent on average, though this figure varied from 73 per cent in Jaguaré to roughly 50 per cent in the central slum tenements and in Vila Nova Esperança.

By way of illustration, below I include the sociogram of interviewee 164 with characteristics very close to the average[8]. The interviewee concerned is a resident of Cidade Tiradentes, female, aged 46, migrant, married for 23 years and unemployed at the time of interview.

---

5   The whole list of calculated measures included: no. of nodes; no. of ties; density; diameter; centralization index; clusterization coefficient; 2-clans/nodes; 3-clans/nodes; no. of spheres; no. of contexts; E-I of spheres; E-I of contexts; efficient size; density of ego network (the latter two testing the effects of the structural holes cited in Chapter 1); normalized average degree; information; per cent outside; local E-I.

6   To test the associations between the social dimensions involved I conducted a factor analysis by principal components. The test with eighteen indicators revealed the existence of five factors with Eigenvalues over 1, explaining 69.7 per cent of the variance. As well as the three dimensions cited, the model indicated cohesion (including degree and densities) and indicators of the ego-centered network. However these other two dimensions proved to be irrelevant in the subsequent analyses of network heterogeneity and their effects on poverty, which is why I concentrate on the first three dimensions in the following chapters.

7   The normalized average degree (average ties per node) was 8.3, the clustering coefficient was 0.46 (which indicates the formation of cohesive groups) and the centralization index was 37 per cent (which indicates the degree to which the network is centered around the ego). The average diameter was 6.3 steps (maximum distance between nodes) and the average density was 0.104 (proportion of possible ties observed). The variation between the fields was fairly small around these averages.

8   50 nodes, 82 ties, normalized average degree of six 13 per cent centralization and 0.50 clustering coefficient.

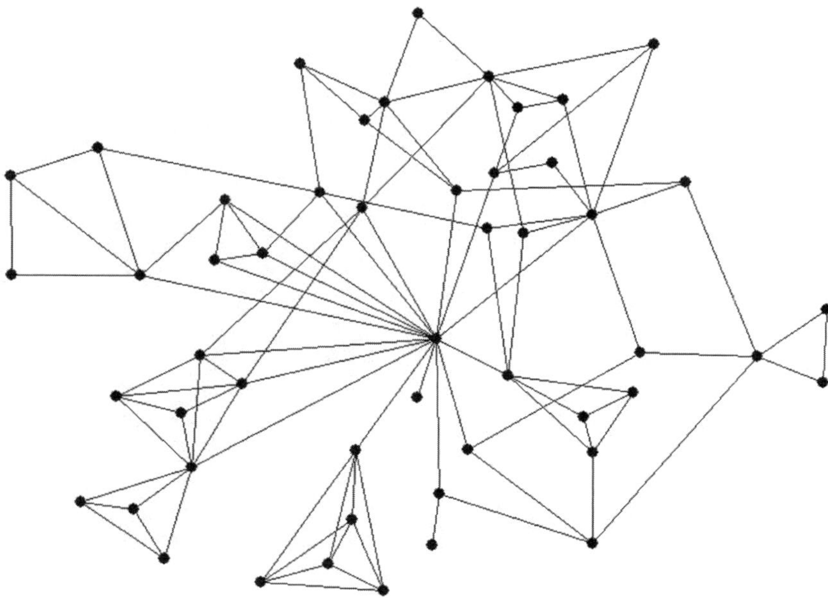

Figure 1   Sociogram of interviewee 164. Source: Author, based on collected empirical data.

Middle class individuals, on the other hand, had very different networks. The average size was much higher – 93 modes and 183 ties, although the variation between individuals was also high – between 25 and 238 nodes.[9]

To illustrate this point, the figure below presents a middle class case close to the cited average values. This is case 93, a woman aged 38, married and working in the administrative sector of a small organization. As we can see by comparing with the previous figure, the network is significantly larger and much more complex

Although it is not the intention of this study to discuss middle class cases, it is worth highlighting an important dimension that separates the networks of individuals who work in activities linked to professional communities and those whose activities involve work-places alone. Professional communities are a type of work sociability sphere that includes sets of mutually associated individuals and organizations engaged in specific practices and professional identities linked to particular areas of activity (Marques 2000 and 2003). The majority of professions involve only work-places, which are spatially localized and involve a much narrower scale than the communities. Among middle class individuals

---

9   The networks have an average diameter of 7.4 steps and a normalized average degree of six ties. The clustering coefficient was 0.56 while centralization was 29 per cent.

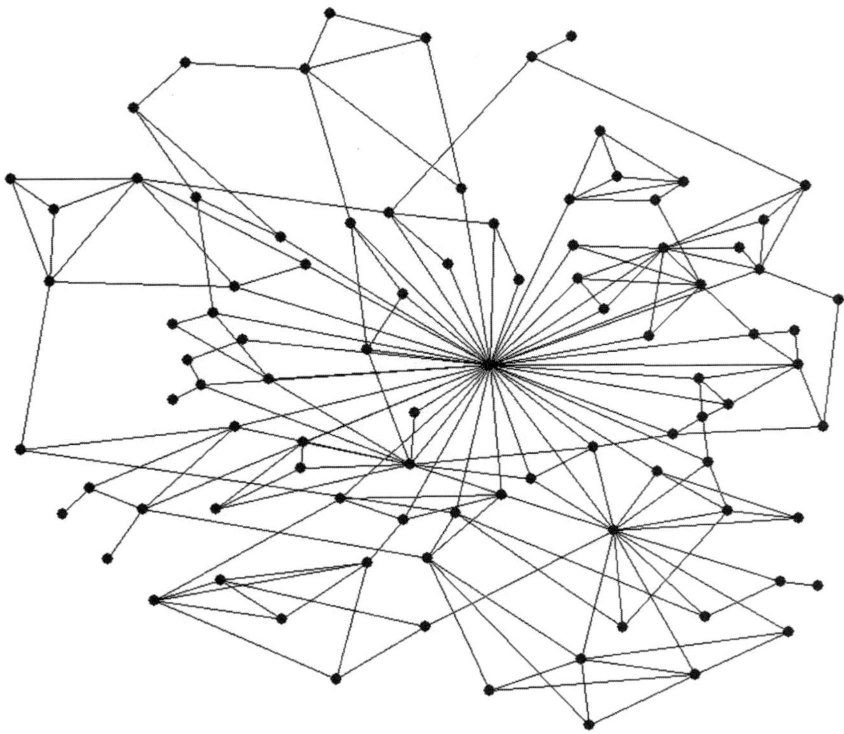

Figure 2.   Sociogram of interviewee 93. Source: Author, based on collected empirical data.

whose activities involve their insertion in professional communities, the average number of nodes was 131 compared to 70 among those people whose jobs were connected to work places only. One possible explanation for this result is that those jobs involving professional communities need to maintain ties active (or latent) for long periods, overlapping in time as layers, whose periods of more intense activation are separated in time, but which coexist in the present of the networks. The phenomenon is practically non-existent among individuals living in poverty, although involves only a part of the middle class individuals. If we compare poor individuals with only the middle class persons who work in work-places, therefore, the above differences become reduced.

Another characteristic of the middle class sample worth highlighting is that their networks are basically associated with people from outside the local area of residence – only around 20 per cent of the individuals present in the networks lived in the same region as the ego. The networks of the former social stratum match with what Wellman (2001) calls personal communities. The proportion of migrants from the same region of Brazil is higher than the proportion found in the networks of people living in poverty – 11 per cent, compared to 8 per cent among the latter – despite the proportion of migrant interviewees being lower (27 per cent compared to 70 per cent among the poor), indicating a greater persistence of sections of their networks existing prior to migration. As we will see in Chapter 7, this is caused by an important relational mechanism associated with the different availability of resources necessary to build and especially to maintain ties in the networks. Gender homophily, on the other hand, was lower than the case of the poor group – on average 55 per cent, compared to 62 per cent.

We can now examine what the data suggests concerning the sociability of individuals living in poverty. The average number of different spheres of sociability was 3.8, with almost no variation between the field sites, though among the interviewees as a whole the figure varied between one and seven. The sphere with proportionally the most individuals, on average, is the family, with 40 per cent, followed by the neighborhood with 32 per cent. The presence of these spheres varies greatly, from non-existent to practically the entire network (97 per cent). The average level of the other spheres is much lower, comprising 9 per cent work sphere, 6 per cent friendship, 5 per cent church, 3 per cent studies and 2 per cent associations.

This low average presence conceals some significant variations between individuals, variations which are in fact crucial to understand the specialization of sociabilities beyond the spheres of the family and neighborhood, which appear as a common denominator of sociability. Hence, for 59 individuals, for example, work accounts for more than 10 per cent of their sociability, while for 29 people from this same group it includes more than 20 per cent of the nodes in their networks. For 37 individuals the church sphere includes more than 10 per cent of the nodes of their network, while for seventeen people this sphere includes over 20 per cent. Something similar happens in the case of the study sphere whose share is over 10 per cent in the case of 28 individuals only. Sociability in associations is more restricted and only fourteen individuals had shares of more than 10 per cent for this sphere. I explore this point more closely in the next chapter, detailing and identifying the types of sociability that exist.

As would be expected, the sociability of the middle class was very different. The middle class had networks with 5.5 spheres and 5.3 contexts on average, indicating a much more pronounced diversification of sociability. The proportion of individuals in the family sphere was similar to that found in the networks of people living in poverty (35 per cent) but in the other spheres the differences were considerable. On average the work sphere included 26 per cent of the individuals from the networks and the friendship sphere accounted for 14 per cent. These were followed at a much lower level by the study sphere with 10 per cent, leisure with 6 per cent and neighborhood with 5 per cent. The church and association spheres represented just 1 per cent (each) of the nodes found in the networks.

In comparison with the networks of individuals living in poverty, therefore, we can affirm that middle class sociability is much more strongly based on work and studies and much less associated with the local neighborhood. Family sphere basically involves the same proportion of sociability in the two social groups.

Among middle class people the most common entry contexts were networks, with 45 per cent, followed distantly by the family with 19 per cent, work with 17 per cent and studies with 11 per cent. Neighborhood corresponded to just 4 per cent and church, association and leisure to less than 1 per cent. Comparatively, therefore, networks were much more important in the expansion of middle class networks, while the neighborhood represented a residual mechanism of network expansion in contrast to the networks of impoverished interviewees. The work sphere was also much more important, as was studying.

It is worth recalling that, as McPherson et al. (2001) emphasize, work places and study locations potentially generate lower homophily and higher social exchange than the neighborhood and family contexts. All of these indicators point to the greater social diversity of middle class networks compared to those of people living in poverty. As we shall see in Chapter 5, these differences in sociability are directly linked to the living conditions of impoverished individuals, also among the poorer sectors.

3. Attributes and networks

As already discussed in the first chapter, networks and attributes are mutually constructed through homophily, membership of organizations and the adoption of specific practices, among other mechanisms. The observation of the associations between networks and basic social attributes such as income, gender and so on, therefore, can help us understand the variability of the networks, as well as start to indicate the mechanisms that determine how networks are constituted and mobilized, a topic analyzed in detail in Chapter 7. The remainder of this chapter is dedicated to this task, discussing the main correlates of networks and types of sociability.[10]

a. Income

Given that creating and maintaining ties involve a variety of processes that imply costs, a relation between an individual's networks and his or her income would be expected, what would be in line with the literature described in Chapter 1. Pursuing this hypothesis, the networks of distinct social groups are subject to what we could call different 'economies of ties.' According to this mechanism, people with fewer economic resources confront greater problems not only in building ties, but also in maintaining them in distinct spheres, leading to a tendency to abandon

---

10   All the relations reported are significant to 99 per cent of significance, save where specified.

entire sections of the network over time. As a result, poorer individuals would tend to have smaller networks that are also less varied in terms of sociability.

However when we analyze only poor individuals, there is no direct relation between per capita income and network indicators (in either correlation or covariance tests). These findings may be related to the small variability in the income of the social group under study. Indeed when we include the middle class in the comparison, enormous differences between the networks emerge, as already discussed.

This mechanism would explain the lower average presence of people from the same region of Brazil in networks of poor migrants, even though migrants are more abundant in this group. In effect, as we shall see below, the majority of migrant individuals living in poverty discard sections of their original networks in a form similar to that described by Jariego (2003). On the other hand, among middle class networks, especially when professional communities are present, the tendency is for older regions of the network to persist, further increasing the difference between the networks. The question, therefore, does not seems to be related simply to migration, but to the type of sociability and the resources available to migrant individuals belonging to different social groups. I return to this point in Chapters 6 and 7.

Sociability, on the other hand, is shown to be directly correlated with average family per capita income, even among the poor alone. When the middle class is introduced into the comparison, this dimension obviously becomes even more associated with income.

Given that the variability in income within the studied group is relatively small, it is worth observing in greater details how the very poor individuals behave. To test this dimension, I separated the interviewees with family per capita incomes equal to or lower than R$ 175, considered as very poor.[11] The very poor included 99 individuals, who tend to have systematically more local networks with fewer spheres and contexts of sociability. However the other characteristics of their networks do not differ significantly from the rest of the poor. The distribution of the spheres suggests a sociability based more on the neighborhood and less on family and work, repeating the findings concerning the original contexts of ties. The very poor also tend to have higher localism. These results match those obtained by Fontes and Eichner (2004) for a low income community in Recife. It is worth adding that, contrary to the usual expectation, church attendance among the very poor is lower than among the other individuals living in poverty.

b. Schooling

According to the international literature, the school is an important location for increasing both the person's ties and the diversity of his and hers network

---

11   This amount corresponded at the moment of the research to the level used by Conditional Cash Transference programs, as indicated earlier.

(McPherson et al. 2001 and Bidart and Lavenu 2005). In the Brazilian case it would be unsurprising if this effect is lower than observed internationally, given the relative social uniformity of the country's public schools, a fact that enhances homophily.

However the information on São Paulo's networks suggests that this effect really does exist and that higher levels of schooling are correlated with larger, more diversified and less local networks in a statistically significant form. Given that income is correlated with the diversity of sociability and with localism, I controlled the effects of schooling on the networks through the interviewees' incomes. The effect continues to exist, showing that there is a concrete relation between levels of schooling, network size and the diversity of sociability. This effect exists both in relation to the interviewees as a whole (including the middle class) and just those individuals living in poverty. The finding adds further weight to the argument that schooling and education play a significant role in reproducing social inequalities and poverty.

As we shall see in Chapter 7, at least two mechanisms are present in this outcome. Firstly the effect of the relatively heterophilic school environment, which tends to increase with the educational level attained (Bidart and Lavenu 2005). On the other hand, the school environment, especially secondary school and university, also produces an effect of relational transition from the homophilic networks of childhood and adolescence, centered on the family and the neighborhood, to the more heterophilic networks of adult life where work and associations, for example, make themselves present.

c. Age and life cycle

The international literature suggests that networks increase until the start of adult life and decrease subsequently over the life cycle, whether due to the dynamic of sociability over the life span (McPherson et al. 2001 and Blokland 2003) or to the impact of important events that transform the networks (Bidart and Lavenu 2005). On the other hand, less homophily is expected in adult networks due to their more intense insertion in spaces outside the neighborhood and family (McPherson et al. 2001). In the case of adolescence, by contrast, greater homophily is expected, given that their networks tend to be more specialized around specific forms of sociability (Bidart and Lavenu 2005).

Taking the interviewees as a whole, the São Paulo results contradict this description, suggesting that there is no direct relation between age in general and a wide variety of network characteristics, including size, diversity of sociability, localism and gender homophily.[12] The data nonetheless indicates the existence of a significant and negative relationship between age and certain types of sociability,

---

12   In actual fact, there are no statistically significant differences in relation to age in any of the measures: numbers of nodes and ties, clusterization, average degree, density, efficient size, localism, fellow migrants, or numbers of spheres and contexts.

in particular the spheres of studying and friendship – the older the individual, the lower the proportion of these spheres in his or her network. The link between this finding and schooling is obvious, but the lower relative presence of the friendship sphere confirms data from the literature concerning the association between increased levels of social isolation and older age groups (Molina and Gil 2005), even though in the Brazilian case retirement does not necessarily play the central role suggested by Bidart and Lanevu (2005).

Additionally, to test the effects of age more precisely, I analyzed the behavior of the indicators by age bands, which revealed a sizeable difference for those under and over sixty years old. Although the number of cases of individuals aged sixty and over is low (14 interviewees) the networks are on average smaller (26 compared to 52 nodes), have fewer ties (46 compared to 107) and fewer spheres of sociability (3.1 compared to 3.9) and contexts (3.7 compared to 4.4). In relation to sociability, the proportion of individuals in the family sphere is higher and those of friendship and studying lower. The network, studying and leisure contexts are less important in terms of acquiring relations while the family is more important. There are no differences in relation to the proportion of individuals in the networks from outside the local area of residence, but the situations of family vulnerability are more frequent. Hence, although the evidence is limited by the small number of cases, the data suggests that old age has pronounced effects on the person's networks, reducing social integration and making contacts and sociability more dependent on the family, in a form similar to the results obtained by Grossetti (2005), Bidart and Lavenu (2005) and Molina and Gil (2005).

On the other hand, the literature also highlights another age group, young people. To test for distinctive characteristics of this group, I compared the individuals aged 21 or under (43 cases) with the rest of those living in poverty. Although no differences were found in the network indicators, the patterns of sociability were very distinct with a higher concentration of individuals in the spheres of friendship and studying and relatively low presences of the work and church spheres. In terms of contexts, there is a lower acquisition of nodes through work and a higher acquisition through studying. In addition young people's networks tend to be more local. Despite the fact that the number of cases is also low for this group, the results confirm the analyses of Bidart and Lavenu (2005) and Grossetti (2005), suggesting the existence of important transformations in the networks when young people progress to adult life. I return to this point in Chapter 7 when I discuss the mechanisms responsible for network transformations.

d. Gender

The international literature (McPherson et al. 2001, Beggs 1986 and Campbell and Lee 1992) prompt the expectation that women's networks are more local and based around kin and neighbors. Analysis of the São Paulo networks suggests an absence of gender differences in relation to network size and other characteristics, including localism. In fact in our case women's networks tend to be a little bit larger than men's, as well as less local and more varied in terms of their sociability, though the differences are not statistically significant. Identical results are obtained if we include just those individuals living in poverty or those from the middle class (all 239 cases).

There are also no differences between men's and women's networks in terms of the variability of sociability, though when we examine the spheres individually, women have smaller proportions of individuals in the spheres of work and leisure and more people in the church sphere. In terms of acquiring ties, the network and church contexts tend to be more frequent and the contexts of family, work and leisure less so. Consequently, the findings contradict the dominant perception of the concentration of female sociability in the private sphere and the domestic context, though the lower presence of the leisure sphere, the higher presence of the church sphere and a more intense acquisition of nodes through the networks are all consistent with the sociability usually attributed to women (Campbell and Lee 1992).

However, Dominguez (2004) suggests that these differences should be understood as associated with culturally constructed roles, and particularly to the different participations in the labor market and not just to gender differences per se. In particular, people working outside the community can be expected to have less local networks, with less involvement of family and neighbors, irrespective of gender. To test these effects, I ignored the cases of pensioners, students and housewives and compared the networks of working men and working women (including the unemployed). The results suggest that among men and women who work outside the community, the differences in spheres of sociability disappear, in keeping with the hypothesis suggested above. These results show parallels with those obtained by Moore (1990) and to some extent by Dominguez (2004), in reference to the United States.

e. Migration

Migration is one of the most important processes in the constitution of low-income urban communities in Brazilian cities. How is it related to the networks and how are the networks associated with the process of incorporating migrants (although in this case national migrants), in Portes's sense (1999)? It is usually assumed that migration destroys an individual's previous network and that the latter slowly reform through a process of incorporation in the new location (Jariego 2003). On the other hand, networks are themselves part of the migratory process, influencing the places to which people migrate and where individuals later become settled (Santos 2005, Martes and Fleischer 2003 and Portes 1999). The information from our networks suggests that the two dimensions are interconnected.

There are no differences between the networks of migrants and non-migrants in terms of network size, relational activity, variability of sociability and localism. The type of sociability, though, does vary slightly and migrants have fewer relations in the spheres of friendship and studying. Their networks tend to present higher gender homophily and, among migrants, a higher proportion of employees used the network to obtain their current job – 80 per cent compared to 52 per cent among non-migrants.

The absence of differences in the networks could mean rapid processes of incorporation or simply the absence of variations linked to migratory status. To test these alternatives, I separated the networks according to how long ago people migrated. This is a hypothetical procedure given that I lack this information for the same people at different moments in time, although I do have data on migrants with different lengths of time living in São Paulo.

The only difference found relates to the presence of migrants from the same region of Brazil in the networks, which does in fact reduce substantially over time, falling from 21 per cent for those who migrated between one and five years ago to 10 per cent for those who migrated more than ten years ago. There are no other differences between networks of recent and long-term migrants.

So although the presence of migrants from the same region of Brazil suggests a process of incorporating migrants in relational terms, all the other data suggests that the phenomenon occurs very quickly or has very little impact on the relational patterns of individuals. Nonetheless, migration may have a different and more localized effect on certain groups of individuals who, for example, live with fellow migrants originally from the same region of Brazil. This final hypothesis is verified when we observe that individuals with over 20 per cent of their network composed of migrants from the same region tend to have substantially smaller and less diversified networks than other individuals. Sociability in these cases is more concentrated on the family to the detriment of work and studying, with the same occurring in relation to the original contexts of the ties. Interestingly 15 per cent of the sample had migrated more than five years ago.

More than suggesting a general pattern of influence on migration, therefore, the data indicates the existence of a group of people whose origin organizes their sociability, even long after migration. These people tend to have smaller and less diversified networks than others.

But what is the role of the networks in the migratory process itself? The interviews confirm the description of the literature on migratory processes guided by the networks of relatives and acquaintances from the home town. Initial evidence of the process comes from the high concentration of interviewees with specific origins, such as the case of migrants from Bahia in Vila Nova Esperança (67 per cent of its migrants) or those coming originally from Pernambuco (23 per cent) and Bahia (46 per cent) in Paraisópolis. Additionally, the interviews revealed the existence of large proportions of interviewees migrating from the same very small village or a cluster of neighboring rural villages. In some cases the networks today include individuals who were neighbors in their original home area who repeat the same neighborhood pattern in São Paulo. This reconstruction of previous patterns of primary sociability has very different features than the form depicted by Jariego (2003) in the case of foreign migrants living in Spain. Maintaining ties with people still living in the original home town is relatively rare, though, probably because of the effects of the economy of ties mechanism described earlier.

This information suggests the constitution of specific spaces of interaction and sociability, at least for some individuals. Consequently migration does not simply represent a process of social dislocation and reinsertion, but characterizes trajectories that provide a type of sociability localized in one place but with individuals from another. This pattern differs from middle class migrants, who almost always succeed in maintaining the various sections of their original networks active.

f. Church attendance

Previous studies on religion and associations reported that regular church attendance increases the chance of individuals being employed and obtaining income, due to the access to social circuits organized in these locations associated with a religious sociability (Almeida e D'Andrea 2004 and Gurza Lavalle and Castello 2004). The data from our interviewees partially confirms these findings. Individuals who attend church more than once a fortnight (78 cases) are on average older than the other interviewees, but tend to have similar levels of income and schooling. The group includes higher proportion of women, housewives and students, but not people with partners, suggesting a certain dissociation between frequenting churches and families. In terms of access to the labor market, those who go to church very frequently tend to be less often unemployed or self-employed, though there is no marked difference in relation to jobs with signed work cards. The differences are fairly small, albeit significant.

There are no differences in the networks of those frequenting church and those who do not in terms of size and localism, but the sociability of the church goers is more diverse. The networks of the latter tend to have fewer people in the leisure and neighborhood spheres, and, obviously, more in the church sphere, as well as tending to acquire more nodes via the church than those who seldom attend.

Hence, individuals with a high rate of church attendance tend to have a more varied sociability and jobs that are a little better than those who do not go regularly. As we shall see in Chapter 5, though, the effect of the sociability concentrated on churches is not unique and expresses a pattern that includes frequenting other organizations with more heterophilic sociability than that of the family, friends and neighbors. The question therefore does not seem to reside in religious sociability in itself, but in the relational effects enabled by less homophilic social spaces.

Given the low frequency of associations, it was not possible to assess their relation to the networks, although the analysis conducted later on suggests a similar effect of reduced homophily.

g. *Space and segregation*

The relation between networks and space is widely known and was already discussed at length in Chapter 1.

Since the distribution of individuals tends to be segregated by attributes, geography becomes one of the main elements responsible for producing 'baseline homophily' – that is, the homophily provoked by increased exposure of a given individual to people from his or her own group (McPherson et al. 2001). The exception to this pattern occurs when moving about the urban region involves relatively low costs, either because of low levels of segregation, the presence of easy transport and communications services or because of the abundance of material resources.

Two consequences arise from this fact. The first identifies localism with homophily and few social bridges, in the sense established by Briggs (2003). The question here, therefore, is determining just how local individuals' networks and contexts of sociability actually are, based on the premise that very local networks have few bridges and, consequently, tend to provide little stimulation for social mobility.

However a second potential influence is associated with the distinct problems and costs involved in constructing external ties faced by individuals living in segregated areas. The question here is the different effects of segregation on individuals' social networks, causing a potential obstacle to the development of networks. If we can observe substantial differences between different localizations in the networks according to segregation, then segregation has an effect on the networks.

On average the networks of people living in poverty contained 63 per cent individuals of the same place of residence, a proportion that varied between 51 per cent in the slum tenements and Vila Nova Esperança and 76 per cent in Paraisópolis. In general, therefore, the networks tend to be fairly local. Just 30 per cent of individuals have networks with more individuals from outside the community than inside. This pattern of localism is reinforced by the information on sociability. Among the leisure activities cited by the interviewees, for example, 53 per cent occurred in the local area of residence. In addition, we should not forget that, as we have seen previously, the networks of individuals living in poverty contain on average 32 per cent and 29 per cent of individuals in the neighborhood sphere and context. For comparative purposes, it should be recalled that average localism among the middle class sample was 20 per cent and the proportions of people in the neighborhood sphere and context were just 5 per cent and 4 per cent, on average. In summary, it can be concluded that the networks of individuals living in poverty tend to be highly localized, closely matching the findings of Fontes and Eichner (2004) in Recife.

Despite this fact, 62 per cent of those individuals in employment work outside the community, confirming that despite localism, opportunities tend to be located in other areas.

But in what way does these networks vary between more or less segregated locations? To analyze segregation, I separated the cases of Cidade Tiradentes, Vila Nova Esperança and Jardim Ângela, all taken as situations of urban segregation, from the cases of Jaguaré, Paraisópolis, Favela Guinle and the slum tenements, taken as non-segregated areas. The classification of the latter two areas requires some explanation. Favela Guinle was included among the less segregated cases despite its distance from the expanded center of the metropolis, due to its proximity to the centre of Guarulhos municipality and to its industrial district. On the other hand, the slum tenements are obviously centrally located, but in a very much different way to other field sites, including the fact that they comprise a circuit of several tenements rather than a territorially bounded community. To avoid introducing bias into the analysis, the tests described below were repeated to include and exclude these two areas.

When we consider the seven study areas (119 non-segregated cases and 90 segregated cases), segregation distinguishes the networks very little. The size and other characteristics of the networks tend to be statistically undifferentiated between segregated and non-segregated areas. On the other hand, segregated places tend to have proportionally higher sociability in the spheres of studies and church, although the absolute differences are again slight. Finally segregated places tend to have slightly more outside people in their networks, though the size of the effect in small, on average. The results proved to be identical when Favela Guinle was removed.

When we remove the slum tenements from the analysis we obtain results that point in the same direction, but provide a firmer basis for their interpretation. Here the size and variability in sociability of the networks remained very similar, as well as their sociability, slightly more concentrated on the spheres of studying and church in the case of segregated locations. However the presence of outside individuals was shown to be significantly higher in segregated areas (40 per cent compared to 31 per cent). Moreover the proportion of people from outside is even higher in Vila Nova Esperança (49 per cent) than Tiradentes (37 per cent), although both are segregated locations, compared to something around 25 per cent in Jaguaré and Paraisópolis. This suggests that the scale of the local area of residence may interact with segregation, additionally stimulating certain individuals from smaller locations to look for relations outside.

We can surmise, therefore, that segregation exerts a less pronounced effect than expected, but that it does work to produce networks for some individuals with larger proportions of individuals from outside the local area of residence. Apparently when the local area is small in size, individuals have even more incentives to construct and maintain external relations. The consequences of these different relational patterns for living conditions and poverty are analyzed in the following chapters, but it is worth emphasizing here that this result suggests that the networks effectively help to integrate and insert socially at least a portion of the more spatially segregated individuals.

Therefore, beyond the importance of specific findings, the overall results suggest a fairly complex pattern of associations between attributes and networks. In fact an important conclusion is that the effect of attributes on networks is mediated by various processes, making it difficult to establish single directions for all the individuals. This result is in keeping with the premises of relational sociology presented in Chapter 1 and indicates that in order to understand the complexity of these associations, we should explore the diversity of the networks and sociabilities. The next chapter is dedicated to this task.

Chapter 4
How do the Networks Vary?

As we saw in the previous chapter, the different characteristics of the networks are influenced by a variety of social attributes, making any single and direct characterization of the networks of people living in poverty fairly difficult. The best methodological procedure, therefore, is to explore precisely the diversity of the existing situations. This chapter proceeds in this direction by constructing typologies of networks based on the information discussed previously.

After a series of experiments I reached the conclusion that it would be better to produce two distinct typologies – one for the networks themselves, classified according to their characteristics, and another for the patterns of sociability of individuals, classified according to the emphasis on particular spheres. While the former tell us about the structures of relations of the individuals, the latter concerns the distinct uses of these structures by individuals in their practices of sociability. Although this separation is merely analytic and methodological (and every network simultaneously implies a pattern of sociability), I opted to separate these two dimensions, since networks and sociability do not always vary together and the construction of a single typology perhaps tends to mask the existing differences.[1] Subsequently, the association of the two typologies allowed me to define the different types of relational patterns existing in the studied cases. In the following chapters we shall see that the types of networks and sociability have a significant influence on living conditions in general and poverty in particular.

The chapter is divided into three sections. In the first, I explore the diversity of networks, developing a typology based on indicators and measures taken from the networks. Next I repeat the exercise for sociability, determining the different types in existence. Finally in the third section I combine the two typologies in order to determine the types of relational patterns present in the networks of individuals living in poverty, as well as the conditions for their presence. The types are illustrated by concrete examples from the field research.

---

1   In an initial exploratory exercise involving just 89 networks (Eduardo Marques, Renata Bichir, Thais Pavez, Miranda Zoppi, Encarnación Moya and Igor Pantoja. "Personal Networks and Urban Poverty: Preliminary Findings." In: Brazilian Political Science Review, Vol 2, No 1 2008), I adopted a single typology of attributes – network and sociability indicators – but the procedure proved inadequate for the 209 networks studied here given their variability.

Types of network

To analyze the variability of the networks, I used the same eighteen indicators discussed in the previous chapter relating to size, cohesion, connectivity, group formation, relational activity, ego-centered structure, variability of sociability and localism.[2] The different cases described by these indicators were then subject to cluster analyses, resulting in five types of networks.[3] The set of indicators is presented in Table 4 in appendix at the end of the book, but the graph below summarizes the differences between the types of networks based on three fundamental dimensions – size, localism and variability in sociability – measured by the number of nodes, the proportion of individuals from outside the area and the average number of spheres of sociability. In the remainder of this section I discuss each type of network in detail.

It should be noted from the outset that the types of network have fairly different numbers of cases – 11 28, 58, 68 and 44 cases, respectively. The most frequent types, therefore, are small to medium sized, followed by the medium sized networks. As we can observe in the graph, the size of the networks and the variability in sociability tend to decrease as we shift from the first to last group. By contrast, the presence of people from outside the local area tends to increase, though not uniformly – the larger networks present higher levels of localism, but the smaller networks also present higher localism than the medium and small to medium sized networks. The intermediary networks combined medium size, low localism and more varied sociability. In the following chapters we shall explore the importance of these differences.

Just to establish a level for comparison, it is worth recalling that the middle class networks had an average of 93 nodes, around 20 per cent of local individuals and 5.5 different spheres of sociability.

The indicators allow us to characterize the types of networks as described below.

a. Large networks, with varied sociability, but fairly local – 11 cases

The large networks are the least frequent. Their size exceeds that of the average size of the middle class networks (131 nodes compared to 93), but their urban insertion and variability in sociability are much lower. The individuals with these kinds of networks have an average family per capita income of R\$ 214 (the lowest among the groups), an average age of 34 and high levels of schooling, considering

---

2   The following indicators were used in the analysis: nodes; ties; density; diameter; average degree; centralization; clusterization coefficient; E_I index of the district; E_I index of the contexts; E_I index of the spheres; no. of 2-clans/no. of nodes; no. of 3-clans/no. of nodes; betweenness; information; efficient size of the ego-net; density of the ego-net; no. of spheres; no. of contexts; proportion of people from outside the area.

3   The analysis used the K-means algorithm in the Spss 13.0 software.

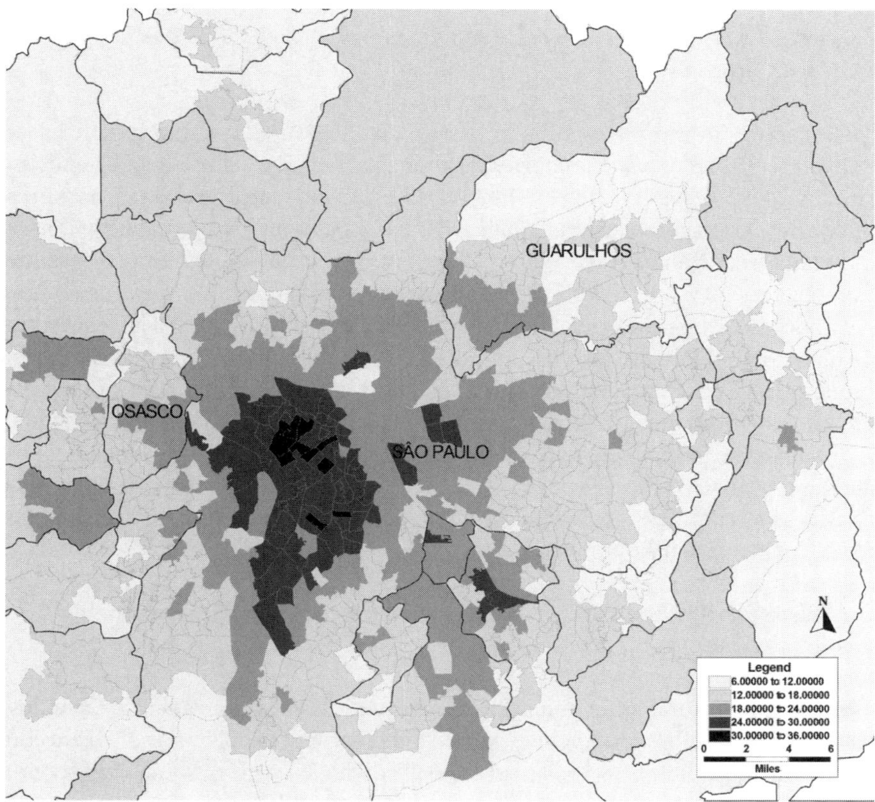

Graph 1 **Size, localism and variability in sociability by type of network. Source: Author, based on collected empirical data.**

the social group in questio: 7.0 years of study. Single adults and women are over-represented in the group, which present the lowest gender homophily among all the types. Young people and students are also over-represented in this type of network. Most of those in employment work outside the community. It is marked by high levels of precariousness, especially in income and in the family. The group includes non-religious people, but among those who are religious the attendance is above average. The large networks are over-represented among segregated individuals and more commonly found in Cidade Tiradentes (where we interviewed more young people), Guinle and Jardim Ângela. All these characteristics should be taken with a degree of caution, though, due to the low sample size. Black individuals are over-represented (perhaps because of the high relative presence of Cidade Tiradentes).

b. Large to medium sized networks with highly varied sociability and high localism – 28 cases

These networks are just a little smaller than the average of the middle class networks (85 nodes compared to 93), although their localism is higher and the variability in sociability lower. People with large to medium sized networks have a low average per capita income (R$ 266), but with high variability.[4] These individuals have an average age of 34 and an education level slightly above the average, around 6.8 years of study. Gender homophily matches the average of the networks as a whole and people with partners are over-represented. The main form of obtaining jobs is the network and those working in the community are over-represented. Self-employed, employees and domestic workers without work cards and owners of small businesses tend to have this type of network more frequently. Individuals are more likely to have no religion when compared to other case types and family-related precariousness is the lowest, but they frequently present work-related precariousness. Networks of this type are more common in Jaguaré, the slum tenements and Jardim Ângela.

c. Medium sized networks with average variability in sociability and low localism – 58 cases

The networks of this type belong to people with family per capita income and characteristics around the average of the studied group: R$ 277, age 38 years and education equivalent to 6.5 years of study. Individuals with this kind of network obtain their jobs through a network more often than the others and the relative average size of households tends to be higher. These networks are more commonly encountered in Guinle, Paraisópolis and Vila Nova Esperança.

d. Medium to small networks with average variability in sociability and low localism – 68 cases

This is the most frequent type of network and generally very close to the average of the indicators. Individuals with medium to small networks have an average family per capita income over the average (R$ 276), 33 years of age and 5.9 years of schooling. Average gender homophily is the highest of all the types of network. Individuals with this type of network tend to be more often housewives, employees with work cards and self-employed. Evangelicals are over-represented in this type of network and family vulnerability is one of the lowest. Localism is the lowest among all the groups.

---

4   The standard deviation is R$ 230. There are four cases with family per capita income over R$600 and 11 with income below R$ 150.

e. Small networks with low variability of sociability and high localism – 44 cases

Finally, small networks are typical of individuals with a relatively higher average age – 40 years (these are the oldest individuals on average) – and lower schooling (5.2 years of study). Nonetheless the group also includes a far from negligible set of very young individuals, once again proving the mediated relation between attributes and networks. The average family per capita income – R\$ 272 – is not the lowest in average terms but the group's standard deviation is the highest (R\$ 321), indicating a high variation in income levels.[5] These networks contain the largest presence of migrants from the same region of Brazil. It is also the group with the highest incidence of both non-religious people and Catholics, although church attendance is the lowest of all the groups. Housewives and the self-employed are slightly over-represented. This type of network is the least frequent in segregated areas with an over-representation of interviewees living in Paraisópolis.

One last point about the types concerns their distribution by segregation condition. The data suggests the absence of any pattern in terms of segregation.

2. Types of sociability

We can now turn to the scenarios of sociability found in the networks. To explore this dimension I submitted the proportions of individuals in the various spheres of sociability to cluster analysis.[6] The result that best fitted the data includes six distinct types of sociability considering the relative presence of spheres.[7] The table below presents the average proportions of spheres by type, as well their respective number of cases. The darker cross-hatches indicate spheres of sociability present in higher proportions than the average, characterizing the type. The lighter cross-hatches indicate sociabilities strongly present in a given type of sociability, even though lower than the average. The highlighted spheres concentrate between 81 per cent and 90 per cent of the sociability for each type. The last row presents the number of cases of each type of sociability while the last column presents the average sociability of the middle class group, which was not used in the construction of the groups and is presented merely as a parameter for comparison. To enhance the table's clarity, percentages equal to or lower than 6 per cent have been hidden.

---

5   In fact the group includes one individual with an income much higher than the rest. Were this person excluded, the average income would be R\$ 225, the lowest of all the types of network.

6   The cluster analysis included all nine spheres considered and used the K-means algorithm of the Spss 13.0 software.

7   Some spheres, such as studies and leisure, do not go as far as to shape or compose specific profiles.

Table 2　　　Types of sociability by spheres of sociability[8]

Spheres	Types of sociability (%)						Middle class (%)
	family	neighbors	friends	church	work	association	
family	64	27	35	30	27	36	34
neighbors	19	54	23	19	25		
friends			33				14
work					33		26
church				34			
association						33	
leisure							
studies							10
others							
No. of cases	65	72	19	17	29	7	30

Source: Author, based on collected empirical data

The two first types of sociability are based mainly on the family and neighborhood – primary and/or local ties – although with inverted emphases. In the third type we have a large concentration of people in the friendship sphere, which may or may not be local, but which also tends to be marked by homophily. The other types of sociability are characterized by the strong presence of relations constructed within institutional or organizational environments – church, work and associations. It is important to stress that although all types of sociability have the majority of their nodes concentrated in primary and potentially more homophilic spheres, in the case of the last three types there is also a substantial amount of relations constructed and maintained in spheres of potentially less homophily.

Although at this point in the text this distinction represents just a hypothesis, it is reasonable to consider that sociabilities based on more organizational spheres lead to patterns of contacts with lower homophily and greater diversity. This is because the contacts constructed in these environments tend to be more strongly based on choices than in the cases of family, neighbors and friendships, more likely to be influenced by the effects of the 'baseline homophily' discussed in the first chapter. We shall see in the following chapters that this hypothesis is indeed confirmed empirically and the presence of these sociabilities is usually associated with better social conditions.

8　Percentages equal to or lower than 6 per cent hidden. The dark gray cross-hatched areas have above average proportions while the light gray cross-hatched areas show important sociabilities within the group, even though lower than average.

Middle class sociability is concentrated primarily in the spheres of friendship, work and studying. The presence of neighbors in the middle class networks is very low, lower even than the group of networks of poor people with the lowest presence in this sphere. The relative presence of the family sphere is similar to the average of the networks of individuals living in poverty.

We now describe the general attributes of the individuals by type of sociability. For each type I highlight just the above average spheres, which in the final instance characterize each type.

a. Sociability characterized by an emphasis on the family – 65 individuals.

The individuals with sociability focused on the family have an average age of 38, very low average schooling (5 years of study) and relatively low family per capita income: R$ 245. The group includes a sizeable number of elderly people and is slightly more female in composition. The presence of migrants from the same region of Brazil in the networks is the highest of all the different types of sociability. Housewives and self-employed workers are the occupational groups that most stood out. Individuals tended to work in the community itself and seldom frequented associations. Most of the people with this sociability are Catholic, but do not go to church regularly. Family-related precariousness among individuals with this type of sociability is lower than those living in poverty as a whole. This type is more frequently found in Paraisópolis, the slum tenements and Jardim Ângela. The average number of spheres of sociability is the lowest of all the groups – just 3.

b. Sociability characterized by an emphasis on the neighborhood – 72 individuals

These individuals have an average of six years of school education, an average age of 34 and fairly low average income, R$ 211. In fact the group presented the highest number of individuals. The trajectories reported in the interviews indicate the existence of various individuals who had migrated several times between São Paulo and their original home towns. Housing and work vulnerabilities were present at higher than average levels with a large number of self-employed workers.

c. Sociability characterized by an emphasis on friendship – 19 individuals

The individuals with this pattern of sociability had the second highest level of schooling among all the groups (7.4 years of study), but the lowest average family per capita income (R$ 186). This was the group with the lowest average age – 30 years – and the highest proportion of young people. It was a fairly common type among the very poor, but not the extremely poor, and tended to be more female than male. Housing, work and overall precariousness levels were very high in this group and students and housewives were over-represented. Concentration on the friendship sphere was over double that found among the middle class sample.

d. Sociability characterized by an emphasis on the church – 17 individuals

The people from this group had an average level of schooling (6.3 years), an average age of 38 and average family per capita income between medium and low, R$ 332. The group included more migrants than the overall average, but practically did not include fellow migrants (3.7 per cent), suggesting a higher than average dissolution and substitution of ties. Employees with and without work cards and pensioners were over-represented. The networks included many more individuals from outside the local area than average. Naturally those frequenting church were heavily over-represented in the group and this was the only sociability where Evangelicals were predominant (76.5 per cent). The individuals with this sociability had above average levels of family precariousness, but all the other precariousness factors were found at low levels. The numbers of spheres and contexts were high – 4.3 and 4.9, respectively.

e. Sociability characterized by an emphasis on work – 29 individuals

Individuals with this sociability tend to have high levels of schooling for the social group in question, attaining an average of 6.6 years of study, an average age of 39 (with few young and elderly people), as well as a high average family per capita income for the social group being researched: R$ 471, the highest among all the sociabilities. The group contained a particularly high concentration of employed individuals with a signed work card (52 per cent compared to an overall average of 16 per cent) working in relatively long-term jobs outside the community (78 per cent). Naturally work and income precariousnesss were lower in this group than the overall average of the interviewees. Jobs in this group had been obtained via networks in a much higher proportion than the other types of sociability (76 per cent). The networks included many more individuals from outside the local area than average (50 per cent) and had fewer migrants and far fewer fellow migrants from the same region than average (just 1 per cent). Individuals who frequented associations were over-represented in this group and the numbers of spheres of sociability and different contexts were high – 4.4 and 4.7, respectively. In this case, the proportion of sociability in the work sphere was even higher than the average of the middle class networks: 33 per cent compared to 26 per cent among the middle class. The individuals with this type of sociability had an above average level of participation in associations (10.3 per cent), suggesting that sociabilities with low homophily tend to become associated.

f. Sociability characterized by an emphasis on associations – seven cases

This type of sociability was shared by just seven individuals. Their average educational level was the highest of all – 8.6 years – exceeding complete primary schooling. Per capita family incomes were also relatively high and reached R$ 390 on average. The networks of individuals with this sociability were the only ones with a gender homophily well below the average (55 per cent). The presence of migrants from the same region of Brazil in the networks was very low (3 per cent). All the individuals worked in the community, though the majority without a work card. Localism was the highest of all the sociability types (just 24 per cent of individuals in the networks were from outside). Obviously those frequenting associations were over-represented among the individuals with this sociability, but less obvious is the high rate of church attendance, reinforcing a dimension indicated in the sociability of work that sociabilities with low homophily tend to be correlated.

But how do the different types of sociability affect the areas under study? The data suggests that although no clear patterns can be discerned by area, there is a certain concentration of less local and less primary sociabilities in more segregated locations, a finding which is fairly counter-intuitive.

Individuals with more primary sociabilities are concentrated in Ângela, Paraisópolis, the slum tenements and Jaguaré – with an emphasis on the family in Paraisópolis, the slum tenements and Ângela, neighbors in Guinle and Jaguaré, and friendships in Jaguaré. Conversely the sociability concentrated in the church sphere occurs more strongly in Vila Nova Esperança and Cidade Tiradentes, while that concentrated in work environments occurs in Guinle and Tiradentes. Finally the sociability centered on associations was more present in Paraisópolis and Tiradentes. Therefore, the less local and less primary types of sociability, more associated with institutional and organizational environments are over-represented in more segregated places.

This result matches the evidence of the previous chapter showing that some segregated individuals have slightly less localist patterns, strengthening the idea that this population has greater incentives for searching for ties that are less homophilic and less local. As we shall see in the following chapters, this hypothesis is not only confirmed, but has also important consequences for social conditions. Among segregated individuals, those who manage to establish less homophilic and less local patterns apparently overcome the isolation of segregation and achieve better social conditions.

3. Combining types of networks and sociability

Having analyzed the variability of networks and sociabilities, we can investigate the existence of combinations among them. Generally speaking, the distribution of types of sociability by type of network indicates the absence of direct associations, repeating the pattern of heterogeneity already discussed in the previous chapter. However, four of the 30 possible situations (crossing five types of network with six types of sociability) appear with greater frequency among the diverse cases: individuals with large networks, but local and primary sociability (13 per cent); with small networks and local and primary sociability (17 per cent); with medium-sized networks and local and primary sociability (44 per cent); and with medium-sized networks and mostly non-local sociability constructed in organizational and institutional environments (16 per cent).[9]

We can surmise that large, medium or small networks with local and primary sociability tend to favor homophily, while medium-sized networks with low levels of local and primary sociability tend to increase the heterophily of individuals' relational patterns. If the hypotheses in the literature concerning the link between network heterophily and social conditions are correct, then the first three situations would tend to be associated with worse living conditions, while the fourth situation would favor access to opportunity structures.

These hypotheses are confirmed in a preliminary fashion by the observation of the social characteristics of the interviewees in each type of relational situation.

Among individuals with large and small networks with local and primary sociability we find an over-representation of younger and older people respectively. In the first case, schooling tends to be higher than average and students and non-migrants were more frequent. In the second case, schooling was low and there was an over-representation of pensioners, housewives and migrants (with a large presence of fellow migrants from the same area of Brazil). Generally speaking, therefore, these relational situations were frequently linked to individuals with low social integration. Both the situations were more frequent in non-segregated areas.

The medium-sized networks with primary and local sociability are the most common situation, close to the average of the studied universe in terms of age and schooling. It is worth highlighting the high presence of migrants, self-employed workers and the unemployed. The majority of those interviewees in employment worked in the local area.

The final situation mainly includes mature individuals with relatively high levels of schooling and better insertion in the work market, including a high proportion of employees with work cards, though accompanied by equally high numbers of self-employed workers and employees without work cards. These individuals often tend to work outside the community. This social situation, therefore, is frequently associated with individuals who are better integrated socially.

In order to illustrate these four situations, I present some examples from the case study in the following.

---

9   Another 10 per cent of cases are distributed among several other residual and intermediary situations.

a. Primary sociability within small networks (101 cases)

Case Number 76 from Vila Nova Esperança illustrates this relational situation. She is a 21 year-old, non migrant young woman, married for two years with someone who was her neighbor. She has finished high school education and is now a housewife, having a per capita family income of only ¼ of the minimum wage.

Her network has 19 nodes 21 ties and three spheres of sociability: family, neighborhood and friendship, all characterized by potential homophily. The most important is neighborhood with 43 per cent of the sociability, followed by family (31 per cent) and friendship (26 per cent). Around half of her network (49 per cent) involves individuals from outside the community.

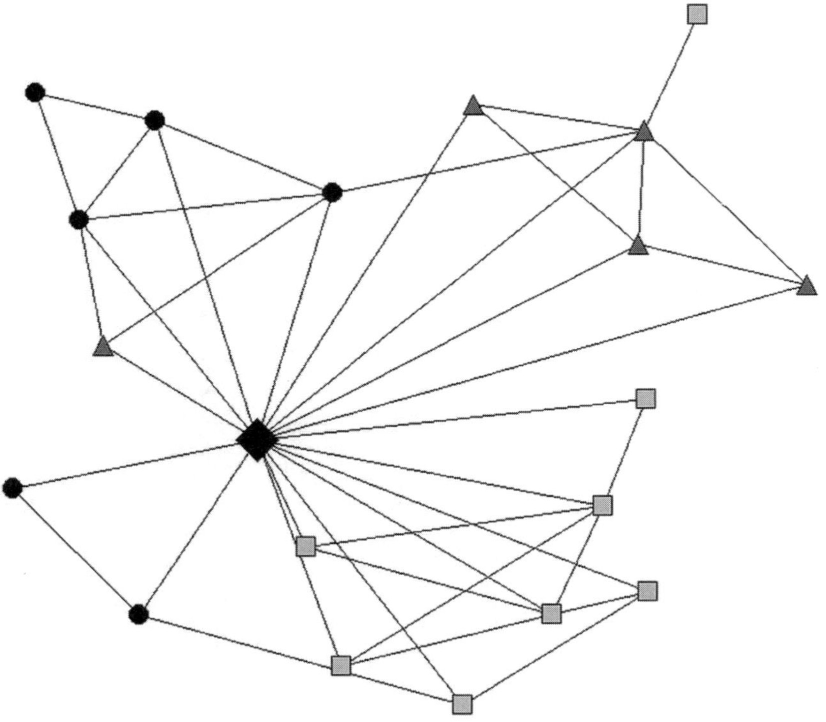

Figure 3   **Case 76, Vila Nova Esperança. Source: Authors' elaboration based on empirical data collected.**

Key: large diamond – Ego; black circles – family; squares – neighbors; triangles – friendship.

b. Primary sociability within medium networks (72 cases)

Case 121 from Paraisópolis is the illustration of this type of network and sociability. He is a 52 year old man who migrated from the state of Alagoas, in the Northeast of Brazil more than ten years ago. He is married whith someone who also works outside the community, as a maid. He studied only until primary school and works now as a registered gardener in luxury condominium near his favela. He is catholic and reports to go to church weakly and for leisure goes to the bar with friends.

His network has 40 nodes, 54 ties and four spheres of sociability. The most important is family with 44 per cent of the sociability, followed by friendship with 31 per cent, neighborhood with 15 per cent and work with 10 per cent. Therefore, 90 per cent of his sociability is concentrated in spheres of highly potential homophily. His network is marked by intense localism, and 90 per cent of his sociability involves individuals who live in Paraisópolis.

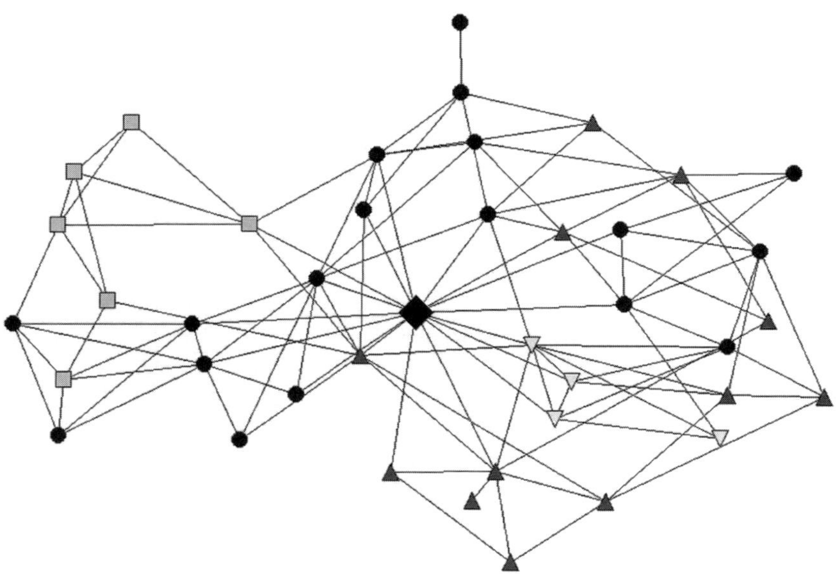

Figure 4   Case 121, Paraisópolis. Source: Authors' elaboration based on empirical data collected.

Key: large diamond – Ego; black circles – family; squares – neighbors; up triangles – friendship; work – down triangles.

c. Primary sociability within large networks (63 cases)

Case Number 75, a 13-year-old girl born in Bahia but who has been living in São Paulo (Vila Nova Esperança) for the last two years is an example of this type of network and sociability. Her parents are still in the Northeast, and she lives with her older sister, helping her to take care of her little baby. She has worked as a maid, but now only studies, in a nearby neighborhood. As the majority of the teenagers, she has many friends, several of them from a Catholic association, although she professes no religion.

Her personal network shows 68 nodes, 66 ties and four spheres: family, neighborhood, study, and church association. The most important sphere is for sure neighborhood, comprising 56 per cent of her sociability. Studying involves 22 per cent and church 13 per cent, while family includes only 9 per cent of the nodes. Around 70 per cent of her network involves individuals who live in the same favela.

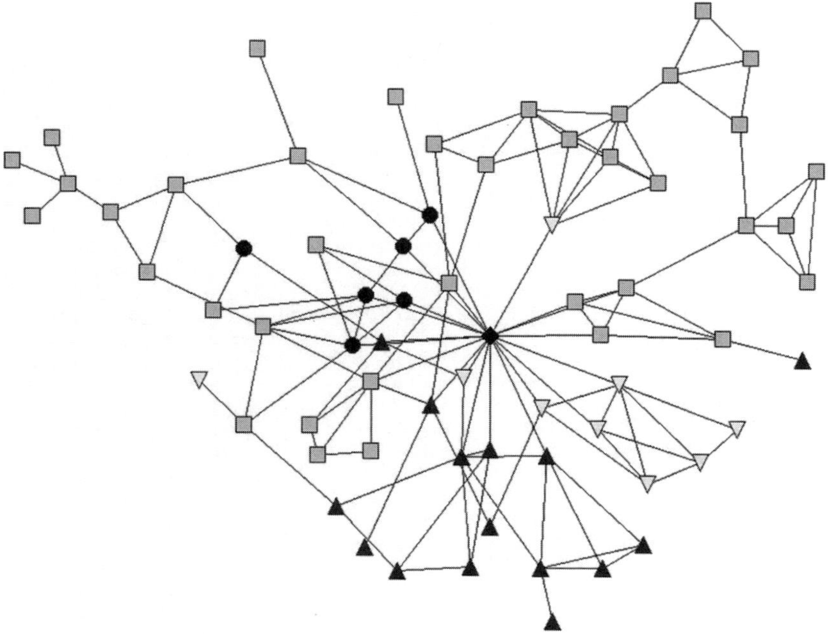

Figure 5   Case 75, Vila Nova Esperança. Source: Authors' elaboration based on empirical data collected.

Key: large light diamond – Ego; black circles – family; squares – neighbors; up triangles – friendship; work – down triangles.

d. Institutional Sociability within Medium Networks (98 Cases)

The example for this type of network and sociability is interviewee 52, a resident of the slum tenements born in Bahia, young (19 years old) and married with two children. He works as a car park attendant (with a signed work card) and has a family per capita income of R$ 115. He studied for five years and states that he is Evangelical, though he adds that he never frequents church. For leisure, he reports playing soccer regularly with friends in a nearby park, what explains the leisure sphere in his network.

His network has 36 nodes, distributed within five spheres – family (39 per cent), work (24 per cent), neighborhood (20 per cent), leisure (9 per cent) and church (8 per cent). Although 59 per cent of his sociability is concentrated in potentially highly homophilic spheres – family and neighborhood, 32 per cent happens inside organizations – work and church. Around 62 per cent of the individuals from his network is from outside the slum tenement circuit. The sociogram is presented below.

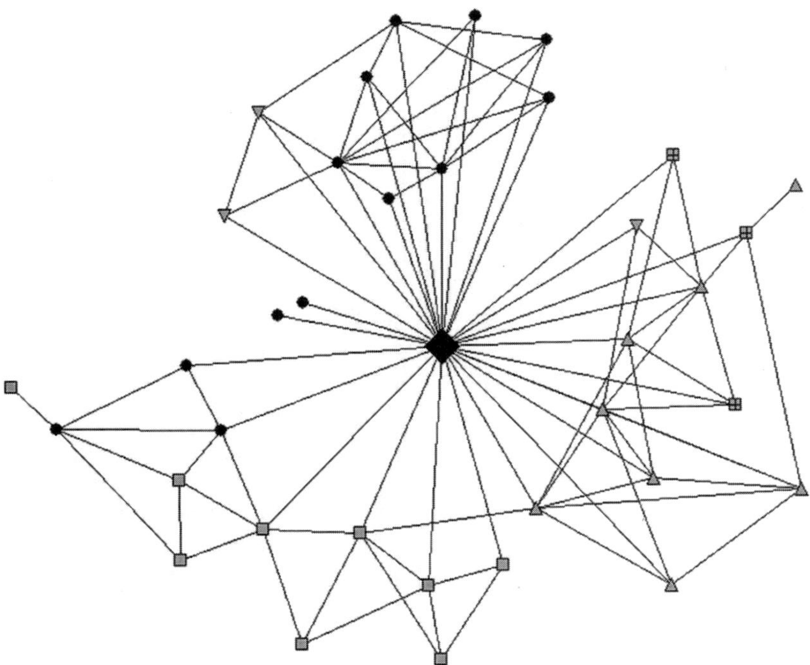

Figure 6   Case 52, Slum tenements. Source: Author, based on empirical data collected.

Key: large diamond – Ego; black circles – family; squares – neighbors; triangles – work; light squares with plus signs – leisure; inverted triangles – church.

So, although networks and sociability vary substantially, it is possible to find distinct and solid patterns. The next chapter explores the consequences of these relational situations and the diversity of the networks for accessing market goods and services that influence individual living conditions.

Chapter 5

Do the Networks Matter for the Access to Markets?

Previous chapters analyzed the characteristics of the personal networks of individuals in poverty, their variability and the sociability contexts that surround them. Departing from these results, this chapter and the following investigate the main consequences of the networks for the social situation of the individuals, specifying the role of networks and sociability in the production (and reproduction) of social situations. In this chapter I analyze the effects of the networks on the access individuals have to goods and services obtained in markets, including the labor market, but also others where goods and services are obtained in economic relationships involving generalized and non-personalized exchanges.

Using quantitative techniques I investigate the associations between relational patterns and some of the most important dimensions in the definition of social conditions via markets: the obtaining of jobs, the obtaining of jobs with certain tenure, social precariousness and monetary income[1]. Work and income are the elements most commonly associated by the literature with poverty, while social precariousness establishes a synthetic measure of negative social conditions, pointing out to the most severe deprivation situations, as we saw in Chapter 2. The analysis involves univariate as well as multivariate analysis using several different techniques, including only individuals in poverty. [2]

It is important to restate that causality between the elements in considered as biunivocal, and if networks influence attributes and social situations, these also influence intensely the production and transformation of social networks. In this sense, networks, attributes and social situations were constructed together through the life trajectories of the individuals, intentionally, caused by other processes, or even at random. So, the distinctions established in this Chapter are merely analytical and social situations and networks construct each other continuously in time.

---

1   Edgard Fusaro, to whom I am thankful, gave me precious assistance in this chapter.

2   All the reported associations have 95 or 99 per cent of significance, except when otherwise indicated.

1. Work

The greater part (66 per cent) of individuals obtained work by means of network contacts.[3] However, what are the main consequences of the networks of individuals for their jobs, and to what extent might the effects be attributed to other variables traditionally considered by the literature? In the test that follows I utilized network measures and included as 'with work' those individuals employed with or without an employment record card, whether domestic or not (74 cases), as well as small business owners (17 cases) and workers in family businesses (just three cases).[4] Considering the characteristics of those activities declared as self-employed work I regarded these activities as representing hidden unemployment, adding them to the ranks of the unemployed, as conforming to those 'without work'.[5] Individuals with work came to 94 (45 per cent of those interviewed), as against 57 without work (27 per cent) and another 58 (28 per cent of the total) in which neither condition applied (housewives, the retired, students).

First off, variance analysis tests with separate network measures. indicated that the variability of the sociability of individuals, as well as localism, had significant effects.[6] The networks of those in work tended to be slightly more local and with a more varied sociability. The size of the networks and other relational measures did not reveal a connection to the work condition.

The types of networks, on the other hand, did not reveal a direct effect upon the individual's likelihood of having work or not.[7] As regards sociability, those individuals with sociability linked to work were more likely to be employed than the others (significant to 95 per cent of significance). The causality at work here

---

3   Guimarães (2004) confirms the networks' preeminence in a 2001 survey carried out in the metropolitan region of São Paulo – 80 per cent of all individuals looking for work affirmed that they had made use of relationships with family, friends and acquaintances. Another survey, carried out in 2004 by the same author, indicated that even amongst those seeking work by means of employment agencies, some 60 per cent affirmed having obtained their previous employment through the network. (Guimarães 2008).

4   Strictly speaking therefore, one cannot call it employment, as the owners themselves are included within this condition. However, I felt that, organized in such a way, the variable would better serve to describe the condition that generates effects upon poverty, that is to say the consideration of the presence, or otherwise, of a relatively stable source of income. Ownership, on the other hand is associated in almost all cases with very small commercial businesses, such as small local bars or tiny shops located in the entrance of the houses' garage.

5   Just to cite a few of the jobs in which the self-employed were engaged, we found nine street peddlers, two occasional florists' assistants, five occasional skip or truck loaders and two paper and aluminum can trash pickers.

6   With respectively Statistic F equal to 3.08 and p-value of 0.048 and statistic F equal to 6.95 and p-value of 0.001.

7   To explore the effect of network types and sociability I constructed a set of crossed tables submitted to statistical tests of nominal variables.

is not even vaguely clear given that it is reasonable to imagine that those with intense work-linked sociability are, or have fairly recently been, employed. This was the only sociability presenting significance individually. However, those individuals with sociability linked to institutional environments – church, work and associations were also significantly more likely to be employed than those with a more local and primary sociability (family, neighborhood and friendship.

To analyze the joint effect of social and relational conditioners I used an exploratory tree classification technique, commonly known as CHAID (Chi-squared Automatic Interaction Detector). The method consists of a set of subsequent tests between a dependent and several predictive variables. In each test, the model chooses, using Chi-square statistics, the independent variable with greatest explanatory power over the dependent variable. The cases are then separated into subgroups according to the chosen independent variable and the test is run again. The process is repeated until no statistical significance is found or until the number of cases in one of the subgroups is too small. The result is a tree of associations, in which each level corresponds to a selected independent variable and each cell represents a social situation, described by the variables.[8]

In the explanation of the 'has work' status eighteen variables were used to get the following dimensions: relational, socio-economic, age bracket, migratory, and spatial.[9] The result is presented in Figure 3 that follows.

As we can see, the incidence of work is 54 per cent in the set of cases considered (disregarding the retired, housewives and students), but reaches 73 per cent amongst

---

8   The method works with double entry tables with the relations between the dependent variable and each predictor testing all possible partitions of the categories choosing that one which represents the largest value for the Chi-squared statistic. The data is grouped according to the chosen partition and a new analysis is performed within each subgroup, with the previous process repeating itself for the dependent variable and the other predictive ones. This process is repeated until the divided groups reach the minimum number of cases stipulated for the analysis. As this is a stepwise method all possible combinations are analyzed, and we can take the variables indicated in the final result as representing the most important conditioners in the explanation of the variability of the dependent variable.

9   The following were used: Relational – 1) number of nodes of the individual network 2) average degree, 3) efficient size of egocentric network, 4) proportion of persons external to the area, 5) total number of spheres, 6) dummy variables with reference to those types of networks with five groups, and 7) dummy variables referencing types of sociability and network, as well as their combinations; Socio-economic – 8) gender of individual, 9) years of study 10) family income per capita 11) attends church or some place of worship more than fortnightly; Age brackets – 12) age of individual 13) pensioner (60 or more years old) 14) young (age less than or equal to 21); Migratory – 15) migrant 16) migrant of more than ten years 17) proportion of contemporaries greater or equal to 21 per cent, Spatial – 18) segregated.

In this case, for reasons that will be obvious, the work-related variables were excluded. Those who do not work cannot work outside, have period of employment, previous employment or be classified within a determined position within the occupation.

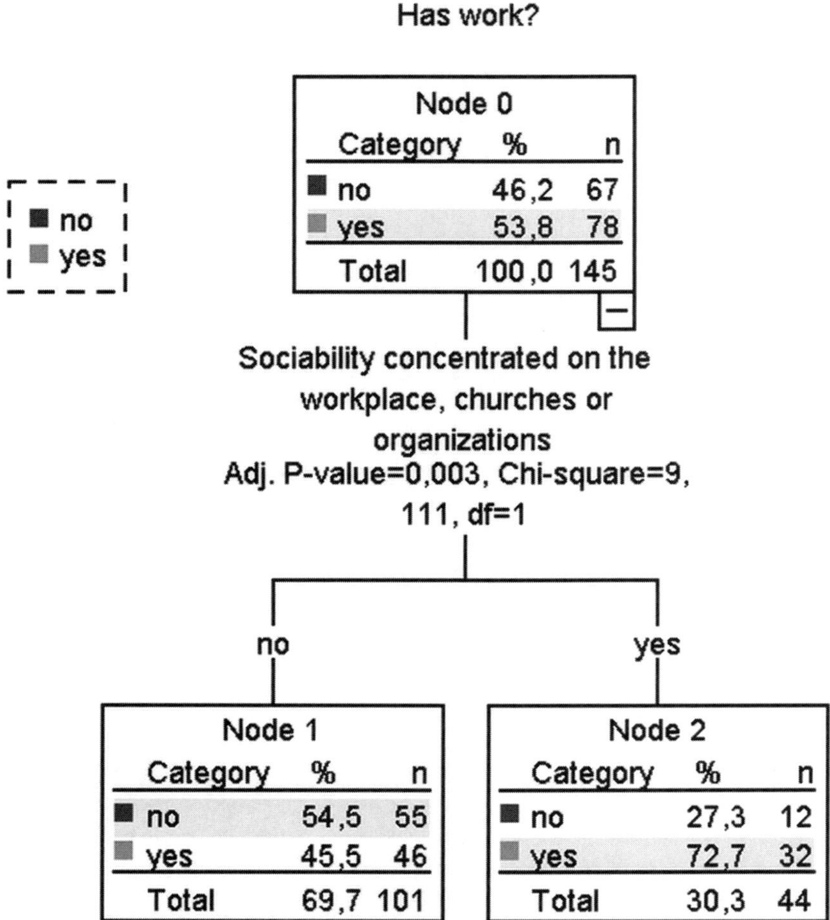

Figure 7   Tree explaining work (CHAID)

individuals with less primary sociabilities whilst falling to 46 per cent in the case of those having more primary and local sociabilities. Thus, the analysis indicates the importance of weakly homophilous sociabilities for the individual's access to employment. It is important to note that the types of sociability present as most important even in the presence of socioeconomic variables considered classic in discussions of the topic. These include: schooling, income, age, migratory status, or the degree of residential segregation to which the individuals in question are submitted.

The result indicates that an individual's sociability type is the key factor in determining whether or not they individuals was in employment. This suggested that more homophilous sociabilities, and those of a more primary nature – family, neighborhood and friendship – tended to generate worse employment-related situations. For obvious reasons, results were the same for sociabilities with an institutional emphasis – church, work and associations, that represent the complement to the prior mentioned. The model correctly explained 62.3 per cent of cases.

As previously discussed, the causality present here is probably multiple, with individuals just as likely to have the sociability they have for having work more frequently, as they are to have work for having this type of sociability. The most propitious approach to the understanding of this association is not to be found in the search for a unique causal direction, but rather in the study of the effects of the mechanisms over both elements throughout the trajectories of individuals as will be discussed in Chapter 7.

2. Protected work

The individuals in question might be employed or not, but they also enjoy very different degrees of stability and protection in their jobs. This is as much the case in access to social benefits as it is in the case of the stability of the connection over time. To test the networks' effect upon the obtaining of better quality jobs I divided the jobs up into 'protected work' – employment with employment record card (domestic or not), small business owners and employees of family businesses, and 'poorly protected work' – employees without employment record card, the self-employed and the unemployed[10]. This latter condition involved some 41 per cent of those interviewed or 59 cases of the set of 145 cases considered[11]. The retired, housewives and students were withdrawn from the analysis (31 per cent of the universe).

The analysis indicated that none of the measures or types of networks impact directly on the obtaining of protected work. On the other hand, those individuals with proportionally greater institutionally based sociability and less local or primary sociability were once again revealed as having greater chances of having protected employment than the others. Within the group of individuals evincing this type of sociability, 57 per cent had protected employment against 34 per cent of those with more local and primary sociabilities[12]. This result appeared again separately for some types of sociability.

With regard to sociabilities, those individuals with a sociability characterized by the neighborhood were less likely to have protected employment - 30 per cent as against 46 per cent in the rest of cases. Sociability linked to work also revealed

---

10   As in the previous case, one cannot, strictly speaking, regard this as a condition of employment. See note 8.

11   This condition represented a previously analyzed subgroup. Six cases were also withdrawn due to a lack of information on protection.

12   All indicated associations have a significance of 95 or 99 per cent.

itself as being of significance for the association with protected work, with those having this sort of sociability being in protected work in 66 per cent of cases as against 34 per cent of those with other types of sociability patterns. As has already been highlighted however, the causal sense remains somewhat unclear.

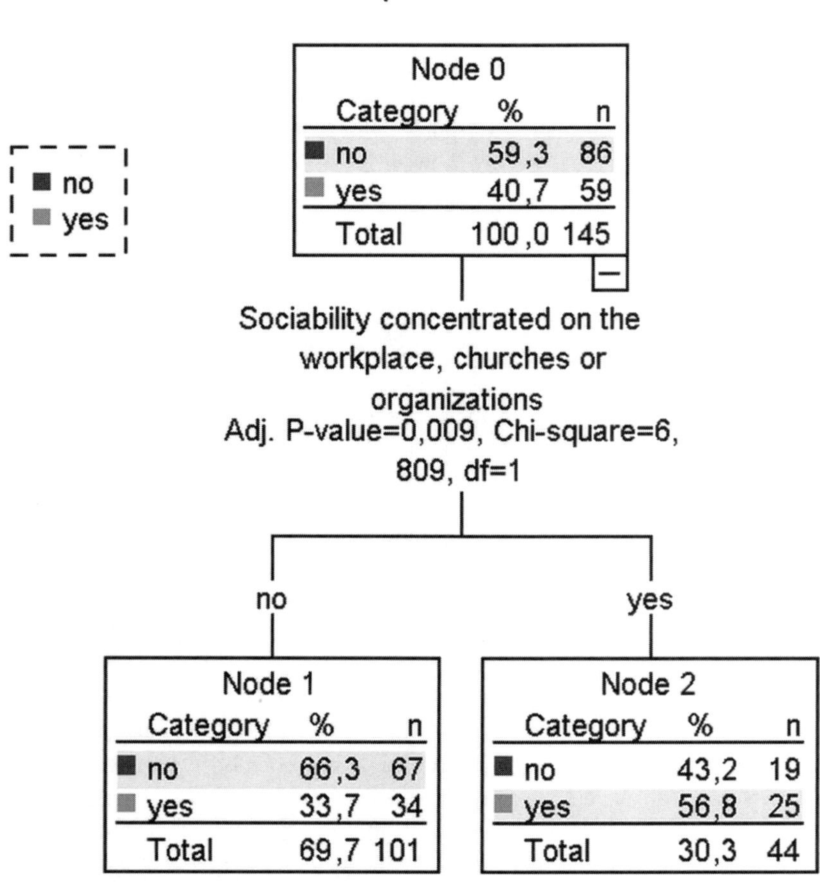

Figure 8   Tree explaining protected work (CHAID)

For the joint analysis of those conditioners of the most protected work I resorted to the same CHAID technique, using 18 variables[13]. The figure that

---

13   Relational – 1) number of nodes of the individual network 2) average degree, 3) efficient size of egocentric network, 4) proportion of persons external to the area, 5) total number of spheres, 6) dummy variables with reference to those types of networks with five groups, and 7) dummy variables referencing types of sociability and network, as well as their combinations; Socio-economic – 8) gender of individual, 9) years of study 10) family

follows presents the relevant information. As result the technique separated those individuals with church or work related sociabilities from the rest (employment sociability also revealed significance separately, although less markedly). The model correctly explained 64 per cent of cases.

As can be seen the incidence of protected work is just 41 per cent amongst those participating in the labor market, but hits 57 per cent amongst those with a church and work based sociability and falls to just 34 per cent amongst those with other types of sociability. Thus, in a similar way to the previous analysis, even in the presence of classic socio-economic variables such as years of study, migratory status, age structure and income, the dimension that most distinguishes those with protected work from those without, is that indicating the existence of a sociability pattern that is weakly primary and potentially less homophilous.

3. Social precariousness

This section tests the associations between social attributes, relational elements and social precariousness[14]. As already discussed, social precariousness was considered as being a situation in which the interviewee evinced at least two of four conditions of precariousness – familial, housing, work-related and income-related[15]. Approximately one third of those interviewed – 30 per cent or 63 of the cases – were found to be in this condition. However, the distribution of the desegregated conditions of precariousness varied considerably, revealing just 12 per cent in familial 16 per cent in housing-related, 60 per cent in precariousness of employment and 29 per cent in income-related.

Although the situations of precariousness did not present a direct connection with the characteristics and types of networks, sociability did show relevance. First of all, those individuals with sociability centered on the neighborhood were more subject to precariousness: 46 per cent of persons with this type of sociability evinced precariousness whereas this fell to just 23 per cent for those with other

---

income per capita 11) attends church or some place of worship more than fortnightly; Age brackets – 12) age of individual 13) pensioner (60 or more years old) 14) young (age less than or equal to 21); Migratory – 15) migrant 16) migrant of more than ten years 17) proportion of contemporaries greater or equal to 21 per cent, Spatial – 18) segregated.

14   I have also tested the associations between attributes, networks and access to the labor market (and to formal jobs). The results are similar to the ones presented here and were omitted due to lack of space. In fact 66 per cent of the jobs were obtained through networks. I refer the reader to Marques (forthcoming) for those results.

15   Were considered precarious: 1) family arrangements with only one adult breadwinner with children under 12 years of age; 2) living in a wooden shack or in a room without a bathroom; 3) being unemployed or underemployed; 4) having per capita family income of less than ¼ of the national minimum salary - R$ 125, at the time, of the threshold of the Bolsa Família program, the Brazilian federal CCT program.

types of sociability. Work based sociability went against this, with only 12 per cent of this group in situations of precariousness against 34 per cent of the rest. Hence, the more local and primary the sociability, the greater is the probability of social precariousness. In contrast, those individuals with sociability concentrated in institutional environments had a reduced probability of precariousness.[16] The analyses also indicate that individuals with average sized networks, and with minimally local and primary sociability, tended to be less subject to situations of precariousness than the others: only 11 per cent of those with these types of relational patterns were in precarious situations as opposed to 35 per cent in other relational situations.

To test the joint effect of attributes and networks on social precariousness I decided to use again CHAID techniques. In our case, seventeen variables expressing relational elements and socio-economic, migratory and employment attributes were used. Since the precariousness variable was constructed considering income, family structure and position within the occupation, these variables obviously could not be included in the model. This was also the case with segregation, since it is highly correlated to housing precariousness in the case of slum tenements. The method indicated three variables as the best solution (the adjusted model correctly explained 69 per cent of cases). The resulting tree follows.

As we can see, the three variables that best explain social precariousness are i) a certain type of network and sociability, ii) whether or not the sociability is family-centered and iii) whether or not the individual is a migrant. The models also included traditional socio-economic variables, such as income, years of schooling and age. As can be seen, precariousness affected 30 per cent of cases, but amongst those individuals with mid-sized networks, low localism and non-homophilic sociability, it fell to 9 per cent (right-hand cell of the first level). So, among the poor, those with less homophilic relational patterns have a less precarious situation.

However, the left-hand cell of the first level indicates that amongst those without this relational pattern, precariousness was found in 34 per cent of cases. Amongst those, the ones with family-centered sociability tended to be in less precarious situations – 23 per cent (in the right-hand cell of the second level), whilst among those who had neither of these two sociabilities it reached 40 per cent (left-hand cell of the second level). Although this is in part generated by the method, since precariousness included a familial dimension, the result nonetheless strongly points towards the role of the family in the reduction of precariousness for individuals with a more homophilic sociability.

This result may appear contradictory, since concentration of sociability within the family was more associated with precariousness in the tree's first level. Notwithstanding, amongst those not having mid-sized networks or with more homophilous and more local sociabilities, those with familial support were less prone to falling into precariousness (second level of the tree), even if not to the

---

16   In all analyses the associations are significant to 99 per cent of significance.

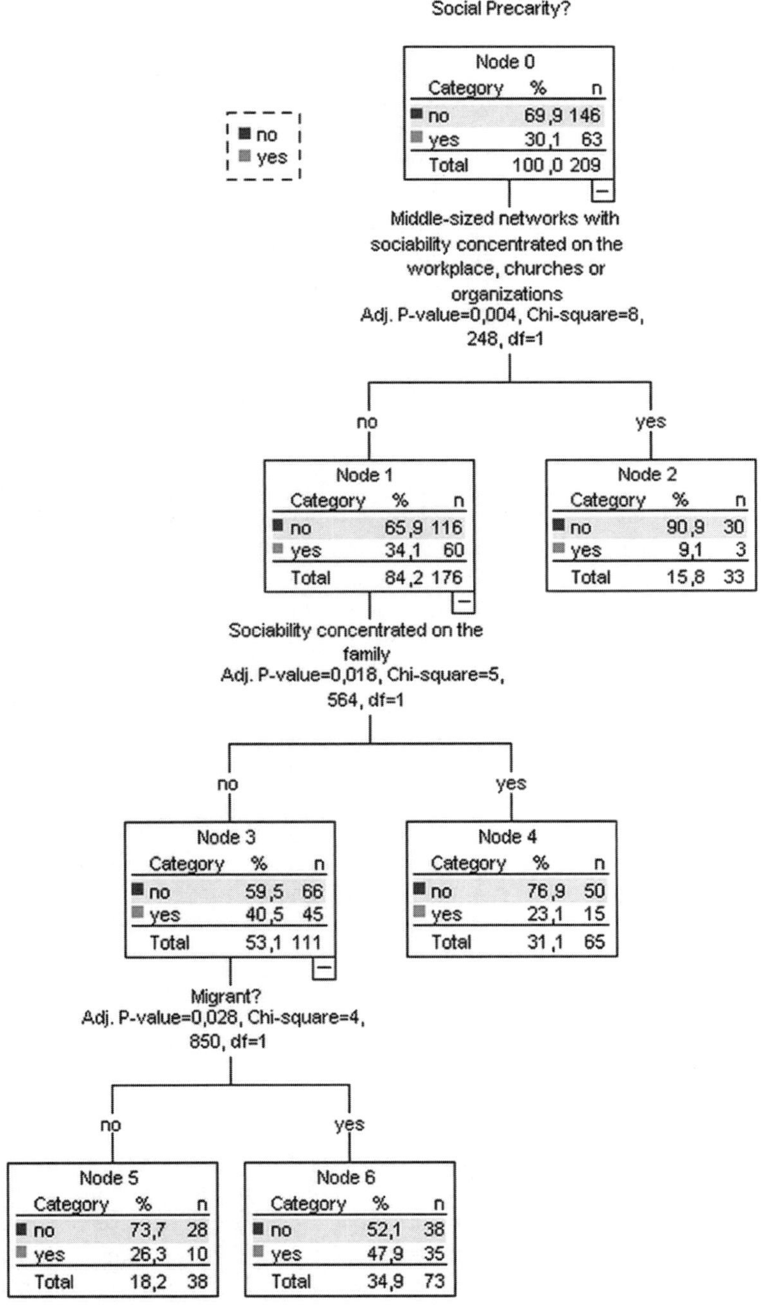

Figure 9   Tree explaining social precariousness (CHAID)

same extent as those evincing the previous sociability (23 per cent against 9 per cent). As we will see in the next Chapter, family ties are, in truth, associated with the solution of daily problems and with access to goods and services produced outside the markets. (Wilson 1987; Gonzalez de la Rocha 2001).

Finally, amongst those individuals who had neither the first level combination, nor familial sociability, migration appears as a discriminatory element (third level of the tree). Precariousness was present in almost half of those migrants with homophilic and local, but not familial sociability (48 per cent right-hand cell of the third level), whilst among those who had this same relational situation, but were not migrants, it was only 26 per cent (left-hand cell of the third level).

At first sight, this might suggest the existence of prejudice against migrants in the local community or in the local job markets. A more detailed analysis, however, suggests that the model is, in truth, delimited to a specific group of individuals of low social integration. The networks of individuals classified in this situation contain large numbers of fellow countrymen, suggesting that migrants with low relational integration in São Paulo are especially likely to find themselves in this condition. The effect cannot simply be attributed to prejudice given that other migrants present a lower presence of fellow countrymen (and are not located in the right-hand cell of the third level). It is worth adding that the situation of individuals who possessed a more homophilic but not familial sociability, and who were not migrants (left-hand cell of the third level), was similar to the ones with family-centered sociability (right-hand cell of the second level), suggesting that both situations of integration – being a local or having family support -, have the same effect on reducing precariousness.

On the whole, therefore, the result indicates that protection against precariousness depends on less homophilic sociability, family support and social integration of non-migrants. It is worth noting however, that the model is hierarchical, and sociability in the family and migrant integration only attenuate precariousness if someone does not have weakly homophilic and little local sociability.

4. Income

Finally, I analyze the association between networks, attributes and the income of individuals in poverty.

First, using univariate analysis, only the variability of sociability, measured by the number of spheres, had a direct effect upon income for the set of cases. Type of network was not associated with income either, but certain types of sociability were. Individuals with sociability based on the church, work or associations tended to have substantially higher incomes – R$390 per capita as against R$225 for those with local and primary sociability. Finally, persons with average networks and organizational sociability (the relational situation that presents least precariousness, as we saw in the last section), had even higher incomes -

R\$430 per capita as against R\$240 for the other relational situations.[17] By and large therefore, the more diversified, less primary and less local the sociability, the greater the income tends to be.

As is usual in this type of analysis, the network measures and the various social indicators were correlated. So, to analyze the combined influence of relational patterns and social attributes upon income, I conducted a series of multivariate analyses using GLM (General Linear Model) models.[18] After performing a series of tests, including socio-economic, sociability and network variables, I ended up with the model that follows.[19] Very similar results were obtained with family income as opposed to per capita family income, albeit with smaller explanatory capacity. As I was not interested in predicting results, but in evaluating the joint influence of the processes and variables upon income, the result can be considered satisfactory.[20] The first five columns present the parameters and the last column shows the effect in Reais of a variation of one unit in each variable on the level of the average per capita familial income of R\$271 (US\$ 140).

---

17   In all these analyses the associations are significant to 99 per cent.

18   This statistical model permits the analysis of a continual dependent variable against both categorical and continuous variables. Differently from conventional regression analysis, the procedure really considers categorical variables instead of recodifying them in dummy variables.

19   Given the assumptions of normality and linearity, I used as dependent variable the square root of monthly per capita family income, which presented the best fit. The model tests the violation of the assumption of equality of the variances of the independent variables. In our case, the significance of the Levene test was of 0.195, suggesting the acceptance of the model.

20   Three outliers were excluded from the model, leaving 206 cases in the analysis.

Table 3   Results of GLM model of family income per capita (square root)

	Effect between subjects	Estimated parameters				Effect on income (R\$) of a change in one unit of the independent variable with the others constants, at the level of average income (R\$271)
	F	B	Standard deviation	t	Sig.	
Corrected Model	24.68					
Intercept	308.46	20.28	1.25	16.28	0.000	
Years of schooling	10.22	0,27	0.09	3.20	0.002	9.0
Persons in the household	53.03	-1.66	0.23	-7.28	0.000	-51.9
Average networks with varied and not local sociability	4.45	1.92	0.91	2.11	0.036	66.9
Interaction between stable income and nº de nodes	13.77	0.04	0.01	3.11	0.002	1.3
Interaction between segregation and nº of spheres	7.11	0.44	0.16	2.67	0.008	14.7

Source: Interviews by the author.

Obs.: N = 206 cases; R^2 of 0.427 and R^2 adjusted from 0.409.

As we can see, the traditional variables, such as individual's schooling and the size of the family (number of persons in the household), presented statistical significance in the explanation of family income per capita, although with opposite effects. The first variable exerts a positive influence on earnings and, as would be expected, individuals with higher levels of schooling tend to have higher incomes. Each additional year of study adds on average, R\$ 9.0 to the average family income per capita of those individuals. It is worth remarking that the analysis only included individuals in poverty, and it is likely that a study of a broader range of social groups would have derived stronger effects from schooling.

The second variable, inversely, impacted negatively on earnings. Basically, the greater the number of persons in the household, the lower the income per head. The effect of the number of persons is not merely numeric (although this variable does enter into the calculation of the dependent variable), given that the earnings of persons other than the ego are included in total family income, just as the networks give access to more persons than just the ego. The model is informing us that the aggregative effects of networks and incomes do not compensate for the dependency effect and dependence grows at a faster rate than the arrival of other income generators or network aggregators. As can be seen in the last column, each extra individual in the home drains R$51.9 per capita from income, a very significant effect.

The relational variables entered the model in three ways. In the first place, a dummy variable, specifying whether or not the individual in question had an average network with varied and not local sociability (centered on the church, work or associations), repeating the results of the previous section. The effect is positive, indicating that income tends to be higher amongst those with these relational patterns, adding, on average, R$66.9 to income, which corresponds to more than seven years of study and to the negative effect of the addition of one extra person to the home. Nevertheless, we have to bear in mind that the type of network and sociability only assumes the values zero and one, whilst the number of years of study varies between zero and twelve and the number of persons in the home from one to nine.

The model also includes two interaction variables with relational dimensions including, in the first place, an interaction between network size and stable income. Stable income is captured by a dummy variable that gains value one in situations that guarantee a more or less regular earnings flow. This includes work with an employment record card, domestic or not, owning a business, and also the retired. Considering the dynamics of the local labor market, I decided to include those without employment cards (domestic or not) as having a stable income, if they had been in their current job for more than a year. Those individuals without stable income were the unemployed and underemployed, as well as those without an employment card but who had recently been employed.[21]

The logic of the interaction is easy to understand. As 'stable income' assumes the value one for those who possess this condition, the interaction term has no effect for those who have unstable income. As can be seen from the last column, for those with stable income each additional node in the network adds R$1.3 to income. As the number of nodes varies substantially, the effect may be considerable. Just for comparison purposes: for those with stable income, each additional ten nodes correspond to an additional R$13 of income.

The last variable shows the positive effect of the interaction between segregation and variability of sociability and complements previous evidences. As segregation acquires a zero value in non-segregated locales, the variability of sociability has no effects on non-segregated individuals. In segregated places, however, each extra sphere adds R$14.7 to the income of the individuals, an effect

---

21   Stable earnings revealed a significant (and positive) correlation to income. However, the analysis showed that the interaction term was also significant and increased the model's explanatory power. Given that, I opted to maintain the interaction instead of the original variable. The consideration of some of those without employment record card as stable followed an excellent suggestion by Nadya Guimarães.

similar to an additional two years of schooling. This is a fairly significant impact given that the number of spheres ranges from one to 7.

The interpretation of the evidence is relatively clear and seems to confirm previous findings. Segregation isolates the individuals territorially, and consequently the best off individuals amongst the segregated will be those with varied sociability, indicating that networks can really help in the reduction of that isolation stemming from segregation. However, this result is only achieved by those able to maintain a varied sociability, with the social situation tending to be worse for those individuals who cannot sustain varied patterns of sociability, thereby increasing the heterogeneity of the situations among the poor. On the other hand, there is no effect on the non-segregated individuals.

5. Summarizing the network effects

Considering the centrality of these results to my argument, I will consolidate them before we proceed. We saw that the differences of the networks among the poor have important consequences for the individuals in terms of access to work, protected work, social precariousness and monetary earnings. The types of network and sociability were strongly linked to the individual's chances of having employment, having employment with some degree of protection as well as to the likelihood of their being submitted to situations of precariousness. In all these cases, the worst conditions were associated with those relational patterns based on primary contacts and more prone to homophilia and localism. Inversely, those with less primary relational patterns, which were more based on organizational environments, tended more frequently to be in work, to have better protected jobs and to find themselves in less precarious social situations. Although the most important conditioner of situations of precariousness is sociability with less homophily and weak localism, precariousness may be attenuated by the presence of sociabilities centered on the family, or aggravated by the status of migrant.

Finally, the individual's income is connected to their schooling and the number of persons residing in the home, traditional variables in the topic's analysis, but also to the individuals' relational patterns, the size of their networks (for those with stable income sources), as well as the variability of their sociability (for those resident in segregated areas). The size of the effects of these variables allows us to confirm the stand-out importance of networks and sociability in the explanation of the income of the poorest.

In all cases, the best conditions were those of individuals with medium-sized networks, evincing little localism and with a sociability constructed around organizational spaces (church, work and associations), which tends to be less homophilous.

Chapter 6

Do Social Networks Matter in Gaining Access to Goods and Services Obtained from Outside Markets?

We saw in the previous chapter that networks and sociability patterns mediate the access to markets and the goods and services provided. However, individuals might (and effectively do) access several goods and services through social support external to the logic of the market (as well as to the State), solving several daily problems and mitigating poverty situations.

Among those may be included from the access to information about job positions to emotional support in situations of personal or family crisis, among several others. The access to the State is also commonly mediated by social contacts. This happens because even considering the most Weberian universalistic logic, the direct delivery of policies involves elements of personalization, as stressed by authors such as Lipzky (1980). As already discussed, this happens especially in moments of intense expansion of services, when information about the policies is relatively opaque and when implementation involves several details and street-level bureaucracies.

The access to the three sources of welfare – markets, State and sociability –, therefore, depends on social contacts and may be influenced by the different configurations of social networks of the individuals. To analyze these elements however, we need very different information than the ones mobilized in previous chapters. In this chapter I use the information collated from in-depth interviews conducted with 20 interviewees from the original pool, and covering a range of types of network and sociability. As described in Chapter 2, I presented the interviewees with their networks as previously drawn up and asked them to discuss how they mobilize those networks in order to obtain varied forms of assistance in their everyday lives. Questions were asked concerning migrations (including intra-urban moves), house-building, small-scale repairs, help looking after children, the elderly or the house, aid in times of ill health, the lending of provisions and money, trust and emotional support, match-making, help finding work and information on politics, services and public policies.

The results reveal the existence of patterns of network mobilization in the act of obtaining social assistance. The structure of the chapter begins by establishing certain conceptual platforms required for the construction of my argument. The second section discusses the types of social assistances provided by and to individuals, with special reference to personal networks. Whenever possible, I give examples from the case study, but citing fictitious names to warranty anonymity.

1. Exchanges, help and trust

This section defines conceptually the core elements involved in these assistance relations, namely: exchange, trust, reciprocity and intimacy. The aim is not to conduct a detailed conceptual discussion of these categories within the social sciences, or to discuss at length the types of relationship that underpin given social situations, as does Blokland (2003), but rather to establish the conceptual bedrock required to understand the subsequent analysis. On the other hand, the study did not attempt to arrive at native categories, but merely to analyze these important processes whilst taking into account the interviewees' own interpretations, without any pretension towards reproducing them.

As suggested by the classic contribution of Homans (1958) 'social behavior is … exchange', but not necessarily based only on rewards and costs and certainly involving only intentionality. In this sense, assistances analyzed here consist of acts of exchange. These exchanges are intrinsically social (Polanyi 1980) and involve the swapping of material and immaterial elements, as well as possessing certain symbolic dimensions. Social help and support automatically involve exchange, as they hinge upon a logic of reciprocity, just like those originally studied by Mauss. In the sense underscored by the anthropological tradition of gift-giving, the elements involved in these exchanges shape whole conjuncts of ample social and symbolic meanings that, in their original formulations, provided interpretive keys to wide-reaching societal elements (Mauss, [1923] 2003) and have been applied to diverse social dimensions ever since (Lanna 1995; Vilela 2001).

Social exchange theory in sociology has already stated the role of norms in the enforcement of reciprocity and the production of trust and social solidarity. At least two types of exchanges are present in social situations. A first type is associated with what the literature calls restricted exchange involving face-to-face exchange situations associated with specific dyads. In these situations, reciprocity is direct and mutual and the accountability of the exchange is immediate (Uehara 1990). The attributes of those involved in the exchange are key in this 'quid pro quo' exchanges and although social norms are important, personalized and specific trust in the reciprocation of the exchange is the central element that explains why each actor uses the relationship for exchanges.

A second type of social exchange has a collective or societal configuration. This describes the several social situations where someone provides something but is reciprocated by others, creating expanded but indirect cycles of reciprocity that may span the whole society, constituting generalized exchange. In these broad systems of exchange, social trust and solidarity are forged (Molm 1990, Uehara (1990) has sustained that these two types should not be understood as opposite but as extremes in a continuum where several combinations might be present.

In this sense, therefore, they differ amongst themselves in terms of their more or less impersonal character, spanning a continuum that goes from generalized or impersonal exchanges to the most personalized and non-transferable (Nunes 1997), in which the attributes of those involved in the transaction are key.

Mercantile exchanges, which can be mediated by money or some other 'currency', are the most intensely impersonal as stressed by Grosseti (2009) and discussed in Chapter 1, even if they always involve social relations and, as such, are mediated by a bevy of social, material and symbolic processes (Weber, [1922] 1999; Polanyi 1980). As will be seen, my results suggest that, in contexts of poverty, in which diverse types of informality abound in mercantile exchange, the level of impersonality should be lesser. In which case, the economy of exchange should prevail in transactions[1].

These transactions involve the exchange of both material goods, such as money, provisions, tools, and other such items, and immaterial goods, such as information, affection, solidarity, emotional support, etc. Furthermore, all such transactions possess clearly symbolic dimensions, such as recognition and prestige. These exchanges do not always involve similar goods or services, and may not necessarily be immediate, which factors indebtedness into the equation of social reciprocity. In a sense, relationship patterns are always exchange networks, not only because of what can be channeled through these relationships, but also through the reciprocity involved and the levels of trust and intimacy that sustain them over time. Additionally, the status of these relations can also be transformed by changing dynamics of exchange, reciprocity and trust, as we shall see further on.

On the other hand, all types of help come at some species of cost to the giver. This cost may include material resources, such as money and goods, but will also involve the time spent in rendering assistance, as well as the operational and emotional investments that entails. Obviously, the costs incurred through these practices are mediated by the existing conditions of reciprocity and can be mitigated, in part, by the types of tie involved. In this sense, the more costly the assistance rendered, the more dependent it will be upon the existence of certain types of tie and levels of trust capable of mediating that reciprocity (offering greater or lesser assurance that one can rely on future payback). However, as I shall show further on, the presence of social reciprocity and trust does not necessarily exclude monetary payment.

By trust I understand the surety that one's expectations regarding a given relationship will be met, whatever they may be. For some interviewees, homophily is a condition of trust – with individuals claiming only to trust those who share their attributes (or behaviors). For others, there are different types of trust, associated with specific social situations. Analysis of the cases suggested that, depending on the situation, expectations vary from relationship type to relationship type,

---

1   I owe the observation of this dimension and its formulation to my conversations with Encá Moya and Valéria Macedo, to whom I extend my thanks.

with each requiring its own capital of trust. Of these types, three were identified: personal, professional and political/associative.

The first of these is the most common and concerns how dependable the ego considers its contacts to be with regard to matters of a personal nature. This is associated with intimacy, but only depends on it in relations of trust, as we shall see. Professional trust is the surety the ego has that its contacts will uphold their part of the bargain in professional activities. This type of trust featured heavily in interviews with small business owners and others who rely on regular work colleagues. Finally, political/associative trust, which appeared less frequently than the other two, involves the assurance that one's contacts will deliver on promises made in relation to activities, alliances and political disputes. In all of these cases, trust may occur in horizontal or vertical relations, being compatible with disparities of power and hierarchy.

Different degrees of trust, in turn, are usually associated with different forms of reciprocity. Most of the time, low-trust assistance is associated with the moral and impersonal reciprocity typical of group belonging, as per what Blokland (2003) calls attachments (after Weber [1922] 1999) – i.e., non-instrumental relationships based on rationality and the value of belonging to groups circumscribed within shared identities. It is also associated with more instrumental relationships based on reciprocity via direct barter; or what Luciano, an interviewee from the Jaguaré shantytown, called 'give-and-take' relationships. Whilst the relationships that bind the former are linked with both rationality (deliberate and conscious action) and values, the latter are based on rational, goal-oriented actions in a manner similar to that defined by Blokland (2003), after Weber ([1922] 1999). At the other end of the spectrum, relations that involve high levels of trust are associated with specific exchanges and reciprocity that may be distributed over time and involve different material and immaterial goods. In this case, the reciprocity is wholly personalized and underpinned by a specific type of personal tie.

In fact, each of these levels of trust demands ties of different strength, frequency of interaction and type. While low trust exchanges (mobilized as generalized exchange) may happen through weak, less frequent and interaction-type ties (in the sense afforded to the term by Degenne 2009), high trust forms of exchange (which depend upon restricted exchanges) claims for stronger, more frequent and denser relational flows.

Intimacy, on the other hand, also rests upon the assurance that the other will uphold his/her part of the bargain, but its focus is on matters of a personal nature that require confidentiality derived from a high degree of trust. In the words of João, a resident of the Cidade Tiradentes housing complex, 'intimacy is an open game'. Unlike trust, intimacy can only feature in relationships in which differences in hierarchy or power remain slight.

In addition to the different costs of providing assistance, other factors that influence access to help – and therefore to the impact it can have on living conditions and poverty – are the array of types of tie and degrees of trust present in relationships.

2. Access to assistance

Information drawn from the interviews suggest that the assistance that mediates access to markets and social support can be grouped according to an overlap between trust, cost and type of reciprocity. Depending on the situation, the reciprocity and trust involved assume a range of shapes and aspects, and the exchange can be more or less personalized. On the other hand, in the specific case of returning each specific favor, the costs, obviously not restricted to monetary dimensions, acquire distinct contents, often mixing prestige, affection, expectation of retribution and money. Another relevant dimension to these costs is the time and personal availability spent in providing the help, as well as its frequency or perpetuity. As such, while relatively little wealth circulates in the world of the poor, the provision of high-cost assistance is very common.

There is an often tenuous line between what is purely a market-structured purchase and what constitutes exchange via social reciprocity, albeit also involving cash payments. In the first case, even though the individuals may know each other, the transaction is purely the purchase of a good or service that could just as well be procured elsewhere. On the other hand, we have social exchanges that may also involve payment, even between very close individuals. Andreotti (2006) found this kind of situation extensively among excluded people in Milan and suggested that this involved 'a sort of monetarization of social networks'. I believe, however, that in this case money is simply one of the dimensions involved in the exchange, which is not generalized, but specific and personalized by the ties of trust involved. I suggest that these cash payments constitute retributions that help reduce the cost of the favor rendered, in addition to such other factors as increased prestige and affection or pay-back for, or the promise of, assistance past or future, in the context of reciprocity.

Considering these dimensions, there are basically three types of observable help: immediate, low-trust and low-cost help; more constant, trust based and costly help; and help involving centrally trust and intimacy. In what follows I will discuss each in detail, illustrated, wherever possible, with examples from the interviews. In general terms, as we move from type one to type three, the required level of trust and tie strength increases, as does the cost incurred. Each type of help is associated with a specific form of reciprocity.

a. More immediate, low-cost forms of help that require low trust

This type would include help in times of ill-health, the lending of tools and provisions, looking after someone's home while they are away, as well as the passing-on of information about services and jobs.

This type of help is typically associated with ties of acquaintance or interactions in Degenne (2009) sense, in which contact may even be frequent but is only superficial and has low strength. It is interesting to add that this kind of help tends to escape from researches focused on social assistance networks, considering the kind of tie that enables these assistances. This is the kind of relationship that Luciano from the Jaguaré shantytown describes as 'Hi, how's it going' relationships. In general, this kind of help occurs in relationships with a low degree of personalization and only distant reciprocity, being close to the description of generalized exchange already established. Most of the ties involved are neighborhood-based (although may be of any kind) and tend to be easily broken, especially through changes of residence. However, they are also easy to replace at the new residence, though the interviewee may express a preference for those at one locale or the other. Fights are also a regular situation in which these ties may be broken. The ties that sustain this kind of help basically function as impersonal supports for relations of reciprocity in the provision of everyday assistance. As such, they require very low levels of trust, and are associated with situations in which reciprocity is tenuous and distant.

At the root of this type of help lies a diffuse sense of solidarity. If we consider that all types of solidarity are associated with identities, in this case we would be talking about a loose identity or sense of pertaining to a large group, such as 'we of the community', 'the poor', 'the women', 'the brothers of faith' or even just 'the human race'. The discourse that emerges from the interviews to justify this kind of aid is associated with this sense of belonging to a wider group. As João from the Cidade Tiradentes housing complex puts it, 'when it comes to being sick, even your enemies have compassion'. Health crises are a perfect illustration for this kind of situation, in which one can often count on the help of neighbors. One of the important situations in which help is provided is lending cars or driving the sick person to the hospital, as in cases related by Lúcia, David, Luciano and Rafaela, from the slums and shantytowns of Paraisópolis, Jaguaré and Vila Nova Esperança, respectively. The ties that channel this kind of aid are normally those that Blokland (2003) calls attachments.

Even though this type of help does not require a base of prior trust, it can be withheld from those who have failed to provide the minimal requirements of reciprocity in the past, whether in a personalized or a generalized form. In the words of João, from Cidade Tiradentes, 'I always used to lend tools, but I don't do it anymore, because people don't return them'. Conversely, the provision of assistance during a health crisis can serve to deepen the relationship between individuals, boosting one's trust in the person who came to one's aid and perhaps even establishing a higher degree of intimacy. So while neither trust nor intimacy are required in order for someone to provide this type of assistance, given its practically impersonal character, both can be positively (or negatively) impacted by the provision (or not) of such help.

Passing on information about employment opportunities can be associated with all three types of help, but it is often conveyed via ties equipped for only immediate, low-cost assistance, especially when it comes to more local vacancies. In its most extreme form, such information can even come from complete strangers. In the case of João, for example, the information that led to his getting a job was given to him in a park by someone he had never met before, while for Ednalva, from the Paraisópolis shantytown, it came from someone she met on the bus. Maria, an unemployed woman from the Jaguaré shantytown, who used to collect recyclables to make ends meet, secured a cleaning job thanks to information from an acquaintance she made when she started to attend a new church. It costs nothing to convey this kind of information and it can be propagated through the weakest possible connections and sometimes even by chance encounters, in a manner similar to the weak ties described by Granovetter (1973).

Specifically in this respect, certain locations where information circulates more freely tend to generate potential intersections between the networks of individuals who barely know each other, if at all. In this case, it is not the effect of the network of any given ego, but rather of specific shared spaces that make it possible to tap the networks of people outside one's own network. Antonio's hairdresser's is a case in point. Antonio is also a pastor and the director of a community organization in Paraisópolis. According to the interviewees, that particular space represents an important venue for information exchange and serves as a point of convergence. The same may occur around individuals who are known to have extensive networks. Rafaela, from Vila Nova Esperança, and Antônio and Jorge, from Paraisópolis, say they are often approached by people, sometimes even strangers, looking for information about job vacancies. All three are, not incidentally, community leaders with involvement in associative activities, what influences the size and the diversity of their relational patterns. In both cases – when the effect comes from organizational environments or from the proximity with a person who has a rich network – the situation is very different from a 'weak ties' effect, since the assistances come from the network of an another person, and not from the ego's weak ties.

Another important key difference in relation to the results of Granovetter's influential work is related to the search for jobs. The author's arguments about the importance of weak ties to the job-seeker are based on the idea that if a given ego has been unemployed for a certain amount of time, any job that does eventually come his way will not come via strong ties – because if these had such potential, he would probably not have remained unemployed for so long. Technically speaking, the argument derives from an empirical regularity observed by Granovetter: if a given ego has a strong relationship with A and another with B, it is highly unlikely that A and B should have no relationship at all. New information is therefore far more likely to reach you through weak ties than through strong ones[2].

In apparent contradiction of Granovetter's findings, a significant number of the higher-quality jobs found by the interviewees came via strong ties, even family ties. However, the evidence largely refers to the first jobs of newly-arrived migrants or first-time job seekers. It all comes down to the fact that, when these

---

2   Obviously, the logic assumes that all other conditions in the job market remain constant and that the networks connected to the ego by strong ties change very little – otherwise new information could well enter through changes in the economic environment or networks, regardless of tie strength.

individuals draw for the first time upon the networks that absorb them (or integrate young adults into the working-world), new information about job opportunities comes from both strong and weak ties. [3] This effect tends to be particularly strong for low-skilled individuals on the brink of survival, for whom virtually any job can make all the difference. I will return to this point in the next Chapter when discussing the relational mechanisms.

Examples of such cases are Ana Luiza, Luciano, João, Rafaela, Lúcia and David, who obtained jobs at important times thanks to information channeled through relatives or other very strong ties. In the case of the first four, these jobs were secured when they arrived in São Paulo after migrating from the Northeast, while for David and Lúcia, it was when they began their working lives in São Paulo in their late teens. In both cases, therefore, strong ties provided crucial job information when entering the local labor market for the first time.

Despite having this point in common, their trajectories (and their consequences) are very different. With the help of a relative, Ana Luíza found a steady job in a clothes shop selling brideswear in the center of São Paulo, but what she really wanted was to become self-employed. After some time working, she learned how to make wedding garlands with the help of some friends and left her job. She has been working from home ever since, drawing upon contacts she made during her time at the shop. In addition to her higher income, she now has control over her own work and no longer needs to commute each day from Vila Nova Esperança to the city center. The case of Luciano is also worthy of mention. After working with his brothers at a bakery in a middle-class neighborhood near Vila Nova Jaguaré, he too started his own business. After a critical period during which he had to contract heavy debts and even sell his house to pay them off, he now finds himself in a highly prosperous situation in relative terms. João, from Tiradentes, also got his first job in São Paulo through a relative – a brother-in-law working at a carpenter's shop. However, João's future turned out to be far less prosperous than those of Ana Luíza and Luciano. Lastly, Rafaela, from Vila Nova Esperança, was helped into work by an aunt at two key moments: first, when she arrived in São Paulo from the Northeast, only to move back a year later; and again when her pendular migration brought her back to São Paulo.

The effects for first-time job seekers in São Paulo appear to be rather similar. David fell out with his father during his late teens and left the family home in Paraisópolis. He secured his first job, in a photography store, with the help of his sister. Lúcia's two sons got their first jobs at a car tire mechanic's workshop near Vila Nova Esperança thanks to her uncle, who had received them in São Paulo after migration and had lent them their first home in the city in a small precarious house in the back of his lot.

---

3   Guimarães (2004) obtained results compatible with this interpretation in two different surveys among jobseekers in São Paulo. Though she did not study their networks directly, the author identified a significant decrease in the importance of the jobseeker's inner circle as the individual got older.

The first two cases – those of Ana Luízia and Luciano – show that future planning can also play an important role in the individual's ability to milk the relational opportunities that arise. The presence or otherwise of this planning is associated with the cultural frames through which the individual sees society and his/her situation, in the sense of Lamont and Small (2008: 8), i.e.: 'an interpretive schema that simplifies and condenses the social reality, selectively choosing and codifying objects, situations, events, experiences, and sequences of action'. In both of the abovementioned cases, the interviewees planned their insertion in accordance with the situations in which they found themselves, and this enabled them to use the knowledge acquired in the bakery and clothes shop to start their own businesses as owner and autonomous professional, respectively.

On the other extreme we find people who adopt a far more passive posture before their futures; a situation well illustrated by João, from Tiradentes, who had long and important relationships with people who were out of work but did little to improve their lot. In his own words, his partner from a nine-year relationship 'didn't fight'. For João, many people 'have no ambition, or maybe it's a lack of gumption or plain laziness. I mean normal ambition, to have a house, a wardrobe to hang your things in'. Yet it is not exclusively a matter of effort, but also one of planning: these people 'only remember to eat when they're hungry. That's not how it works; that you just remember to plant when you're already hungry'. I believe that this behavior can be viewed not simply as the product of choices, but also as the adaptive result of an accumulation of precarious situations experienced over the course of certain peoples' lifetimes, thus reducing their degree of freedom.

Another aspect worth mentioning is help in gaining access to public services and policy benefits. The information does not suggest the existence of personalized help involving electoral reciprocity in obtaining public services and policy benefits, contrary to what is asserted in the vast literature on political clientelism. Confirming the results of earlier studies on access to public services and policy benefits in São Paulo (Figueiredo, Torres and Bichir 2006), there was no evidence of intermediation, whether personal, political or of any other form, associated with relations of electoral reciprocity.

This tendency is connected with the universalization of access to the most basic public services and policy benefits, as already demonstrated in specific studies on the theme (Figueiredo, Torres and Bichir 2006; Figueiredo *et al.* 2005, for example). However, that does not mean that social exchanges associated with such access do not exist, but rather indicates, in counterpart, that such benefits have been reformulated as rights as opposed to electorally negotiable currency. This distinction is conceptually important, as the tradition of studies in this area is to assume the presence of political clientelism wherever access to these benefits involves some form of exchange. As we know, social relations involve exchanges, which paints as somewhat naive the interpretation of the institutionalization of public policies as a social unraveling of the relations between the State and society.

Suffice it to recall all the social dimensions involved in the implementation of public policies through street-level bureaucracy as enumerated by Lipsky (1980).[4]

The crux of the matter is what circulates in exchanges associated with policy access, not how socially 'disincarnate' those exchanges may or may not be. Clientelism is defined by the establishment of relations in which help toward access to policy benefits is exchanged for electoral support. And it is precisely this dimension that is affected by the universalist expansion of access to public policy benefits, seen as the electoral value of this support plummets when the benefits are understood to be – and more importantly, are felt to be – rights of the citizen.

As such, even in the absence of clientelism in the classical sense, the interviews frequently presented cases of institutional referrals that were personal in character. One such case was that of Carlos, a young resident from a São Paulo favela, and his school principal, who had him transferred to a better school. This also occurred with Marta, another resident of the slums, who managed to get onto a computer course thanks to the mediation of the director of the municipal crèche attended by her son. Along similar lines, policy technicians can serve important functions with regard to other public initiatives, explaining procedures and forwarding people for attendance, as in the case of community health agents (Lotta 2010). Furthermore, contacts with community networks and associations also help channel this kind of assistance, especially in the personal networks of the poor or the elderly. In one of the study areas, the local parish priest doubled as a powerful social and political leader, occupying the role of mediator between the local sphere and the formal universe of the institutions.

As these exchanges involve reciprocity, individuals that produce such mediation frequently achieve projection and distinction, especially among the poorer and the elderly, who depend more on this kind of support. However, in all of these cases, it is more a case of making information available and providing assistance with red tape (which can pose a huge obstacle to this social group) than of intermediation in the classical sense, associated with forms of reciprocity with some electoral return.

b. More constant, crucial, trust based and costly help

This type of help includes chronic situations of ill-health that require constant attention; daily child care; housework; help with migration; and loans of small sums. In all of these cases, it amounts to a relatively costly (though not necessarily financially so) activity for the provider. The cases studied indicate that there is often payment involved, even for people very close to the recipient (siblings,

---

4   It is worth highlighting the parallels between this reasoning and Karl Polanyi's criticism (1980) of the free market as a field of economic relations disincarnate of social relations. Both the market and the State are constitutive parts of society, shot-through with ties of the most varied kinds, and can be separated from it only analytically, and only provisionally, even then. The ontology of relations between the State and its immediate surroundings (as well as with the market), however, cannot ignore its wider insertions.

parents, good friends, etc), in a similar way as the one found by Andreotti (2006). Following the interviewees, I see these payments as a way of mitigating the burden of cost incurred by the helper. But such exchanges should not be misconstrued as any old mercantile transaction, as they involve reciprocity, depend upon trust, and cannot be canalized by any type of tie, what definitively localizes them far from generalized exchange. In this sense, the provision of this kind of assistance in a purely mercantile and de-personalized form constitutes something quite different. In the case of the middle class, such costly help is frequently sourced from the market, through crèches, nannies, nurses, builders and bank loans. In the case of the poor, market-mediated hirings are limited to specialist construction services. All other forms of assistance are provided socially and in accordance with the logics of reciprocity and trust.

Looking after the kids while the parents go out to work is a service usually rendered by family members, including elder siblings or neighbors, with or without cash payment. In the case of Jorge, from Paraisópolis, the task was always a paid one carried out by a sister-in-law, while for Maria, from the poorest area of Jaguaré, it was her neighbors who took care of the kids, also on a paid basis. Maria once remarked: 'no-one does that for free'. Jorge and his wife never needed anyone to look after the children on a daily basis, but his sister-in-law does the school-run in return for a monthly payment. On the other hand, some cases did relate childcare by neighbors with weak connections to the family involved, leading to frequent accounts of mistreatment. Hence trust is such an important dimension in this kind of assistance, although many people have nobody in a position of trust to assume the task and have to mobilize estrangers.

Care for the seriously ill also involves high costs and levels of trust. The same can be said of post-natal care for women with newly-born children. In these cases, it is almost always the family that provides the support. When a post-natal mother lives far away from her family and does not have a strong personal network to draw from, she tends to move back to the family temporarily, even if this means going to worse living conditions. In a case reported by Carlos, his sister, who lives in a good house outside the slum, moved back to the family shack during the later stages of a high-risk pregnancy, sharing a room with the interviewee, his brother and their mother.

It has to be noted that, contrary to the process of communitarian self-help housing construction widely narrated in the literature during the 70s and 80s (Kowarick 1979), no cases arose of mutual community help in house-building. While some interviewees said their houses were originally built in this way (partially or completely), the vast majority of these descriptions, and all descriptions of more recent events, indicates the hiring of builders or some collective, but not community effort. By collective process I understand the assistance of a small but select group based on personal reciprocity, which is quite different from community processes, which involve the participation of a large number of people and rest on the fundamental principle of identity or solidarity. In most of the cases identified by the study, the construction was carried out by family members and close friends, with some payment being made, especially to those rendering specialist services (electrics and plumbing), though these were almost always hired from the market at local prices and in an impersonal manner. The cases of Jorge, Lúcia and Rafaela are illustrative. Jorge, a community leader in Paraisópolis, received help from only his wife's uncle and his brother-in-law when building his house, but he had to pay them. Lúcia also received help from in laws and her son, while Rafaela had only her husband and brothers to help her build their wooden hut in Vila Nova Esperança. Rafaela has since sold the hut to her sister and now lives in a brick house purchased with what she managed to save of her pay as a cleaner.

One of the aspects to feature most regularly in the results is assistance with migrations, particularly taking people in and helping them find their first job in the new city. Sometimes the person receiving the migrant, usually a member of the family or close friend from the old hometown, actually covers the costs of the migration, whether on condition of repayment or otherwise. Some people specialize in this type of help. Lúcia, from Vila Nova Esperança, spoke of how her uncle regularly received migrants arriving at the João XXIII neighborhood, both on a paid basis and free of charge. He even built some housing units at the back of his lot so he could rent them out. Other people, such as the aunt of Rafaela from Vila Nova Esperança, do not charge for this assistance. This aunt, once a recipient of such help herself, has put up various other members of the family. Her house is a 'kind of hostel', says Rafaela.

The accounts also showed that pendular migrations are fairly common. For example, Luciano, from Jaguaré, José, from the slums, and Rafaela, from Vila Nova Esperança, all migrated between São Paulo and their hometowns on various occasions. Numerous other interviewees spoke of returning migrants. José, from the slums, and João, from Tiradentes, told of relatives who had come down to São Paulo only to fail to adapt and return home. In João's words, they 'don't settle here, because south of the Northeast it's another country. It's all very different'.

There were also many cases of intra-city moves, often involving assistance from friends or relatives in other parts of the city. These moves may be spurred by conflicts with the family that had originally taken the migrant in, or by the pursuit of better urban and professional insertion. However, the migrant's first base would seem to be pivotal in determining professional direction and developing an urban employment track-record and an initial personal network. I will return to this point in the next Chapter when discussing the relational mechanisms.

Finally, there are also small cash loans, with interviewees mentioning having lent or borrowed sums of between R$1.00 and R$10.00 (US$ 0.5 and US$ 5.0). Most of the time these loans are made by and to family members or close friends, be they from the neighborhood, work or church. Obviously, 'you ask those you know can afford it', says João from Tiradentes. In other words, the lenders are close ties who are slightly better off financially. There may also be a certain sense of shame involved. João, who lives alone and has no family support to draw from, said that he has sometimes preferred to go to loan sharks than run the risk of 'being turned down by someone I respect, which would be the death of me'.

In the case of shop owners, these requests would appear to be relatively common, confirming results found by Andreotti (2006) in Milan. Luciano, from Jaguaré, however, says that he only lends to 'sound family men and women with well-consolidated families. Basically, only to decent folk'. The practice is therefore subject to a moral filter, otherwise 'the money might go on drink, gambling or to feed addictions'. Many of the interviewees said the borrowers always pay the money back, therefore maintaining the lender's trust and keeping the doors open for future assistance. For shop owners who lend money, the main interest seems to be in keeping good relations with the clientele. According to Luciano, 'that person is a client, and you don't want to upset the pie', but there is also a very specific reciprocity, as 'they are there in the day-to-day, helping out', buying products. One important symbolic dimension here is the distinction and respect earned by the regular lender. Jorge, who is a community leader in Paraisópolis, as well as a shop owner, says that 'getting the money back varies a lot from person to person. There are debts I don't even call in'. In this case, there is clearly an intrinsic asymmetry of relations (and in some cases even of hierarchy), based on a reciprocity in which the formation and preservation of prestige play a central role.

As this type of help involves trust and is personalized, individuals who provide it are hard to replace. As such, severed or reduced contact with them (increased physical distance, a shrinking economy of ties or various forms of rupture) can result in a deterioration of conditions of support and create social vulnerability (in extreme cases, even ostracism). Newly-arrived migrants also tend to suffer from the difficulties experienced in securing this kind of help, given their low degree of social insertion. The interviews revealed that this was one of the prime benefits to be gained from taking in migrant relatives. In addition to the proverbial 'wanting the best for one's family', as in the case of João from Tiradentes, who said he 'brought [a relative] down, because I saw, and still see, a lot of progress in São Paulo', the formation of a physically expanded nuclear family can make life a lot easier, affording not only emotional comfort, but also access to this kind of help, and that described in the following section.

c. Help that involves trust and intimacy

This type of help involves loans of large sums of money, serving as a confidant, or providing emotional and political support (for those involved in electoral politics, community organizations or unions). The ties that channel this kind of assistance hinge upon trust and intimacy. Most of the time, this level of trust involves social, political or even moral homophily.

Some interviewees involved in commercial activities mentioned loans of significant sums of money. In these cases, the loans had a strong mercantile motivation, despite being interest-free, as they were associated with the purchase of a stake in partnerships. However, there was clearly a strong aspect of trust involved, as is common in commercial partnerships, especially given the degree of informality characteristic of this particular social sphere, where ties in the economy are pervaded by the economy of ties. This trust rests upon a homophily of behavior, as described by McPherson *et al.* (2001). The ego will not necessarily lend money to those who are close to him, but largely only to those with a similar character to his own, and who can therefore be considered trustworthy in matters of commerce and employment. Hence many of these cases are devoid of intimacy, involving people whose only interaction is within the public sphere.

For confidences and emotional support in more personal matters, the situation is rather different. These cases generally involve what Luciano from Jaguaré describes as 'spicy' themes, or the kinds of moment Lucia from Vila Nova Esperança termed 'times of precision'. The first dimension of homophily in these matters is gender – women confide in women and men in men. The exception would appear to be among the young, where friends will sometimes have confidants of the other gender. However, the highly selective nature of this support means only very few individuals will qualify as providers of this kind of assistance, even among those closest to us.

Another requisite for the establishment of relationships of extreme confidence is the absence of asymmetry, as it would seem that only very balanced relationships allow for this sort of help. In this sense, relationships of confidence with certain family members may be out of the question, as the kind of proximity may actually disqualify them as possible confidants or providers of emotional support (though there are exceptions). An example of where this may not be viable is between parents and children in traditional or patriarchal families, in which hierarchy and authority are pillars of the relationship grammar. That said, confidant relationships between mothers and teenage or adult daughters would seem to be very common and a key source of emotional support for both. As already discussed, while trust may be present in relationships of authority, intimacy is not, tending, therefore, to be the preserve of equals. I believe this dimension is not exclusive to the social group analyzed here.

An additional element worth underscoring in relation to issues of secrecy and emotional support is behavioral homophily, or, to use the words of João from Tiradentes, 'when you see eye to eye'. To quote Luciano from Jaguaré: 'for me, trust is when someone has the same habits as you, likes the same things as you, has the same fiber as you, frequents the same places as you and has the same tastes as you'. Hence it is far more likely that we will deposit trust in people who share our beliefs, behaviors and practices. Examples of this abounded, including youths confiding in peers with whom they had a lot in common, homosexuals confiding in other homosexuals, evangelical Christians in other evangelical Christians, and so on. This selectiveness seems to be connected with the fact that, as these issues are often of a personal nature, they will involve moral judgments mediated by the existence of a homophily of behaviors and ideas. This homophily potentizes a sharing of languages and repertoires that makes it easier to understand the issues under discussion, what for sure reinforces group identity and solidarity, but also homophily in itself, turning the group denser, but more closed to the outside. [5]

For those interviewees involved in union or party-political life, there was another specific form of trust – political trust -, leveraged by a homophily of ideas based on shared political views. These relationships are sometimes hierarchised, such as between a leader and the members of the group he or she leads. While there will often be trust in these relationships, there will rarely be personal trust or intimacy. As David, a young man from Paraisópolis, explains: 'when it comes to politics I find it hard to bring up [personal] matters, as these people expect you to show a certain capacity, a certain strength, and so I keep it to myself, as I wouldn't feel comfortable about them knowing my weaknesses'. The grammar of hierarchical relationships is less than compatible with intimacy.

In the case of more costly, trust-based help, depletion in the number of people in one's network capable of providing such assistance can create even more dramatic problems than in the other two categories dealt with above. This whittling may occur due to changes of address, but also due to a breach of trust or loss of intimacy, leading to a reduced base of support, especially of the emotional variety. In extreme cases, this can even occur within the family environment. This is exactly what happened to Cristina, a 24 year-old unemployed mother of three from Tiradentes. At the time of our first interview, she was living with her husband's family. A year later, she had been beaten by her husband, fallen out with her in-laws and moved back with her parents, along with her third child. Her two other children, now aged nine and 11 (by other fathers), had already been raised by her mother, but, in this case, it was not so much a matter of help with childcare as de facto adoption, with Cristina having relinquished all say over the kids' upbringing.

Cristina claims that her family can't stand her husband, the father of her third child, an unemployed gang member who frequently beat her. Whenever she was beaten by him, her brothers would do the same to her husband, but she always ended up going back to him. After this had happened several times, she lost all moral credit with her family, leaving the ties unbroken but drained of the contents she (and the family) would have expected of them. And so, today, even though she lives in the family home, the interviewee is not on speaking terms with most of the family members, who treat her with visible disdain. For a person in a situation like this, ties capable of channeling emotional support and trust-based assistance are practically obliterated. Cristina is basically on the threshold of despair. As she says herself, the only person who continues to help her is a resident of the same building who took pity on her (diffuse and depersonalized solidarity). Nevertheless, the bonds of family have proved so strong that her parents continue to feed her and give her a home.

On the other hand, the content of the ties in a given personal network can also change, increasing potentially the number of providers of costly, trust-based assistance. This may happen due to the dynamic of the relationships themselves,

---

5   Many thanks to Renata Bichir for drawing my attention to this dimension.

but also as a product of the delivery of assistances, since help in a moment of crisis may built trust and turn an acquaintance into a close friend. I will return to this situation in the following chapter while discussing the relational mechanisms.

Chapter 7

How do the Networks Matter: Network Mobilization and Relational Mechanisms

The information obtained through the interviews made profoundly clear the existence of causal regularities associated with the mobilization of sociability in resolving day-to-day issues, as well as in the individual's devising of strategies. Analysis of this information may help enumerate the relational mechanisms that contribute to the production of poverty (or its mitigation) and of the effects demonstrated above. These are not regularities of the networks or of individual elements, but rather social mechanisms in the sense already discussed, which have an impact upon the networks and their availability when it comes to individuals solving their daily problems.

As we already discussed in the first chapter, social mechanisms are middle-range regularities observable empirically, that are part of our analytical models and that may be considered as the specific causal triggers that lead to certain recurring social outcomes. In the case of relational mechanisms, these regularities are associated to networks, their sociability patterns, as well as their mobilization in the individuals' daily lives. With their analysis we may pass from the investigation of correlations between attributes and processes, in Mahoney (2001)´s sense, as in the case of the discussion of neighborhood effects, to the construction of causal explanations, specifying the way the associations observed in the previous chapters are produced. In the specific case of poverty studies, the delimitation of mechanisms allows us to go beyond the somewhat normative discussion of the social capital produced through networks to the specification of how the different mobilization of relational structures may lead regularly to certain results, under certain conditions.

The regularities observed in the data suggest the existence of mechanisms that:

1. influence the formation of networks and individual sociability, at the same time as they
2. impact social action and mediate access to opportunities.

This distinction is merely analytical and, in practice, the two effects occur concomitantly and in association over the course of an individual's life, resulting in specific configurations of attributes and relations. This is the reason why it is impossible to find simple causalities between the acquisitions of attributes and the construction of networks, when understood as disconnected processes. Most of the time, the accumulativeness behind these mechanisms goes some way toward setting in motion those vicious circles that lead to the persistent reproduction of inequalities, in Tilly's formulation of the term (2005).

The literature on social stratification proposes a distinction between inequality of results and inequality of opportunities. The former concerns different living conditions, while the latter refers to the varying probabilities of individuals achieving a certain social level, given their respective social origins. Relational mechanisms interfere in both. By directly reducing access to the goods, services that promote welfare, the mechanisms contribute to the production (or reproduction) of unequal results. Additionally, since their mediation of the individual's access to opportunity structures is far from uniform, they help constitute inequalities of opportunity. As relational mechanisms generate a combined effect on these two types of inequality, I will make no distinction between them through the chapter.

As we will see, some mechanisms differentiate between the networks of the poor and those of the middle class, while others generate heterogeneity among the poor by creating different patterns of access to markets and social assistance, influencing the reproduction of inequalities. Various mechanisms present a circular and cumulative functioning, reproducing situations of poverty among individuals. To analyze these elements is the aim of this chapter. Since the presentation of these mechanisms involves mainly an effort of synthesis, the analytical level is more abstract than in previous chapters and I reduce the references to the cases to their minimal. In general, however, the presentation of the mechanisms will remind the reader of empirical quantitative findings of previous chapters and of specific situations cited in the last chapter.

The chapter is divided into two sections. In the first section I discuss the process of network transformation in time, investigating the main elements associated with change. The second section presents the mechanisms that impact urban life conditions in general and poverty in particular.

1. Changes in the networks

The networks were treated in the quantitative phase of the research as relatively static relational structures. This is due, in part, to the focus of the study, but also to the fact that networks were not mapped at more than one moment in time, which would have made it possible to present a temporal panel. However, the qualitative data shed some light on the changes that had occurred to these networks since our first meetings, approximately a year before the second interview. Without hoping to make a detailed investigation of the network transformations, this section systematizes what was learned about these changes, thus dynamizing what we have discussed thus far.

Network changes can be more localized and conjunctural in nature, or more structural, associated with lifecycles or the types of relational environment to which the individual has access. These changes can either create (or destroy) relationships or change the environment in which these occur, thus contributing to the alteration of the contents of these ties. As a result, not only the sizes and structures of the networks may change, but also the types of tie and the practices of sociability may be transformed, with important consequences for social exchanges, as we saw in previous chapters.

The most general process of network change is the life cycle of the individuals (Bidart e Lavenu 2005), already discussed in Chapter 3. This is basically a tendency toward change of a very general character that can be counterpoised by a number of other factors, but which will also exercise its own influence upon us all. In general terms, during childhood, the individual has a relatively small network based on primary ties, starting with the family and working out through the neighborhood and family friends. Throughout adolescence, networks expand greatly, especially through the intermediation of the school environment and the neighborhood, with a heavy influx of new foci acquired through established contacts (network) and the spheres of friends and neighbors. Each school level has specific characteristics in terms of the social composition of the individuals available for making connections, as well as concerning features of the social setting of the organization that influence the formation and the maintenance of ties, as we learned from Small (2009). Leaving the school environment and entering the world of work alters networks substantially, usually paring them back while also making them more heterophilic. Other important events will also alter networks, such as migrations, changes of address, marriage and separation, and parenthood, as highlighted in the literature in Chapter 1. As individuals age, their networks tend to shrink, partly as they retire from the world of work, but also because of reduced physical mobility and cessation of former activities (Bidart e Lavenu 2005). Consequently, networks become smaller and more concentrated upon the family, the neighborhood and friends. It is interesting to note that similar patterns were observed in ego-centered networks, at least in the case of surveys conducted in Rio de Janeiro and São Paulo (Marques and Bichir 2010).

Other localized processes also have an impact over these general, trend-based changes. Several basic types of network transformation and building process could be identified. The first and more obvious one is associated with the death of a contact, what may have devastating effects in the access of the individual to goods and services. In one case, the death of a godmother whose social position was way above poverty, almost disconnected the individual from his main sources of money and social support, since she was his only connection with the rest of his family, who disapproves his way of life.

It is important to state that, except for death, the exit of a node in an network may also represent only what we call latency – in which the contacts are not cited during the interview, but did not effectively leave the network. The latency of relations, therefore, is mediated by the combination between the type and the intensity of the ties. These ties may be mobilized again later, especially in the case of family ties and strong friendships.

Secondly, networks are severely altered by geographical displacements through change of address, especially so among the poor, since their networks are more heavily based on neighborhood interactions and relations. Depending on the physical distance of the move, this can affect even intimate and strong ties, though it works more readily upon relationships of acquaintance, which are usually more fluid. As one interviewee from a slum in São Paulo put it, these are the 'Hi there' relationships. In the case of this study, many of our interviewees lost (or gained) somewhere between 5 per cent and 10 per cent of their networks in a single year through the comings and goings of these more superficial contacts, especially within the neighborhood. Evidently, migratory processes are involved in this dynamic and cause deep-set alterations, but intra-urban moves work in the same direction. This type of change affects the poor much more severely than the middle-class, given their greater dependency on space in weaving their relations and the greater difficulty they face in meeting the costs of maintaining these ties, as we shall see forthwith.

A third dynamic of recurring change concerns growing heterophily among the individuals present in a relationship, normally wrought by an upgrading or downgrading of their living conditions (as cases of social mobility in the strict sense were very rare in the studied cases), generating greater social distance among individuals who were close before. In many interview cases, we could detect a distancing between the ego and a given alter in what could be characterized as Bourdieu's (2007) social space. This usually occurred due to a change in social condition or a minor geographical move that led the individual to a different social environment. In this latter situation, an ego's contact may move to another part of the same shantytown, a geographically minimal distance away, but to a part or area that has a relatively richer or poorer social composition, thus inhibiting the ego from maintaining those contacts. The effect here is not related to the social movement of the individual in question, but to the stigma or social distinction attached to certain locations, which reflect positively or negatively upon the individual, thus boosting heterophily (even if the people in question continue to share the same characteristics) and hampering the maintenance of contacts. The drifting-apart stemmed from the awkwardness of the tie itself created by stigma, particularly a territorial stigma in the case of changes of residence. The presence of territorial stigmas in the sense used by Wacquant (2008) therefore has a considerable effect on the possibilities of forging and maintaining ties.

Fourthly, members can be included or excluded from networks because of conflicts or disagreements and newly acquired knowledge. Conflicts, however, do not always lead to rupture, even when quite serious. Cases were encountered in which individuals had experienced serious conflicts with the ego, but given the type and intensity of the tie involved (family or close friends, for example), returned to the network or ended up providing crucial assistance in a time of crisis. In the words of one young resident of a shantytown in São Paulo: 'things may one day go back to how they were. Time heals an awful lot'. These are latent cases in the terms already cited.

There were also found alterations caused by changes in organizational or relational environments, seen as the formation or nurturing of ties depends on the organizational environments in which they occur. In this sense, the networks are influenced by organizational characteristics such as being places of common interest and practices or just of attendance and generating interaction with higher or lower degrees of competition or cooperation (Small 2009). Frequenting new environments and abandoning old ones creates or repels opportunities for contact. This is the case, for example, with switching classes at school, job moves, or joining a new religious congregation. Such changes affect the conjunct and tend to occur constantly. They may also render relations latent only to be reactivated later, much like in the mending of bridges after a conflict.

A finnal driver of change is not associated with the structure of the networks, but with the contect of the social ties that bind the nodes together. The content of the relationships are in constant and intense process of transformation. This is not a case of ruptures, or of the construction of ties, but rather of changes in their types. Generally speaking, the interviews indicated that this dynamic is associated with the complex processes of building trust and intimacy. These processes are very similar to those discussed in such instigating fashion by Blokland (2003), about how types of social action in the Weberian sense transform with changes in relationship contents. In relation to our prime interest here, breaches of trust or a cooling of relations have an impact upon the kinds of support individuals can expect to receive from their networks. Likewise, the provision of certain types of assistance can build trust, complicity and intimacy and raise certain relationships to a whole other level. One example is when an acquaintance helps someone at a crucial time, as in a serious health crisis. The newfound confidence and intimacy this builds will help transform the type of tie the ego and the alter had prior to that event, confirming one of the mechanisms we will discuss in the following. In this important dynamics, therefore, the ties remain in the network and its structure does not change, but the contents of the ties are transformed, with important consequences to what can flow through them.

2. Mechanisms

The mechanisms that shape networks and mediate their mobilization can be broken down into two large groups in pursuit of clearer presentation. The first includes the causal triggers that produce a differentiation between the networks of individuals living in poverty and those of their middle-class counterparts, while the second explains much of the network variability observed among the poor.

a. Distinguishing between middle-class and poor networks

When poor and middle-class individuals are young, there is no substantial difference between their networks in terms of their structure, size and sociability: they all tend to be large, with many friends and acquaintances connected by weak ties. Homophily is very present for both groups, although obviously the content of homophily is different – middle class teenagers for the first and poor youngsters for the second. During this period, the process of growing up remains the most important operation in play up until adolescence. This indicates that it is from that point on that the mechanisms start to work intensely, triggering a widening gulf between the relational patterns of these social groups as they make the transition into adulthood. I refer here to the differentiated effects of *school sociability and labor market socialization* between these social groups, and especially of the existence of a transition toward professional networks in the case of the middle-class. It is not only a question of higher educational level per se, but of the relational effects of the middle-class spending longer periods of time in educational institutions that will have later impacts on their insertion within the workplace. Beyond the well-known lower degree of homophily in the school environment (when compared with the family or the immediate neighborhood), there is a second and even more important effect. In comparison with the middle-class, there is a relational discontinuity in socialization for the workplace among the poor. In order to better understand this issue, we shall take a look at the changes in relations and networks that occur during the transition from adolescence to adulthood.

In general, this transition is marked by changes in the ties from local homophily and primary bonds to more external and mixed connections formed within institutional environments, for both the poor and the middle-class. School is one of the forums for the transition from certain types of more primary and local spheres (family, the neighborhood, friends) to less local and more secondary types (church, workplace, unions, associations). The school structure itself reflects this dimension, as secondary school tends to be much less homophilic (and less geographically local) than primary school. As such, throughout the maturing process, people gradually develop the attributes of the adult world at the same time as they acquire the network patterns that go with it. For the middle-class, this occurs in slow, parallel fashion, with their place of study (and stage of life) ushering the transition along. In the case of the poor, the world of studies does not occupy similar importance, with educational careers being briefer and overlapping with events of an adulthood that commences sooner, perhaps through teenage pregnancy, an early entrance into the job market in low-skilled tasks or precocious marriage.

However, the crux of the issue would seem to me to lie in the much rarer presence of university environments, and other such spaces of gradual relational preparation for the professional world, in the work-bound socialization of the poor. It is on the university campus that the middle-class starts forming its professional networks, seen as the domain of study, third-level at least, represents a slow relational transition toward the specialized job market. This happens slowly during the several years of university study during which middle class youngsters construct and consolidate ties with future professionals of their own fields. At the end of this period, they have a significant part of their networks composed by professionals, with which they will establish activities and from whom they will expand their connections and networks.

Individuals living in poverty, even when they do complete high-school, still face considerable relational discontinuity when they emerge into the job market, as their schoolmates will be dispersed across a far broader spectrum of occupations. Socialization for the world of work, in this case, occurs in practice (and normally in the activities the individual manages to find, but did not choose), without the (lengthy) mediation of an university environment in which relationships can be forged. Nothing could be farther removed from the world of Granovetter's job-seekers (1972) - middle-class individuals with college degrees who search for high skilled jobs in specialized labor markets.

Professionalizing technical courses have a similar effect and can prove important to the few underprivileged individuals who get to attend them, but the result is certainly less intense due to the shorter course length and peripheral nature of the professions associated with those courses in their respective fields. This is because professional fields are organized internally by categorical differences between activities associated with socially constructed frontiers between degree and non-degree level occupations, such as those between doctors/dentists/nurses, on one hand, and nursing assistants and technicians on the other. This frontier is the pervasive distinction between manual and non-manual labor as internalized by the health profession, and it builds and reproduces persistent inequalities in the sense described by Tilly (2005). One of the reproductive dimensions of these inequalities in daily life resides in the operations of the networks (built upon the different trajectories of professional socialization) inside each of these professional fields, but greatly apartheid in each side of these categorical frontiers.

However, another large scale mechanism is superposed upon this, differentiating, over time, the networks of individuals in conditions of poverty from those of the middle class. It is what I call the *economy of ties*, which concerns the economic, emotional and temporal costs and personal efforts that go into creating and, particularly, maintaining ties: keeping contact, making visits, doing things together, etc. Apparently, certain individuals find it much more difficult to bear these costs and, therefore, experience far greater limitations in building and, especially, maintaining them. Due to that, whole portions of the networks of people living in poverty are abandoned periodically, slipping into a period of latency, only for the individual to find, later on, that they cannot be reactivated. In more extreme cases, relationships may end up being entirely forgotten. This mechanism operates constantly and regularly leading to the loss of part of the individual's relational structure, gradually whittling away and impoverishing the spectrum of sociability therein contained. As a result, their networks tend to be based more intensely on recent ties than the middle class networks.

While this mechanism can potentially affect all networks, it tends to attack those of the poor most intensely, especially the migrant poor. Migration (including intra-urban migration) creates additional costs when it comes to maintaining ties, but while poor migrants will often shed a substantial percentage of their networks through the migratory process, middle-class migrants manage to keep more of their former local network alive and active. On the other hand, the non-migrant poor face an effect somewhat similar to that experienced by the migrant when it comes to maintaining ties, even if the phenomenon has a more peripheral effect on the constitution of their relational structures.

The aggregate effect of these mechanisms is that middle-class networks are larger and richer in terms of sociability and represent an overlapping of networks from various periods of life and different spheres. Poor people's networks, on the other hand, are smaller, less varied and generally newer, as accumulations over time are fewer and a much more expressive number of contacts and spheres of sociability being jettisoned with far greater regularity.

b. Distinguishing networks of people living in poverty

A second set of mechanisms makes distinctions between the networks of the poor, making them increasingly more heterogeneous over the individual's lifetime, regardless of his/her attributes.

The differentiations among the poor begin from the *relational entry on the job markets* by migrants (and young non-migrants), with lasting effects on their future lives. On one hand, this mechanism concerns the fact that the migrant poor depend on the ties available to them at their place of arrival, especially those provided by the people who encouraged or facilitated the move, be they family members or other close contacts. Their first jobs are usually obtained through these ties, which will also influence the kind of activities these people go into, as their professional socialization tends to occur 'on the job'. As such, the opportunities open to the migrant are largely derived from their relationships with individuals already present at their place of arrival – or places, in the case of those who move on soon after touching first base. These first activities and contacts tend to influence the conditions the individual lives under shortly after his/her arrival, especially in virtue of their low degree of professional specialization prior to obtaining their first jobs in the new city. This creates a certain dependency upon occupational specialization, with the future very much hinging upon the spread of relational opportunities encountered upon the migrant's arrival. The interesting thing is that these are largely incidental, as migrants have no control over (and little knowledge of) what they will find at their destination in spatial and relational terms, often having only a very sketchy idea of the social situation and occupational activity of the individuals who directly assist them in the move.

I do not want to give this or any other mechanism an air of determination. All mechanisms trigger processes and by doing so increase the probability of certain events occurring and, in some cases, do so in a manner that is dependent upon the individual's trajectory. In the case of relational opportunities encountered upon arrival in a new city, the interviews identified cases of individuals who found themselves arriving into rich relational structures that enabled them to find good quality occupations. Less fortunate individuals, however, arrive into totally unskilled and low-paid jobs, and are forced to enter future circuits of low-quality employment. In these cases, Granovetter's logic of weak ties does not apply, as for the new arrival, or the first-time job-seeker, job-related information provided by strong ties is strategic to obtaining a decent placement.

Something similar happens with non-migrant first-time job-seekers. Given the relational discontinuity in the poor's educational trajectory mentioned earlier, the first job placement of poor youngsters is frequently the result of relational opportunities provided by individuals with whom a given ego has some tie, which, at this phase of life, is most likely to be a family member or neighbor. Likewise, in this context, those first professional activities will tend to derive from the network of some third party and therefore lie beyond the individual's control. It is needless to repeat the importance of these first job placements to the individual's future professional life. Some cases suggest that those who get their first jobs through connections established inside organizations tend to have a better professional initiation. In this case, the entrance to the labor market receives the effect of the lower homophily present in organizations, as we will see in a moment.

At least in part, the issue is also related to the attributes of the individual, via homophily, seen as migrants from better backgrounds tend to be brought to new countries/cities through networks of individuals with similarly good backgrounds (or, in the case of non-migrants, families of a similar type). These people also tend to live in better areas and be connected to people who are more established and better-inserted professionally speaking. However, this dynamic incorporates a significant parcel of chance, especially for migrants, and is by no means deterministic, although tends to generate durable and significant inequalities similar to those described by Tilly (2005). This effect is produced by the formation of monopolies of opportunities for the few privileging individuals from the same social group and urban location, as identified by Kaztman (1999), while others remain trapped in spatial and relational environments marked by the absence of resources and opportunities.

Obviously, the same elements highlighted earlier on concerning the differences between middle-class networks and those of the poor also produce differences among and within the latter. As such, the relational structures of poor youths entering into adult life will also be marked by their different *school sociability and labor market socialization*. Consequently, youths who manage to enroll on third-level courses (just as, to a lesser degree, second-level and technical schooling) will tend to surpass the others, not only due to the effects of education and professional formation already dealt with in the literature, but also through the relational mechanism mentioned above. It is worth underscoring here that this mechanism may superpose positively or negatively with the earlier one, either reducing the isolation experienced by the young job-seeker who finds his/her first placement through opportunities offered by limited relational networks, or increasing it.

Likewise, along the life trajectories of the poor, *the economy of ties* makes its presence felt in varied ways. The interviews were replete with accounts of the abandonment of significant parcels of individual networks, and the individuals living in poverty better equipped to bear the costs of maintaining their contacts tend to accumulate larger, more diversified networks that retain contacts from distinct social moments. Inversely, those with fewer resources tend to accumulate relational disadvantages, leading to latency and a certain ongoing network die-back. Needless to say, this accumulation of disadvantages is wholly regressive, as the poorer the individual, the more intense the effects of the mechanism.

Another important mechanism also impacts upon the opportunities individuals have to draw on their networks for assistance, and it works in a similar fashion to the economy of ties. This mechanism concerns an *association between trust and homophily*. As we have seen, individuals tend to trust their fellows, and the most costly or chronic forms of help are usually given only to those we trust. In the words of one interviewee: 'for me, trust is when someone has the same habits as you, likes the same things as you, has the same fiber as you, frequents the same places as you and has the same tastes as you'. Hence it is far more likely that we will deposit trust in people who share our beliefs, behaviors and practices.

The importance of homophily grows even more in relations based on some degree of intimacy, as in emotional support and confidences. Examples of this abounded, including youths confiding in peers with whom they had a lot in common, homosexuals confiding in other homosexuals, evangelical Christians in other evangelical Christians, and so on. This selectiveness seems to be connected with the fact that, as these issues are often of a personal nature, they will involve moral judgments mediated by the existence of a homophily of behaviors and ideas and associated with the presence of intimacy in the relationship. This homophily potentizes a sharing of languages and repertoires that makes it easier to understand the issues under discussion.

This association tends to create vicious circles in the provision of the types of more costly and trust based support only to those closest to oneself (the second and third types of assistance cited earlier), i.e., people similar to oneself and belonging to the same groups (for example, coming from the same place, having the same religion or personal behavior), thus reducing the circulation of repertoires and information, even among the poor. The outcome for the poorer among the poor is, once again, an accumulation of disadvantages and reinforced isolation. It is reasonable to imagine that this phenomenon also occurs among the middle-class, but in that case it leads to a monopolization of opportunities in the sense of Tilly (2005), among groups as among individuals. With regard to the poor, given their restricted access to opportunities, it again contributes to an 'imprisonment' of some individuals within situations of low access to help, goods and services, whether via the market or otherwise, contributing to the incessant reproduction and compounding of inequalities.

The results indicate that, in the case of individuals who inhabit segregated locales, another mechanism introduces even greater heterogeneity. We have seen that on average, some individuals in segregated places manage to have highly varied and less local sociability, and those are the ones who have better living conditions among the segregated, including income. This effect is completely absent among the non segregated. So, here another mechanism of differentiation comes to bear, as, *for segregated individuals, the connection with opportunities is mediated by the variability of the individual's sociability and by the different degrees of localism* present in their networks. As the effect of social isolation does not apply to people who do not live in segregation, heterogeneity of sociability will have no direct effect on their revenues, suggesting that rich networks tend to counterweight the isolational effect of spatial segregation.

While this constitutes an important mechanism in the generation of heterogeneity within segregated groups, it tends to reduce the explicative capacity of the category of segregation per se. However, it is not a question of the absence of the effect of segregation, as a superficial quantitative analysis of the difference between the segregated and non-segregated might suggest, for example, but rather one of the effects of a combination between segregation, localism and variability of sociability in the individual's day-to-day strategies. This result is very important, as it confirms the research hypothesis on the conjunctive relevance of segregation and networks on conditions of poverty, though in a complex and indirect way. As both networks and segregation mediate the individual's access to opportunity structures, the only way to consider the phenomenon is by considering them in conjunction.

In addition to the relational opportunities encountered among migrants, built along the course of the individual's schooling or rendered viable by sociability, individuals have access to other 'windows of opportunity' for relational patterns that grant them access to lower localism and homophily. In addition to the opportunities that stem from network contacts (derived from the elements discussed above), there is also the potential effect of other networks being tapped by a given ego, even if these are not actually incorporated into his/her own. The cases studied suggest the existence of a mechanism that produces this contact through *attending certain locations or belonging to certain organizations in which a great deal of information circulates.* Frequenting such places gives one access to information filtered through the networks of other individuals who also frequent those locales or organizations, but who may not belong to the network of the ego in question. The results corroborate Small (2009) when he lists the effects that different organizations have on the formation and maintenance of ties. The question here does not lie in the networks themselves, nor in their weak ties such as in Granovetter's work, but in the fact that certain places congregate people with diverse and rich networks which an ego can access merely by frequenting the same places, without actually belonging to any of those networks. These are meeting places such as public squares, but also hairdressers, or churches and associations. Not all meeting places have the same impact nor have meeting places of the same kind, as it largely depends on the type of people who frequent them, creating a very local effect. There is a lot of randomness in the encounters of the networks, although the characteristics of some organizations – more or less competitive environments, or more or less issue oriented, for example – certainly influence the probability of those encounters (Small 2009). In general, the more homophilic the frequenters, the less effective is the mechanism. Through this mechanism, individuals with very local and highly homophilic networks can gain access to information disseminated through others, perhaps wider networks.

The effect of this mechanism is obviously associated with the core evidence discussed in previous chapters, namely that people with sociabilities constructed in organizational environments, such as work, church or associations, tend to enjoy a better social situation. But the description of the mechanism is ampler than that and includes a new element associated with these meeting points, and not necessarily only organizations. The degrees of homophily present in different places will probably play a definitive role in mobilizing this mechanism.

Regardless of the relational opportunities available to individuals, however, the dynamic of social assistances in the daily lives of the individuals discussed in the previous chapter can improve or worsen the situation of potentially available assistance, as these *assistances change the types of tie* that connect the individuals among themselves. Offering help can boost the levels of trust or intimacy in a relationship, turning acquaintances who lend an occasional hand into friends upon whom one can rely for more constant and costly assistance. One example of a situation that can create this kind of change is the provision of help at a time of crisis. One case recounted by a mother of two in a tenement illustrates the situation. Her neighbor, recently moved in with no connections in the tenement, had three small children and no-one to look after them when she went to work. As she left the kids locked all day in a room, one of the other neighbors called child support and the police arrived to investigate. The interviewee went to fetch the kids from the room and hid them from the police, saying that the denunciation was a hoax. Since that day, the interviewee and the mother of the children have become very close friends and help each other reciprocally.

Conversely, other changes could have a negative impact and cause the relationship between individuals to deteriorate, dissipating the stock of contacts that could potentially provide more costly and constant help. This can happen through changes of address, with a subsequent drifting away from now latent contacts, but it can also stem from conflicts and a loss of trust, or even due to the death of alters who occupy important positions in the network. However, we have seen how certain ties are too strong to allow for definitive rupture, with contact slipping into a lingering latency, as often happens among family members. Even in these cases, however, the result is a loss of support all the same. In both cases, the issue is not the transformation of network structures, which can stay the same, but the contents of those structures, with major consequences for the benefit that can be expected from them.

Lastly, it is worth highlighting the conjoint effect the mechanisms have over the course of an individual's life trajectory, something which appears to be important to the analysis of the poorer among the poor. Some of the accounts I heard indicate that the mechanisms discussed here may *gradually restrict the choices* available for some individuals, making their life trajectories strongly path dependent in the sense described by Pierson (2004). A result of this process is that the individual is drawn further and further away from the best opportunities while living in situations that become increasingly more confined in social terms. This path dependency does not signify an imperative of constrained action, as the individuals continue to make choices in their daily lives. What it does mean, however, is that the array of options available to the individual can become increasingly limited over the course of certain trajectories, distancing them from other social situations, once relatively similar. This process represents an aggregated mechanism for the production of heterogeneity among the poor, but one which operates through the accumulation of effects, being therefore very regressive and impacting more strongly the poorer among the poor.

However, I would like to underline another element associated with this, and which backs it up, insofar as it concerns action. One can speculate that cognitive mechanisms akin to those described by Elster (1998) are constantly operating upon lifetime trajectories, adapting the individual's interpretations of his or hers social condition to the situations experienced in their daily lives. For some people at least, this means that their perspectives and views on the world are socially shaped so as to adapt to ever more restrictive dead-end situations that shrink their autonomy, alternatives and choices. I refer to certain cultural elements, widely understood as frames (Lamont and Small 2008) that shape the backdrop to the narratives through which individuals understand and give meaning to their own lives to themselves and to others. Once installed, these frames inform practices differently and influence the strategies individuals put into action, as well as the goals they set in relation to sundry quotidian dimensions of their lives, including the labor market. In doing so, they embrace or reject the opportunities their networks can bring to them through earlier mechanisms.

However, it is essential to underscore that I am not referring here to collective cultural elements, but to cultural referentials that inform individual actions in different ways and which are influenced by specific lifetime trajectories. In this sense, this mechanism pits itself against the prevailing views in the literature that thematizes the so-called culture of poverty in a homogeneous and socially wide-reaching way and works toward differentiating individuals and attaining an understanding this social group as complex, diverse and heterogeneous (Lamont and Small 2008). It is also worth highlighting that these frames constitute necessary conditions, but are not themselves sufficient for action. While they can tell us a lot about average individual behavior, they do not allow us to comprehend why some individuals informed by them act in a certain manner while others do not. The analytical gain in understanding the effect lies in grasping the modal variations within these behaviors.

In sum, the cultural frames of some individuals are impacted in adaptive form by cumulative trajectories of destitution associated with negative events, not to mention disastrous choices on the part of the individuals, that combine to construct spirals of precariousness. In the most extreme cases, those in which individuals find themselves at the limits of survival, many descend into situations in which they start to thematize their lives in fatalistic terms, thereby restricting even further their capacity to act.

Needless to say that once again, as with other earlier mechanisms, we see here the reproduction of durable inequalities in the sense outlined by Tilly, reinforcing social situations in a circular manner, especially when several mechanisms operate in conjunction.

Conclusion

This book began by stating the importance of integrating both social networks and spatial segregation in the study of poverty. The proposal was based on the assumption that living conditions (and forms of deprivation) are caused by lack of attributes from the part of individuals, as well as from broad economic and societal processes, but also by the presence and the functioning of several middle level structures that mediate the accesses of those individuals to those broad structures of opportunity. The evidences presented in the last chapters fully confirmed the importance of relational and spatial structures in the reproduction of poverty situations. They led us, however, beyond the simple confirmation of the hypothesis, adding new elements to the understanding of poverty. In this conclusion, I summarize these elements, recalling their relevance to the construction of a relational approach to the study of poverty considering the debates on the subject. After that, I conclude by discussing the impact of the results on the construction of public policies for combating poverty that incorporate the relational elements discussed here.

In analytic terms, bringing these relational patterns to the centre of the investigation of poverty situations enabled the construction of an intermediary level of analysis. This approach differs from both the structuralist and holistic interpretations of poverty, which derive this condition directly from structural dynamics, usually those of the economy and labor market, or from individualist and atomist approaches, which conceive poverty to be simply the result of individual attributes and personal behaviors and decisions. A large swathe of the debates about Brazilian and Latin American cities were and continue to be polarized by these two approaches.

The study of the relational dimensions of poverty, however, is not intended to eclipse the importance of actors or broader systematic or macro social processes, but to link them to the concrete contexts that encompass individual subjects and through whom they operate. A central focus on these relational contexts may enable integrating the studies of poverty with the studies of the poor, incorporating the practices, daily lives and cultural sphere of individuals in a systematic form, but going beyond the simple reliance on broad descriptive categories such as vulnerability and citizenship. The use of the two concepts, very common for many of those debating the issue in Brazil and Latin America, can produce interesting interpretations, but relinquishes the task of explaining the phenomenon by failing to specify precisely the elements involved in the reproduction of poverty.

The social capital tradition brings alternatives to these approaches, since it also focuses on middle range elements. But instead of using a concept marked by several diverse meanings, as well as centered in the positive effects of the elements under study, I prefer to focus directly on relations and sociability. In this sense, the study of networks and sociability is more precise even than the consideration of social capital transmitted through the networks. This is because it allows for the analysis of relational patterns without a priori assumptions concerning the greater or better quality of certain patterns, particularly since the latter are taken to be intrinsically unintentional, or at least only partially intentional. Here the question is not one of classifying ties as strong or weak, or conceiving their diverse roles in the construction of bridges or bonds, but of investigating what the relational patterns of individuals are like, how they are mobilized by the people implicated and what consequences they bring to them.

Consequently, the role of social relations in the reproduction of poverty is not limited to the presence of certain types of relations or networks. Networks are only structures and, as such, they represent passive relational configurations with only potential impact over social phenomena. Their mapping needs to be integrated with an investigation into their mobilization in people's day-to-day sociability. In this sense, the same networks might be used differently by different individuals, or even by the same person in diverse circumstances.

In fact, networks and sociability are part of the overall set of elements that form the living conditions of individuals in a multidimensional sense, produced slowly over the life trajectory of the individuals through processes that constitute at the same time their relational patterns and their attributes. These processes involve the combination of strategies guided by various forms of rationality, with chance, decisions of other individuals and relational constraints provoked by the age cycles, marriage, migration, intra-metropolitan relocations, sociability practices, the frequency of certain locations, among several other processes. The outcomes of these processes accumulate over time and constitute individuals as they are at any given moment.

For this reason, it is impossible to understand these processes considering direct causalities from attributes to networks, from networks to attributes or, even worse, from space to attributes, as does a substantial part of the neighborhood effects literature. Causality must be understood as multiple, and can only be reached by the study of the relational mechanisms associated with both network production and mobilization.

Departing from this analytical point of view, we may find several social regularities in sociability and relational structures, regardless of the specificities of each network. In a first and more general level, networks vary, on average, according to the considered social group. This suggests that the present discussions on community and social support must be specified socially, and whether communities are localized or personal depends on about whom we are talking about. The networks of individuals living in poverty, for example, tend to be smaller, much more local and less varied in terms of sociability than those of middle class individuals. Consequently networks do not eliminate social differences and inequalities, on the contrary they reproduce them, and can only be understood in this light.

We have seen that they also vary substantially according to the life situations and moments in which individuals find themselves. And these differences between networks, as well as their diverse mobilizations, are exactly the elements that help us to understand the diversity of social situations, even among the poor. This diversity is produced by the complex effects of the diverse attributes and processes, not only by such factors as schooling, age and sex, but also by the decisions and strategies pursued over the course of a person's life, as well as by the occurrence of events and dynamics beyond individual control. In general, our exploration of the diversity of networks has shown that poor people have both small and large networks with local and primary sociability, and relatively non-local medium-sized networks with a sociability focused on organizational environments, potentially marked by lower homophily. These variations were strongly associated with the interviewees' social conditions and poverty. As we have seen, having a job, being in a vulnerable situation and earning higher or lower incomes are all influenced by the types of networks and sociability of the individuals in question. Generally speaking, the results reinforce the importance of non-local, less homophilic relational networks constructed with important participation of organizational environments.

Hence, social homophily appears as a key dimension with wide-ranging consequences, but should not be understood as merely representing the existence of ties between social groups, since these are practically non-existent, at least in the case of São Paulo. Small variations in social homophily may also produce important effects, which confirm the literature's findings about the problems brought by the increasing homogeneity of black and latino neighborhoods in US cities. However, various processes may work as sources of homophily, leading to similar isolation effects, considering the case. We must cite at least localism, restricted sociability (as opposed to variegated sociability), high presence of primary sociability spheres and spatial segregation. It is the combination of these sources of homophily that characterizes the networks in types. These types are associated differently with social conditions. and with poverty in particular.

Social situations also depend on networks because they mediate access to a variety of socially provided basic goods and services necessary for the welfare of individuals. As part of the dynamic of these social exchanges, we were able to observe that different levels of trust present in the relationships and costs of help delivering are interwoven, encompassed by the logic of social reciprocity (material, immaterial and symbolic) and incorporating varying degrees of personalization. Various of these elements involve strong causal circularities that persistently reproduce inequalities in a durable way by creating greater difficulties for individuals with a more vulnerable social insertion to access more chronic and costly forms of help.

But perhaps the most valuable contribution of this book is the precise delimitation of a set of mechanisms that help shape networks, mediate their use by individuals and influence their strategies and actions. These mechanisms differentiate networks and generate heterogeneity between and among social groups and individuals, thus influencing the reproduction of inequalities. The mechanisms involve distinct dynamics for accessing education, especially at university level, the forms of covering the costs of producing and maintaining ties, the spatial dimensions of migration in the city, the transformations in the types of ties, and the combined effects of the variability in sociability and segregation. Various mechanisms present circular and accumulative character, reproducing poverty situations and inequalities between individuals. Other mechanisms create opportunities or enable strategies for individuals to escape these vicious circles, as in the case of the greater variability in sociability of some segregated individuals, or in the continuous transformation of types of ties due to the rendering of assistances. However, at least in the case of some individuals, these mechanisms accumulate disadvantages through their life trajectories, gradually narrowing their options and leading in many cases to loss of hope and the acceptance of fatalism.

Finally, the joint consideration of networks and segregation has helped us explore the potential effects of integration and isolation (sometimes combined in contradictory ways) of the relational and spatial structures, considered in an undifferentiated and fairly imprecise form by a sizeable part of the literature on the topic. Most of the debate assumes, albeit implicitly, that physical contiguity corresponds to relations. As we have seen, a first spatial dimension of the phenomena involves localism. Individuals with higher localism present worse social conditions since they tend to have more restricted access to material and immaterial goods and services. This dimension may be present in areas that are well integrated into the urban fabric as well as in spatially isolated locations, which leads us to the second spatial element: segregation.

The relation between segregation and networks proved to be less direct and more complex than imagined by a significant proportion of the literature on urban poverty. Segregated areas do not present smaller, less varied and more local networks, contradicting a direct relation between relational and spatial patterns. On the other hand, among spatially isolated individuals, those who present more varied sociability tend to have better social conditions, suggesting that networks really may counterweight the effect of the social isolation produced by segregation. But this occurs in the case of some segregated individuals only, thus increasing the heterogeneity both among segregated groups and among the poor in general.

Since policies for combating poverty are based on our representations of the phenomenon, all these questions have important practical consequences in terms of State action. To gain a better understanding of the relation between public policies, poverty and networks we need to replicate studies like this in other social contexts, as well as develop specific analyses of the impact of public policies on relational patterns, which suggests a fruitful ample future research agenda. The findings of this book, however, suggest a number of aspects that point towards various directions for future action and provide warnings on how not to proceed.

Obviously the discussion of the impact of social networks on policies does not in any way mean replacing traditional social policies. In addition to the importance of the networks, the analyzed data reaffirms the importance of universal social policies in overcoming poverty, including the indication of previously undescribed relational effects. This influence is evident, for instance, in the case of the economy of ties mechanism and sociability in the sphere of studies. Given the strength of the mechanism associated with the teaching environment, promoting access to higher education among the poorest sectors of the population tends to have very important relational effects beyond those associated with attributes, enabling transitions from the networks of adolescence to those of adult life (and the world of work) similar to those experienced by young middle class people, with impacts that go far beyond the objectives of the policies.

Moreover the central role played by labor market dynamics is also clear, particularly the promotion of more stable and protected jobs, as expected. Combating poverty cannot be achieved without traditional social policies, or indeed macro-economic policies that promote large numbers of high quality jobs. While these dimensions are important in general, they become even more essential in the areas where there is a large concentration of people living in poverty, especially segregated locations.

In a very general sense, the absorption of networks as an active element of state policies implies the need to consider them in a diffuse form, incorporating relations into policies. This dimension relates both to traditional social policies, such as education and healthcare, and to those developed more recently, such as conditional cash transfer schemes and micro-loans.

However, since the networks influence the presence of poverty situations, public policies can interact directly with them or consider them effectively. Firstly, during implementation, policies can take advantage of particular types of networks existing in poor communities. Although some policy sectors have already discovered this dimension, it is still considered implicitly and has only started to be disseminated. Given that some personal networks are deeply embedded into the relational fabric of communities, their integration with state policies can help the latter to achieve their aims, both by enabling policies to reach their users more precisely, and by helping to customize them, including in terms of language, culturally mediating the relations between the State and the communities. However the success of this strategy seems to depend on mobilizing individuals within the communities with particular relation patterns, given the great diversity found within the existing networks. The integration of these individuals and organizations with state policies involves specific challenges considering the way bureaucracies and state organizations work.

In addition it may make sense to explore initiatives for combating poverty that influence networks or counterweight certain mechanisms. However we need to keep in mind that an overwhelming proportion of the networks and forms of sociability will continue to be constructed outside the policies, what suggests that the effects of these initiatives will tend to be much slower than usually considered. It should also be recognized that such policies are much more likely to generate interactions rather than relations. Nevertheless, policies of this type may produce positive effects by helping poor individuals to cope with the negative effects of some mechanisms, although the results presented here indicate various caveats in relation to this point.

It is not just a question of stimulating the formation of ties in general, since large but local networks based on primary ties contribute little or nothing to changing the social situation of the individuals concerned. This fact is important since the majority of the initiatives now being implemented involve increasing the density of the local social fabric with the aim of strengthening the community. This type of initiative may even help community dynamics, but will not help the residents improve their social situations, given the relational dimensions of poverty.

Generally speaking, the elements that should be encouraged are associated with less homophilic and local sociabilities which can generate contacts with individuals different from ego. This would produce effects on a number of the conditioning factors and mechanisms observed. As we have seen, greater variability in sociability tends to increase the person's access to information and better opportunities, especially for segregated individuals, as well as making a wider range of individuals and spheres available for providing help and access to social goods and services.

These results highlight the advantages of social contexts in which contacts between individuals are frequent and in which different social groups live on a day-to-day basis. In broad terms, this indicates an opposite direction to the isolationist and segregating social and urban contexts that produce the impoverishment of public spaces, such as those that have shaped various urbanistic and local government proposals over a recent period. Although it is impossible to affirm the positive effect of integrating urban contexts on networks in any mechanical way, the sociability of closed condominiums and shopping centers, for example, certainly runs counter to the development of the less homophilic relational patterns with a more varied sociability analyzed over the course of this book. The constitution of urban spaces with less segregation and more heterophilic encounters, by contrast, would tend to generate positive relational effects.

However, depending on the objectives of the policies concerned, different networks should be stimulated in distinct forms. The only individuals who tend to benefit from merely local (and homophilic) initiatives are the practically isolated (such as the elderly), whose networks are so small that their mere expansion can produce important effects in terms of access and social support. This is basically the direction taken by initiatives promoting places for older people to meet and interact currently being implemented by public authorities and by aid organizations. In the case of other individuals, by contrast, the size of the networks does not seem to be particularly relevant.

This is especially true in the case of young people, given that these individuals already tend to have large, but predominantly local and homophilic networks. In this case the question may involve encouraging contacts outside the community, which may in turn allow for relational transitions from youth networks to adulthood networks in which organizational environments have considerable presence. This strategy is potentialized by the intense sociability of the universe of poor young people, which is usually restricted to the spheres of the family and neighborhood. In this case, in conjunction with the promotion of external contacts, it would be essential to reduce the costs involved in maintaining contacts.

For the majority of people, though, the development of public initiatives for combating poverty that make use of networks needs to promote non-local ties with less homophily, such as those constituted in institutional environments. In segregated areas the need is to stimulate the development of a variety of non-local networks for wider groups of individuals, as well as reduce the costs of maintaining ties. In the specific case of employment, the development of job agencies with integrated information on work, but distributed in a radically decentralized form within the communities, could help reduce the effect of the mechanism of the initial localization of migrants and the entry of young people into the job market, allowing access to information and non-local relational structures to be distributed more equitably.

However a central element completely absent from current public initiatives seems to reside in the fact that the creation of non-local and mostly non-primary ties may still be insufficient to respond to the issue in a dynamic way. If the economy of ties mechanism discussed previously is really relevant, another important line of action involves reducing the costs of maintaining ties, especially those that are less local and less homophilic, which as well as tending to be destroyed very easily. In this case the need is to impede the constant destruction of sections of the network, or to ensure that this occurs in a more diluted form, generating an accumulation of ties closer to the kind observed among wealthier social groups. For this to happen, reducing the costs of communication and transportation would seem to be essential to developing and maintaining richer and more diversified networks among poor people. Improvements in the amount of free time poor individuals have to construct and maintain ties are also obviously important.

However the findings presented here indicate that the networks result from slow and long-term processes of accumulating and rupturing ties, meaning that public programs that aim to dynamize networks must be long-lasting, based on institutionalized implementation structures, and will probably produce effects over relatively long-term time scales.

References

Almeida, R. and D´Andrea. 2004. T. Pobreza e redes sociais em uma favela paulistana. Novos Estudos Cebrap, São Paulo, 68: 94-106.

Almeida, R. and D´Andrea, T. 2005. Estrutura de oportunidades em uma favela de São Paulo Marques, E. and Torres, H. São Paulo: segregação, pobreza urbana e desigualdade social. São Paulo, Ed. Senac, p. 195.

Alsayyad, N. and Roy, A. 2006. Medieval modernity: on citizenship and urbanism in the Global era. Space and Polity, Vol, 10 (1): 1-20.

Andreotti, A. 2006. Coping strategies in a wealthy city of Northern Italy. International Journal of Urban and Regional Research, Vol. 30 (2): 328-345.

Arretche, M. 2000. Estado federativo e políticas sociais, Rio de Janeiro, Ed. Revan.

Arretche, M. 2001. Federalismo e relações intergovernamentais no Brasil: A reforma dos programas sociais. Dados – Revista de Ciências Sociais, Rio de Janeiro, Vol. 45 (3): 431-457.

Arretche, M. 2002. Federalismo e relações intergovernamentais no Brasil: a reforma de programas sociais. Revista Dados, Vol.45, N. 3.

Auyero, J. 1999. 'This is a lot like the Bronx, isn't it?' Lived experiences of marginality in an Argentine slum. International Journal of Urban and Regional Research, Vol., 23 (1): 45-69.

Auyero, J. and Swistun, D. 2009. Flammable: environmental suffering in an Argentine shantytown. Oxford: Oxford University Press.

Baeninger, R. 2011. Crescimento da População: desconstruindo mitos do século, 20. In: São Paulo: Miradas Cruzadas. Sociedad, política y cultura, edited by L. Kowarick, L. and E. Marques. Quito, Ecuador: Editorial Olacchi.

Baltar, P. 2002. Mercado de trabalho na região metropolitana de São Paulo dos anos 90: modificações na estrutura ocupacional. XIII Encontro Nacional da Abep.

Baltrusis, N. 2005. Mercado imobiliário informal e o processo de estruturação da cidade: um estudo sobre a comercialização de imóveis em favelas na região metropolitana de São Paulo. FAU/Usp, PhD thesis.

Barros, R.; Henriques, R. and Mendonça, R. 2000. A estabilidade inaceitável: desigualdade e pobreza na Brasil. In: Henriques, R. Desigualdade e pobreza na Brasil. Rio de Janeiro, Ipea, p. 21.

Barry, B. 2005. Why social justice matters. London, Polity.

Bastani, S. 2007. Family comes first: Men's and women's personal networks in Tehran. Social Networks, 29: 357–374.

Bearman, P. and Parigi, P. 2004. Cloning headless frogs and other important matters: conversation topics and network structure. Social Forces, Vol. 83 (2): 535.

Bearman, R.; Moody, J. and Stovel, K. 2004. Chains of affection: the structure of adolescent romantic and sexual networks. American Journal of Sociology, Vol. 110 (1): 44-91.

Beggs, J. 1996. Revising the rural-urban contrast: personal networks in nonmetropolitan and metropolitan settings. Rural sociology, 61:306-325.

Berquó, E. and Cavenagui, S. 2006. Fecundidade em declínio: breve nota sobre a redução no número médio de filhos por mulher no Brasil. Novos Estudos Cebrap, 74: 11-15.

Bian, Y.; Breiger, R.; Davis, D. and Galaskiewicz, J. 2005. Occupation, class and social networks in urban China. Social Forces, 83(4): 1443-1468.

Bichir, R. 2006. Segregação e acesso a políticas públicas no município de São Paulo. Dcp/Usp: MSc dissertation,

Bichir, R. 2009. Determinantes do acesso à infra-estrutura urbana no município de São Paulo. Revista Brasileira de Ciências Sociais, Vol., 24 (70), p. 75-89.

Bichir, R.; Torres, H. and Ferreira, M. 2005. Jovens no município de São Paulo: explorando os efeitos das relações de vizinhança. Revista Brasileira de Estudos Urbanos e Regionais, Vol. 6 (2): 53-70.

Bidart, C. 2009. En busca del contenido de las redes sociales: los 'motivos' de las relaciones. Redes – Revista hispana para el análisis de redes sociales, Vol. 6 (7): 178-202.

Bidart, C. and Lavenu, D. 2005. Evolution of personal networks and life events. Social Networks, 27 (4): 359-376.

Bird, K. and Pratt, N. 2004. Fracture points in social policies for chronic poverty reduction. London, Overseas Development Institute/Chronic Poverty Research Centre, Working Paper, 242.

Blokland, T. and Savage, M. 2008. Social capital and Networked urbanism. London: Basil Blackwell.

Blokland, T. 2003. Urban Bonds. London, Basil Blackwell.

Bógus, L. and Taschner, S. 1999. São Paulo como patchwork: unindo fragmentos de uma cidade segregada. Cadernos Metrópole, 1: 43-98.

Boltvinik, J. 1998. Poverty measurement methods: an overview. Poverty Elimination Program, UNDP.

Bonduki, N. and Rolnik, R. 1982. Periferia da Grande São Paulo – Reprodução do espaço como expediente de reprodução da força de trabalho. In: Maricato, E. A produção capitalista da casa e da cidade no Brasil industrial. São Paulo, Ed. Alfa-Ômega, 117-132.

Borgatti, S. and Everett, M. 1998. Network measures of social capital. Connections, 21 (2): 27-36.

Borgatti, S.; Everett, M. and Freeman, L. 2002. Ucinet for Windows: software for social network analysis. Cambridge, Analytic Technologies.

Bourdieu, P. 1986. The forms of capital. In: J. Richardson (org) Handbook of Theory and Research for the Sociology of Education. New York: Greenwood: 241-258.

Bourdieu, P. 2007a. A distinção: crítica social do julgamento. São Paulo, Edusp.

Bourdieu, P. 2007b. La miseria del mundo. Buenos Aires, Fondo de Cultura Económica.

Brasileiro, A. 1976. Região Metropolitana do Rio de Janeiro: Serviços de interesse comum. Brasília, IPEA/IBAM.

Bréville, B. 2011. Trente-cinq ans de politique de la ville Regards sur l'actualité, No 367.

Briggs, X. 2001. Ties that bind, bridge and constrain: social capital and segregation in the American Metropolis. Segregation and the city, Lincoln Institute for Land Policy.

Briggs, X. 2003. Bridging networks, social capital and racial segregation in America. Cambridge, KSG Faculty Research Working Paper Series.

Briggs, X. 2005. Social capital and segregation in the United States. In: VARADY, D. Desegregating the city. Albany, Suny Press.

Briggs, X.; Popkin, S. and Goering, J. 2010. Moving to opportunity: the story of an American experiment to fight poverty. New York: Oxford University Press.

Bueno, L. 2000. Urbanização de favelas. FAU/Usp, PhD thesis.

Burt, R. 1992. Structural holes: the social structure of competition. Cambridge, Cambridge University Press.

Burt, R. 2004. The network structure of social capital. In: Sutton, R. and Staw, B. Research in Organizational Behaviour. New York, Jai Press, Vol., 22.

Cabanes, R. and Georges, I. (ed.) 2009. São Paulo, debut de siécle: La ville d'en bas. Paris: L'Harmattan.

Caldeira, T. 2000. Cidade de Muros. São Paulo, Ed. 34, 2000.

Camargo, C. (ed.) 2976. São Paulo, 1975 – Crescimento e pobreza. *São Paulo, Ed. Loyola.*

Campbell, K. and Lee, B. 1992. Sources of Personal Neighbor Networks: Social Integration, Need, or Time? Social Forces, Vol. 70 (4): 1077-1100.

Cardoso, F. and Faletto, E. 1973. Dependência e desenvolvimento na América Latina: ensaio de interpretação sociológica. Rio de Janeiro: Zahar Ed.

Carvalho, I. and Pereira, G. (ed.) 2006. Como anda Salvador. Salvador, Edufba.

Carvalho, I.; Souza, Â. and Pereira, G. 2004. Polarização e segregação socioespacial em uma metrópole periférica. Cadernos CRH, Vol. 17(41): 281-297.

Case, A. and Katz, L. 1991. The Company You Keep: The Effects of Family and Neighborhood on Disadvantaged Youths. Princeton, Nber Working Paper W3705.

Castells, M. 1983. A questão urbana. Rio de Janeiro, Paz e Terra.

Cechi, C.; Molina, L. and Sabatini, F. 2008. Is social capital a policy tool against poverty and inequality? A discussion of development strategies in rural India. Available at: http://www.socialcapitalgateway.org.

Cem. 2004. Mapa da Vulnerabilidade Social da População da Cidade de São Paulo. São Paulo, Cem/Pmsp.

Chamboredon, J-C and Lemaire, M. 1970. Proximité spatiale et distance sociale. Lês grands ensembles et leur peuplement. Revue Française de Sociologie, XI:3-33.

Chinelli, F. 1980. Os loteamentos da periferia. In: Valladares, L. Habitação em questão. Rio de Janeiro, Zahar: 49-64.

Coleman, J. 1988. Social Capital in the Creation of Human Capital. The American Journal of Sociology, Vol. 94: 95-120.

Curley, A. 2009. Draining of gaining? The social networks of public housing movers in Boston. Journal of social and personal relationships, Vol, 26 (2-3): 227-247.

Curley, A. 2008. Deconcentrating poverty: program effects on neighborhood diversity and social cohesion. Conference paper for Housing Studies Association. York, UK: University of York.

D´Andrea, T. 2004. Redes sociais em Cidade Tiradentes. Final research report. São Paulo, Cem-Fapesp.

Davis, M. 1992. A cidade de quartzo: escavando o futuro em Los Angeles. São Paulo, Scrita Ed.

Davis, M. 2006. Planeta favela. São Paulo: Boitempo Editorial.

De la Rúa, A. 2005. Proceso de identificación política mediante redes transnacionales de amistad. In: Redes: enfoque y aplicaciones del análisis de redes sociales (ARS), edited by J. Porras, J. and V. Espinoza, Santiago do Chile, Universidad Bolivariana, p. 153-173.

Degenne, A. 2009. Tipos de interacciones, formas de confianza y relaciones. Redes – Revista hispana para el análisis de redes sociales, Vol. 16 (3): 63-91.

Di Méo, G. 1991. L'homme, la societé, l'espace. Paris, Anthropos.

Diani, M. and McAdam, D. 2003. Social movements and networks: relational approaches to collective action. Oxford: Oxford University Press.

Dias, L. and Silveira, R. 2005. Redes, sociedades e territórios. Florianópolis, Edunisc.

Domingues, S. 2004. Estrategias de movilidad social: el desarrollo de redes para el progreso personal. Redes, Vol.7 (1). Available at: http://revista-redes.rediris. es/pdf-vol7/vol7_1.pdf.

Draibe, S. 1989a. O Welfare state no Brasil: características e perspectivas. In: Ciências Sociais Hoje, 1989. Rio de Janeiro: ANPOCS/Ed. Rio Fundo.

Draibe, S. 1989b. As políticas sociais brasileiras: diagnósticos e perspectivas. In: Para a década de 90: prioridades e perspectivas de Políticas públicas. Ipea: Políticas sociais e Organização do Trabalho No. 4. Brasília: Ipea/Plan.

Dujisin, R. 2008. Multitudes y redes en la caída de Milosevic Redes – Revista hispana para El análisis de redes sociales, Vol. 15: 94-105.

Dujsin, R. and Jariego, I. 2005. Las puentes interlocales: las redes personales de los universitarios alcalareños en Sevilla. In: Redes: enfoque y aplicaciones del análisis de redes sociales (ARS), edited by J. Porras and V. Espinoza. Santiago do Chile, Universidad Bolivariana, p. 183.

Duren, N. 2006. Planning à la Carte: the location patterns of gated communities around Buenos Aires in a decentralized planning context. International Journal of Urban and regional research, Vol. 30 (2): 308-327.

Durham, E. 1988. A sociedade vista da periferia. In: KOWARICK, L. As Lutas Sociais e a Cidade. Rio de Janeiro, Paz e Terra, p. 169-192.

Durlauf, S. 2001. The membership theory of poverty: the role of group affiliations in determining socioeconomic outcomes. In: Danziger, S. and Haverman, R. Understanding poverty. New York, Russell Sage.

Durston, J. 2003. Capital social: parte del problema, parte de la solución, su papel en la persistencia y en la superación de la pobreza en America Latina y Caribe. In: Atria, R.; Siles, M.; Arriaga, I.; Robison, L. and Whiteford, S. Capital social y reducción de la pobreza en America Latina y Caribe: en busca de un nuevo paradigma. Santiago do Chile, Cepal, p. 147-161.

Elster, J. 1987. Marxismo, funcionalismo e teoria dos jogos. Lua Nova, 17:163-189.

Elster, J. 1998. A plea for mechanisms. In: Hedstrom, P. and Swedberg, R. Social Mechanisms: An Analytical Approach to Social Theory. Cambridge, Cambridge University Press: 163-196.

Emirbayer, M. 1997. Manifesto for a relational sociology. American Journal of Sociology, 103 (2): 231-317.

Esping-Andersen, G. 2000. Fundamentos sociales de las economías postindustriales. Barcelona, Ariel.

Esping-Andersen, G. 2002. Towards the good society, once again? In: Why we need a new welfare state? Oxford University Press.

Fainstein, S.; Gordon, I. and Harloe, M. 1992. Divided cities: New York and London in the contemporary world. London, Basil Blackwell.

Faria, V. 1980. Divisão inter-regional do trabalho e pobreza urbana: o caso de Salvador. In: Bahia de todos os pobres, edited by G. Souza and V. Faria. Petrópolis, Vozes/Cebrap: 23-40.

Faria, V. 1992. A Conjuntura Social Brasileira: Dilemas e Perspectivas. Novos Estudos Cebrap, 33:103-114.

Fawaz, M. 2008. An unusual clique of city-makers: social networks in the production of a neighborhood in Beirut (1950-75). International Journal of Urban and regional research, Vol. 32 (3): 565-585.

Feltran, G. 2008. Fronteiras de tensão: um estudo sobre política e violência nas periferias de São Paulo. Unicamp: PhD thesis, Campinas.

Feltran, G. 2009a. 'Travailleurs' et 'bandits' dans La meme famille: manières de dire et signification politique In: São Paulo, debut de siécle: La ville d'en bas, edited by R. Cabanes and I. Georges. Paris: L'Harmattan.

Feltran, G. 2009b. Notes sur lês 'debats' du 'monde du crime' In: São Paulo, debut de siécle: La ville d'en bas, edited by R. Cabanes and I. Georges. Paris: L'Harmattan.

Ferrand, A. 2002. Las comunidades locales como estructuras meso. Revista Hispana para el Análisis de Redes Sociales, Vol. 3(4). Available at: http://revista-redes.rediris.es.

Figueiredo, A.; Torres, H. and Bichir, R. 2006. A conjuntura social brasileira revistada. Novos Estudos Cebrap, 75:173-184.

Figueiredo, A.; Torres, H.; Limongi, F.; Arretche, M. and Bichir, R. 2005. Final report – Resarch project 052 – Rede de Pesquisa e Desenvolvimento de Políticas Públicas: REDE-IPEA II. draft.

Filgueiras, F. 2004. Una mirada critica al assets-vulnerability approach. Santiago do Chile, Cepal, draft.

Fiori, J. and Kornis, G. 1994. Além da queda: economia e política numa década enviesada. In: Guimarães, R. and Tavares, R. Saúde e sociedade no Brasil dos anos 80. Rio de Janeiro, Relume Dumará: 1-31.

Fischer, C. and Shavit, Y. 1995. National differences in network density: Israel and the United States. Social Networks, 17(2): 129-145.

Fontes, B. and Eichner, K. 2004. A formação de capital social em uma comunidade de baixa renda. Redes: Revista Hispana para el Análisis de Redes Sociales, Vol. 7 (2). Available at: http://revista-redes.rediris.es

Frank, A.; Pereira, L.; Germani, G.; Graciarena, J. 1969. Urbanização e subdesenvolvimento. Rio de Janeiro, Zahar Ed.

Freeman, L. 2004. The development of social network analysis. Vancouver, Empirical Press.

Freidenberg, J. 2000. Growing old in El Barrio. New York: NYU Press.

Ganzeboom, H; De Graaf, P.; Treiman, D. 1992. A Standard International Socio-Economic Index of Occupational Status. Social Science Research, 21:1-56.

Gilbert, A. (ed.) 1996. The mega-city in Latin America. The United Nations University. Available at: http://unu.edu/unupress/unupbooks/uu23me/uu23me00.htm#Contents,

Gomes, S. and Amitrano, C. 2005. Local de moradia na metrópole e vulnerabilidade ao emprego e desemprego. In: Marques, E. and Torres, H. São Paulo: segregação, pobreza e desigualdades sociais, São Paulo, Ed. Senac: 169-180.

Gonzalez de la Rocha, M. 2001. From the resources of poverty to the poverty of resources? The erosion of a survival model. Latin American Perspectives, 28: 72-100.

Grafimeyer, Y. 1996. La ségrégation spatiale. In: Paugam, S. L'éxclusion: L'état des savoirs. Paris, Éditions la découverte: 209-215.

Granovetter, M. 1973. The strength of weak ties. American Journal of Sociology. Vol. 78 (6): 1360-1380.

Granovetter, M. 2000. A theoretical agenda for economic sociology. Stanford, draft.

Greenbaum, S.; Hathaway, W.; Rodriguez, C.; Spalding, A. and Ward, B. 2008. Deconcentration and social capital: contradictions of a poverty alleviation policy. Journal of Poverty, Vol. 12 (2): 201-228.

Grosseti, M. 2005. Where do social relations come from? A study of personal networks in the Toulouse area of France. Social Networks, 27(4): 289-300.

Grosseti, M. 2007. Are French networks different? Social Networks, 29(3): 391-404.

Grosseti, M. 2009. Que es una relación social? Un conjunto de mediaciones diádicas. Redes – Revista Hispana para el análisis de redes sociales, Vol, 16 (2): 44-62.

Gugler, J. and Gilbert, A. 1982. Cities, poverty, and development : urbanization in the Third World. Oxford: Oxford University Press.

Guimarães, N. 2009a. Desemprego, uma construção social: São Paulo, Paris, Tóquio. Belo Horizonte: E. Argumentun.

Guimarães, N. 2009b. À procura de trabalho: instituições do mercado e redes. Belo Horizonte, Ed. Argumentun.

Guimarães, R. and Tavares, R. 1994. Saúde e Sociedade no Brasil dos anos 80. Rio de Janeiro, Relume-Dumará.

Gurza Lavalle, A. and Castello, G. 2004. Benesses desse mundo: associativismo religioso e inclusão socioeconômica. Novos Estudos Cebrap, 68: 73-93.

Gurza Lavalle, A.; Castello, G. and Bichir, R. 2007. Redes y Capacidad de Acción en la Sociedad Civil. El caso de São Paulo, Brasil. Redes – Revista Hispana para el Análisis de Redes Sociales, 12: 1-38.

Gutierrez, A. 2008. Redes e intercambio de capitales en condiciones de pobreza: dimensión relacional y dimensión vincular. Redes – Revista hispana para el análisis de redes sociales, Vol. 14 (4): 1-17.

Hanneman, R. and Riddle, M. 2005. Introduction to social network methods. Riverside, CA, University of California.

Hannerz, U. 1983. Explore la ville. Paris, Les Éditions de Minuit.

Harris, R. and Wahba, M. 2002. The urban geography of low-income housing: Cairo (1947-96) exemplifies a model. International Journal of Urban and Regional Research, vol, 12 (1):58-79.

Hedstorm, P.; Sandell, R. and Stern, C. 2000. Meso-level networks and the diffusion of social movements. American Journal of Sociology, 106 (1): 145-172.

Heinz, J.; Laumman, E.; Nelson, R. and Salizbury, R. 1997. The hollow core: private interests in national policy making. Cambridge, Harvard University Press.

Hoffman, R. 2000. A mensuração da desigualdade e da pobreza no Brasil. In: Henriques, R. Desigualdade e pobreza no Brasil. Brasília, Ipea.

Hoffman, M. and Mendonça, S. 2003. O mercado de trabalho na região metropolitana de São Paulo. Estudos Avançados, 17 (47): 21-42.

Homans, G. 1958. Social Behavior as Exchange. American Journal of Sociology, 63: 597-606.

Iceland, J. 2006. Poverty in America: a handbook. Berkeley: University of California Press.

Immergut, E. 1998. The Theoretical Core of the New Institutionalism, Politics and Society, 26(1): 5-34.

Jacobi, P. 1989. Movimentos sociais e Políticas Públicas: demandas por saneamento básico e saúde: São Paulo, 1978-84. São Paulo, Ed. Cortez.

Januzzi, P. and Januzzi, N. 2002. Crescimento urbano, saldos migratórios e atratividade residencial dos distritos da cidade de São Paulo: 1980-2000. Rio de Janeiro, draft.

Jargowsky, P. e Yang, R. 2006. The underclass revisited: a social problem in decline. Journal of Urban Affairs, Vol., 28 (1): 55-70.

Jargowsky, P. 1997. Poverty and Place: ghettos, barrios and the American city. New York, Russel Sage.

Jariego, I. 2002. Tipos de redes personales de los inmigrantes y adaptación psicológica. . Redes: Revista Hispana para el Análisis de Redes Sociales, Vol. 1(1).

Jariego, I. 2003. A general typology of the personal networks of immigrants with less than, 10 years living in Spain. XXIII Sunbelt Conference.

Jariego, I. 2006. Geografías del desorden: mallas de paisaje. El entramado de relaciones de los inmigrantes. Sevilha, draft.

Jha, S.; Rao, V. and Woolcock, M. 2007. Governance in the Gullies: democratic responsiveness and leadership in Delhi's slums. World development, Vol. 35 (2): 230-246.

Johnson, J. 1994. Anthropological contributions to the study of social networks: a review. In: Wasserman, S. and Galaskiewicz, J. Advances in social network analysis: research in the social and behavioral sciences. New York, Sage Pub.

Johnson, R. and Wichern, D. 1992. Applied multivariate statistical analysis. New Jersey, Prentice Hall.

Kadushin, C. 1995. Friendship Among the French Financial Elite. American Sociological Review, 60: 202-221.

Kadushin, C. 2004. Some basic network concepts and propositions. In: Introduction to Social Network Theory. New York, Cuny, Draft.

Kadushin, C. and Jones, D. 1992. Social networks and urban neighborhoods in New York City. City e Society, Vol. 6 (1): 58-75.

Kazepov, Y. (ed.) 2005. Cities of Europe: chaging contexts, local arrangments and the challenge to social cohesion In: Cities of Europe. Londres: Basil Blackwell.

Kaztman, R. 1999. La dimensión espacial en las políticas de la superación de la pobreza urbana. Montevideo, draft.

Kaztman, R. and Retamoso, A. 2005. Spatial segregation, employment and poverty in Montevideo. Cepal Review, 85: 125-142.

Keyder, C. 2005. Globalization and social exclusion in Istanbul. International Journal of Urban and regional research, Vol, 29 (1): 124-134.

Kirschbaum, C. 2006. Campos organizacionais em transformação: o caso do Jazz americano e da Música Popular Brasileira. FGV, PhD thesis.

Knoke, D. 1990. Political networks: the structural perspective. New York, Cambridge University Press.

Knoke, D.; Pappi, F.; Broadbent, J. and Tsujinaka, Y. 1996. Comparing policy networks: labor politics in the U.S. Germany, and Japan. Cambridge, Cambridge University Press.

Kowarick, L. 1979. A espoliação urbana. Rio de Janeiro, Paz e Terra.

Kowarick, L. 2009. Viver em risco: sobre a vulnerabilidade socioeconômica e civil. São Paulo: Editora 34.

Kuschnir, K. 2000. O cotidiano da política. Rio de Janeiro, Zahar.

Lago, L. 2002. A lógica segregadora na metrópole brasileira: novas teses sobre antigos processos. Cadernos Ippur/UFRJ, Vol. 16: 155-176.

Lahire, B. 2003. Do habitus ao patrimônio individual de disposições: rumo a uma sociologia em escala individual. Revista de Ciências Sociais, Vol. 34 (2): 7-29.

Lammont M. and Small, M. 2008. How culture matters for the understanding of poverty: enriching our understanding. In: Harris, D. and Lin, A. The colors of poverty. New York, Russell Sage Foundation.

Langenbuch, J. 1971. A estruturação da grande São Paulo. Rio de Janeiro: IBGE.

Lanna, M. 1995. A dívida divina. Troca e patronagem no Nordeste brasileiro. Campinas, Ed. Unicamp.

Lanna, M. 2000. Nota sobre Marcel Mauss e o ensaio sobre a dádiva. Revista de Sociologia e Política, Vol. 14: 173-194.

Laumann, E. and Knoke, D. 1987 The organizational state: social choice in national policy domains. Madison, The Wisconsin University Press.

Lazo, O. 2003. O mundo é amplo e alheio: dos Andes a São Paulo. Publicações Braudel Papers, 28.

Lee, R. Ruan, D. Lai, G. 2005. Social structure and support networks in Beijing and Hong Kong. Social Networks, 27: 249–274.

Le Galès, P. 1996. Politiques urbaines en Europe. In: Paugam, S. L'exclusion: l'état des savoirs. Paris, Éditions la découverte : 554-562.

Le Galés, P. 2005. Elusive urban policies in Europe. Kazepov, Y. (ed.) Cities of Europe. Londres: Basil Blackwell.

Lelévrier, C. 2011. Politique de la ville : quelle réforme ? Regards sur l'actualité, No 367.

Levitas, R.; Pantazis, C.; Fahy, E.; Gordon, D.; Loyd, E. and Patsios, D. 2007. The multi-dimensional analysis of social exclusion. Bristol: Department of sociology and School for social policy.

Lin, N. 1999a. Building a network theory of social capital. Connections, Vol., 22(1): 28-51.

Lin, N. 1999b. Social networks and status attainment. Annual Review of Sociology, 25: 467-87.

Lipsky, M. 1980. Street-level Bureaucracy; Dilemmas of the Individual in Public Services. New York, Russell Sage Foundation.

Long, N. 1999. The multiple optic of interface analysis. Unesco background paper on Interface Analysis, Available at: http://www.utexas.edu/cola/insts/llilas/content/claspo/PDF/workingpapers/multipleoptic.pdf.

Lonkila, M. and Salmi, A. 2008. El colectivo obrero ruso y La migración. Redes – Revista hispana para el análisis de redes sociales, Vol, 15: 32-47.

Lonkila, M. 2010. The importance of work-related social ties in post-soviet Russia: the role of co-workers in the personal networks in St. Petersburg and Helsinki. Connections, Vol. 30(1): 46-56.

Lotta, G. 2006. Saber e poder: Agentes Comunitários de Saúde Aproximando Saberes Locais e Políticas Públicas. São Paulo: Fgv, MSc dissertation.

Lotta, G. 2010. Implementação de Políticas Públicas: o impacto dos fatores relacionais e organizacionais sobre a atuação dos burocratas de nível de rua no Programa Saúde da Família. São Paulo: Dcp/Usp, PhD thesis.

Mahoney, J. 2001. Beyond correlation analysis: recent innovations in theory and method. Sociological Forum, Vol. 16(3): 575–593.

Mailllochon, F. La invitación al matrimonio. Una aproximación a las redes de sociabilidad de la pareja. Redes – Revista Hispana para el análisis de redes sociales, Vol, 16 (5), 2009: 128-158.

Maloutas, T. Segregation and residential mobility: spatially entrapped social mobility and its impact on segregation in Athens. European Urban and Regional Studies, Vol. 11(3):195-211, 2004.

Maloutas, T. 2007. Segregation, social polarization and immigration in Athens during the, 1990s: theoretical expectations and contextual difference. International Journal of Urban and Regional Research. Vol. 31 (4): 733-58.

Marcuse, P. 2996. Space and race in the Post-fordist city: the outcast ghetto and advanced homelessness in the United States today. In: MINGIONE, E. Urban poverty and the Underclass. London, Basil Blackwell: 176-194.

Marcuse, P. 1997a. The enclave, the citadel and the ghetto: what has changed in the post-fordist U.S. city. Urban Affairs, 33: 228-264.

Marcuse, P. 1997b. The ghetto of exclusion and the fortified enclave: New patterns in the United States. American Behavioral Scientist, Vol. 41 (3): 311-326.

Maricato, E. 1987. Política habitacional no regime militar. Rio de Janeiro, Paz e Terra.

Maricato, E. 2003. Metrópole, legislação e desigualdade. Estudos Avançados, Vol. 17(48): 151-166.

Marques, E. 2000. Estado e redes sociais: Permeabilidade e coesão nas políticas urbanas no Rio de Janeiro. Rio de Janeiro, Ed. Revan/Fapesp.

Marques, E. 2003. Redes sociais, Instituições e Atores Políticos no governo da cidade de São Paulo. São Paulo, Ed. Annablume/Fapesp.

Marques, E. 2010. Redes sociais, segregação e pobreza. São Paulo: Ed. Unesp/Cem.

Marques, E. 2011. Do social networks matter in gaining access to goods and services obtained from outside markets? International Sociology, Vol. 41: 10-27.

Marques, E. and Bichir, R. 2011. Redes de apoio social no Rio de Janeiro e em São Paulo. Novos Estudos Cebrap, 90: 65-83.

Marques, E.; Bichir, R.; Pavez, T.; Zoppi, M.; Moya, E. and Pantoja, I. 2008. Personal Networks and Urban Poverty: Preliminary Findings. Brazilian Political Science Review, Vol., 2(1): 10-34.

Marques, E; Bichir, R, and Scalon, C. 2010. Residential segregation and social structure in São Paulo: continuity and change since the 1990s São Paulo: Centro de Estudos da Metrópole, draft.

Marques, E. and Saraiva, C. 2005. As políticas de habitação social, a segregação e as desigualdades sociais na cidade. In: São Paulo: segregação, pobreza e desigualdades sociais, edited by E. Marques and H. Torres. São Paulo, Ed. Senac: 267-290.

Marques, E; Scalon, C. and Oliveira, M. 2009. Comparando estruturas sociais no Rio de Janeiro e em São Paulo. In: Ensaios de estratificação, edited by C. Scalon. Belo Horizonte: Argumentum Ed.

Marques, E. and Torres, H. 2005. (ed.) São Paulo: segregação, pobreza e desigualdades sociais. São Paulo, Ed. Senac.

Marsden, P. 2005. Recent developments in network measurement. In: Carrington, P.; Scott, J. and Wasseman, S. Models and Methods in Social Network Analysis. Cambridge, Cambridge University Press.

Martes, A. and Fleischer, S. 2003. Fronteiras cruzadas: etnicidade, gênero e redes sociais. São Paulo, Paz e Terra.

Martine, G. 1995. A trajetória da urbanização brasileira: especificidades e implicações. Trabalho apresentado no seminário Processo Brasileiro de Urbanização: diagnóstico global. Ministério das Relações Exteriores, Belo Horizonte.

Martine, G. and Diniz, C. 1997. Economic and demographic concentration in Brazil: recent inversion of historical patterns. In: Urbanization in large developing countries: China, Indonesia, Brazil and India. Oxford: Oxford University Press.

Massey, D. and Denton, N. 1993. American Apartheid – Segregation and the Making of the Underclass. Harvard University Press.

Mauss, M. 2003 [1923]. Ensaio sobre a dádiva. Forma e razão da troca em sociedades arcaicas In: Sociologia e Antropologia. São Paulo, Cosac Naif.

McCarty, C. 2005. Structure in personal networks. Journal of Social Structure, Vol. 3:1-19.

McPherson, M.; Smith-Lovin, L. and Cook, J. 2001. Birds of a feather: homophily in social networks. Annual Review of Sociology, 27: 415-444.

Mingione, E. 1994. Life strategies and social economies in the Postfordist Age. International Journal of Urban and Regional Research, Vol, 18 (1): 24-45.

Mingione, E. 1996a. Urban poverty and the underclass. New York, Blackwell Publishers.

Mingione, E. 1996b. Urban poverty in the advanced industrial world: concepts, analysis and debates. In: Urban poverty and the underclass. New York, Blackwell publishers: 3-40.

Mingione, E.2005. Urban social change: a socio-historical framework of analysis. In: Kazepov, Y. (ed.) Cities of Europe. London: Basil Blackwell.

Miraglia, P. 2008. Apresentação. Dossiê Segurança Pública. Novos Estudos Cebrap, 80: 5-8.

Miraglia, P. 2011. Homicídios em São Paulo – guias para a interpretação da violência urbana. In: São Paulo: Miradas Cruzadas. Sociedad, política y cultura, edited by L. Kowarik and E. Marques. Quito, Ecuador: Editorial Olacchi.

Mische, A. and White, H. 1998. Between Conversation and Situation: Public Switching. Dynamics Across Network-Domains. Social Research, 65: 696–724.

Mische, A. 2007. Partisan Politics: Communication and Contention Across Brazilian Youth Activist Networks. Princeton: Princeton University Press.

Mizruchi, M. and Schwartz, M. 1987. Intercorporate relations: the structural analysis of business. Cambridge: Cambridge University Press.

Molina, J. 2005. Localizando geográficamente las redes personales. Redes: Revista Hispana para el Análisis de Redes Sociales, Vol. 8 (5). Available at: http://revista-redes.rediris.es.

Molina, J. and Gil, A. 2005. Reciprocidad hoy: la rede de las unidades domésticas y serviços públicos de dos colectivos de Vic (Barcelona). In: PORRAS, J. and ESPINOZA, V. Redes: enfoque y aplicaiones del análisis de redes sociales (ARS). Santiago do Chile, Universidad Bolivariana: 303-327.

Molina, J.; Lerner, J. and Mestres, S. 2008. Patrones de cambio de las redes personales de inmigrantes en Cataluña. Redes – Revista hispana para el análisis de redes sociales, Vol, 15: 48-61.

Molm, L. and Collet, J. 2007. Building solidarity through generalized exchange: A Theory of reciprocity. American Journal of Sociology, Vol. 113 (1), 205-242.

Moody, J. 2001. Peer influence groups: identifying dense clusters in large networks. Social Networks, 23: 261-283.

Moore, G. 1990. Structural determinants of men's and women's personal networks. American Sociological Review, Vol. 55: 726-35.

Morenoff, J. 2003. Neighborhood mechanisms and the spatial dynamics of birth weight. American Journal of Sociology, Vol. 108(5): 976-1017.

Morris, L. 1994. Informal aspects of social divisions. International Journal of Urban and Regional Research, Vol, 18 (1): 112-126.

Moser, C. 1998. The asset vulnerability framework: reassessing Urban Poverty Reduction Strategies. World Development, Vol., 26(1): 1-19.

Moya, E. 2003. Repensando a questão social: trajetórias de algumas interpretações nos Estados Unidos, França e Brasil. Dcp/Usp, MSc dissertation.

Musterd, S. and Murie, A. (ed.) 2002. The spatial dimensions of urban social exclusion and integration. Amsterdam. Available at: www.frw.uva.nl/ame/urbex.

Musterd, S.; Murie, A. and Kesteloot, C. (ed.) 2006. Neighborhoods of Poverty: Urban Social Exclusion and Integration in Comparison. Basingstroke: Palgrave.

Nakano, K. 2002. Quatro COHABs da zona leste de São Paulo: território, poder e segregação. São Paulo: Fau/Usp, MSc dissertation.

Neri, M. 2000. Políticas estruturais e combate à pobreza no Brasil. In: HENRIQUES, R. Desigualdade e pobreza na Brasil. Rio de Janeiro, Ipea: 503-528.

Nijman, J. 2006. Mumbai's mysterious middle class. International Journal of Urban and Regional Research, Vol. 30 (4): 758–775.

North, D. 1990. Institutions, institutional change and economic performance. Cambridge, Cambridge University Press.

Nunes, E. 1986. Carências urbanas e reivindicações populares: notas. In: Anpocs. Ciências Sociais Hoje: 1986. São Paulo, Anpocs/Cortes Ed, p. 37.

Nunes, E. 1997. A gramática política do Brasil. Brasília, Enap/Zahar.

Olagnero, M.; Meo, A. and Corcoran, M. 2005. Social support Networks in impoverished European neighbourhoods. European Societies, 7(1): 53-79.

Ortiz, M.; Hoyos, J. and Lopez, M. 2004. The social networks of academic performance in a student context of poverty in Mexico. Social Networks, 26: 175-188.

Osterling, K. 2007. Social capital and neighborhood poverty: toward an ecologically-grounded model of neighborhood effects. Journal of Human Behavior in the social environment, Vol, 16(1/2): 123-147.

Padgett, J. and Ansell, C. 1993. Robust action and the rise of the Medici (1400-1434). American Journal of Sociology, 98 (6): 1259-1319.

Pamuk, A. 2000. Informal institutional arrangements in credit, land markets and infrastructure delivery in Trinidad. International Journal of Urban and Regional Research, Vol., 24 (2).

Paugam, S. 2005. Les formes élémentaires de la pauvreté. Paris, Puf.

Pavez, T. 2006. Políticas públicas e ampliação de capital social em comunidades segregadas: o programa Santo André Mais Igual. São Paulo: Dcp/Usp, MSc dissertation.

Pereira, V. 2005. Classes sociais e culturas de classe das famílias portuenses. Porto: Ed. Afrontamento.

Perlman, J. 2011. Favela. Four Decades of Living on the Edge in Rio de Janeiro. Oxford: Oxford University Press.

Perillo, S. and Perdigão, M. 1998. Cenários migratórios recentes em São Paulo. In: Anais do X Encontro Nacional da Abep: 773-790.

Perri 6. 1997. Escaping poverty: from safety nets to networks of opportunity. London, Demos.

Pierson, P. 2004. Politics in time: history, institutions and social analysis. Princeton, Princeton University Press.

Pinçon-Charlot, M.; Preteceille, E. and Rendu, P. 1986. Ségrégation Urbaine: Classes sociales et Équipament colletifs région parisienne. Paris, Ed. Anthropos.

Pnud/Ipea. 1998. Desenvolvimento Humano e Condições de Vida: indicadores brasileiros. Brasília, Pnud.

Pnud/Onu. 2003. Human Development Report. Available at www.undp.org/hdr2003/

Pochman, M. and Amorim, R. 2003. Atlas da exclusão social no Brasil. São Paulo, Cortez.

Polanyi, K. 1980. A grande transformação. São Paulo, Editora Campus.

Policy Research Initiative. 2005a. Social capital in action. Canada Federal Government. Available at: http://policyresearch.gc.ca.

Policy Research Initiative. 2005b. Social capital as a public policy tool. Canada Federal Government. Available at: http://policyresearch.gc.ca.

Portes, A. 1999. Migrações internacionais: origens, tipos e modos de incorporação. Oeiras, Celta Editora.

Power, A. 1996. Area-based poverty and resident empowerment. Urban Studies, 33 (9): 1535-1564.

Preteceille, E. 2003. A evolução da segregação social e das desigualdades urbanas: o caso da metrópole parisiense nas últimas décadas. Caderno CRH, 38: 27-48.

Preteceille, E. 2006. La ségrégation sociale a-t-elle augmenté? La métropole parisienne entre polarisation et mixité. Societés Contemporaines, 62: 69-93.

Preteceille, E. and Cardoso, A. 2008. Rio de Janeiro y São Paulo: ciudades duales? Comparación com Paris. Ciudad y Território, XL (158): 617-640.

Preteceille, E. and Ribeiro, L. 1999. Tendências da segregação social em metrópoles globais e desiguais: Paris e Rio de Janeiro nos anos 80. Revista Brasileira de Ciências Sociais, Vol. 14 (40): 143-162.

Putnam, R. 1995. Bowling Alone: America›s Declining Social Capital. Journal of Democracy, Volume 6, (1).

Putnam, R. 1996. Comunidade e democracia: a experiência da Itália moderna. Rio de Janeiro, FGV Editora.

Ragin, C. 1987. The comparative method: moving beyond qualitative and quantitative strategies. Berkeley, University of California Press.

Ramos, D. and Lazo, A. 2004. A vulnerabilidade econômica das famílias residentes na região metropolitana do Rio de Janeiro no período, 1991-2000. XIV Encontro Nacional da Abep.

Rao, V. and Woolcock, M. 2001. Social capital and risk management strategies in poor urban communities: what do we know? Available at: http://poverty2.forumone.com.

Ribas, R. and Machado, A. 2007. Distinguishing chronic poverty from transient poverty in Brazil: developing a model for pseudo-panel data. Brasília, International Poverty Centre. Available at: http://www.undp-povertycentre.org

Ribeiro, C. 2007. Estrutura de classe e mobilidade social no Brasil. São Paulo, Edusc/Anpocs.

Ribeiro, R. 2002. Segregação, acumulação urbana e poder: classes e desigualdades na metrópole do Rio de Janeiro. Cadernos Ippur/UFRJ, Vol. 16:79-103.

Roberts, B. 1994. Informal Economy and family strategies International Journal of Urban and Regional Research Vol. 18 (1): 6-23.

Roberts, B. 2005. Globalization and Latin American cities. International Journal of Urban and Regional Research, Vol., 29(1): 110-123.

Rocha, R. And Urani, A. 2007. Posicionamento social e a hipótese da distribuição de renda desconhecia. Brasil: quão pobres, quão ricos e quão desiguais nos percebemos?. Revista de Economia Política, Vol., 27 (4): 595-615.

Rocha, S. 2003. Pobreza no Brasil: afinal de que se trata? Rio de Janeiro, Ed. Fgv.

Rocha, S. 2006a. Pobreza e indigência no Brasil: algumas evidências empíricas com base na Pnad 2004. Nova Economia, Vol. 16, (2): 265-299.

Rocha, S. 2006b. Renda, Mercado de trabalho e escolaridade: alguns aspectos sobre o papel de São Paulo no contexto do país. Rio de Janeiro, Iets, draft.

Ross, S. 2001. Employment access, neighborhood quality and residential location choice. Artigo apresentado no International seminar on segregation in the city. Lincoln Institute, Boston, draft.

Ruan, D.; Freeman, L.; Dai, X.; Pan, Y. and Zhang, W. 1997. On the changing structure of social networks in urban China. Social Networks, 19: 75-89.

Sabatini, F. 2001. Transformação urbana e dialética entre integração e exclusão social: reflexões sobre as cidades latino-americanas e o caso de Santiago do Chile. In: Oliveira, M. Demografia da exclusão social. Campinas, Ed. Unicamp: 165-84.

Sabatini, F.; Cáceres, G. and Cerda, J. 2001. Residential segregation pattern changes in main chilean cities: scale shifts and increasing malignancy. Lincoln Institute of Land Policy, draft.

Sabatini, F. 2004. Medición de la segregación residencial: reflexiones metodológicas desde la ciudad latinoamericana. In: Cáceres, G. and Sabatini, F. Barrios cerrados en Santiago de Chile: entre la exclusión y la integración residencial. Lincoln Institute of Land Policy / Universidad Catolica de Chile: 277-293.

Sader, E. 1988. Quando novos personagens entram em cena. São Paulo, Paz e Terra.

Salcedo, R. and Torres, A. 2004. Gated communities in Santiago: wall or frontier? International Journal of Urban and Regional Research, Vol, 28 (1): 27-44.

Salgado, E. 2000. O loteamento residencial fechado no quadro de transformação da metrópole de São Paulo. São Paulo: Fau/Usp, MSc dissertation

Sampson, R. and Morenoff, J. 1997. Ecological perspectives on the neighborhood context of urban poverty: past and present. In: Understanding poverty, edited by S. Danziger and R. Haverman. New York, Russell Sage.

Sampson, R. and Raudenbush, S. 1997. Neighborhoods and Violent Crime: A Multilevel Study of Collective Efficacy. Science, 277 (5328): 918 – 924.

Santos, C. and Bronstein, O. 1978. Meta-urbanização: o caso do Rio de Janeiro. Revista de Administração Municipal, Vol., 25(149): 6-34.

Santos, C. 1981. Movimentos urbanos no Rio de Janeiro. Rio de Janeiro, Zahar.

Santos, C. 1982. Processo de crescimento e Ocupação da Periferia. Rio de Janeiro, Ibam.

Santos, C. 1985. Loteamentos na periferia metropolitana. Revista de Administração Municipal, Vol. 32 (174): 22-39.

Santos, G. 2005. Redes e território: reflexões sobre a migração. In: Redes: sociedades e territórios, edited by L. Dias and R. Silveira. Florianópolis, Edunisc.

Santos, J. 2005. Uma classificação socioeconômica para o Brasil. Revista Brasileira de Ciências Sociais, Vol., 20 (58): 27-45.

Santos, W. dos. 1979. Cidadania e justiça. Rio de Janeiro: Ed. Campus.

Santos, W. dos. 1988. Gênese e apocalipse: elementos para uma teoria da crise institucional latino-americana. Novos Estudos Cebrap, No, 20.

Scalon, C. 2006. Relatório Final de Bolsa de Professora Visitante. São Paulo: Cem/Fapesp, draft.

Saraiva, C. and Marques, E. 2005. A condição social dos habitantes de Favelas. In: São Paulo: segregação, pobreza urbana e desigualdades sociais, edited by E. Marques and H. Torres. São Paulo, Ed. Senac: 143-170.

Schneider, M.; Scholz, J.; Lubell, M.; Minduta, D. and Edwarsen, M. 2003. Building consensual institutions: networks and the National Estuary Program. American Journal of Political Science, 47 (1): 143-158.

Scott, J. 1992. Social Network analysis. Newbury Park, Sage Publications.

Seade. 1995. Arranjos familiares e ciclos de vida das famílias metropolitanas de São Paulo entre, 1985 e, 1993. Estudo especial: Pesquisa de Emprego e Desemprego – PED. São Paulo, Seade/Dieese. Boletim da PED, 118 suplemento.

Seade. 2000. São Paulo: Século XXI. São Paulo, Alesp/Seade.

Sen, A. 2000a. Desenvolvimento como liberdade. São Paulo: Companhia das Letras.

Sen, A. 2000b. Social exclusion: concepts, application and scrutiny. Development Paper, 1. Manila, Asian Development Bank.

Silva Telles, V. and Cabannes, R. (ed.) 2006. Nas tramas da cidade, trajetórias urbanas e seus territórios. São Paulo: Humanitas.

Silva, L. 1992. O que mostram os indicadores sociais sobre a pobreza na Década Perdida. Relatório de pesquisa Ipea. Rio de Janeiro: Ipea.

Simmel, G. 1972 [1908]. El cruce de los circulos sociales. In: Sociología, 2. Estudios sobre las formas de socialización. Alianza Universidad: 41-75.

Simmel, G. 1973 [1902]. Metrópole e Vida Mental. In: Velho, O. O fenômeno urbano. Rio de Janeiro, Zahar: 11-48.

Skocpol, T. 1984. Vision and method in historical sociology. Boston, Cambridge University Press.

Skocpol, T. 1985. Bringing the state back in: strategies of analysis in current research. In: Evans, P.; Rueschmeyer, D. and Skocpol, T. Bringing the state back in. Cambridge, Cambridge University Press: 3-43.

Small, M. 2004. Villa Victoria: the transformation of social capital in a Boston Barrio. Chicago: Chicago University Press.

Small, M. 2009. Unanticipated gains: origins of network inequality in everyday life. Oxford: Oxford University Press.

Small, M. 2008. Lost in Translation: How Not to Make Qualitative Research More Scientific. In: Lamont, M. and White, P. Report from Workshop on Interdisciplinary Standards for Systematic Qualitative Research. Washington, DC, National Science Foundation. Available at: http://home.uchicago. edu/~mariosmall/Documents/Lost.pdf.

Small, M. and Newman, K. 2001. Urban poverty after the Truly disadvantaged: the rediscovery of the family, the neighborhood and culture. Annual Review of Sociology, 27: 23-45.

Smith, H. 2003. Housing networks in San Jose, Costa Rica. Habitat International, 27: 83-105.

Smolka, M. 1983. Segregação social no espaço: definição do objeto de análise. In: Estruturas intra-urbanas e segregação social no espaço: elementos para uma discussão da cidade na teoria econômica. Rio de Janeiro: Ipea/Anpec: 1-26.

Soares, R. 2009. Estado, segregação e desigualdade: Um estudo sobre o impacto das políticas de habitação a partir das redes sociais da favela Guinle, Guarulhos. São Paulo: Dcp/Usp, MSc dissertation. Available at: http://www.teses.usp.br/teses/disponiveis/8/8131/tde-03112009-162339/.

Soares, S. 2010. Pnad, 2009 – Primeiras análises: distribuição de renda entre, 1995 e, 2009. Comunicado Ipea, 63. Available at: http://www.ipea.gov.br/portal/images/stories/PDFs/comunicado/101005_comunicadoipea63.pdf.

Sposati, A. 1996. Mapa da exclusão/inclusão social da cidade de São Paulo. São Paulo, Educ.

Taschner, S. 1990. Habitação e demografia intra-urbana em São Paulo. Revista Brasileira de População, Vol. 7(1): 3-34.

Taschner, S. 2002. Espaço e população nas favelas de São Paulo. Trabalho apresentado no XIII Encontro Nacional da Abep.

Tavares, R. and Monteiro, M. 1994. População e condições de vida. In: Guimarães, R. and Tavares, R. Saúde e sociedade no Brasil dos anos 80. Rio de Janeiro, Relume Dumará: 43-71.

Thatcher, M. "Aids, education and the year 2000!" (Interview to Douglas Keay), Women's Own magazine, October 31 1987, pp8-10

Tilly, C. 1992a. Big structures, large processes huge comparisons. New York, Russell Sage foundation.

Tilly, C. 1992b. Prisioners of the State. Historical sociology, No, 133.

Tilly, C. 2000. La desigualdad persistente. Madri, Manatial.

Tilly, C. 2001. Mechanisms in political processes. Annual Review of Political Science, Vol. 4: 21-41.

Tilly, C. 2005. Identities, boundaries and social ties. Boulder, Paradigm.

Toledo, B. 2004. São Paulo: três cidades em um século. São Paulo: Cosac Naif.

Torres, H. 2005a. A fronteira paulistana. In: São Paulo: segregação, pobreza urbana e desigualdades sociais, edited by E. Marques and H. Torres. São Paulo, Ed. Senac: 101-125.

Torres, H. 2005b. Políticas sociais e território: uma abordagem metropolitana. In: São Paulo: segregação, pobreza urbana e desigualdades sociais, edited by E. Marques and H. Torres. São Paulo, Ed. Senac: 297-317.

Torres, H. 2005c. Medindo a segregação. In: Marques, E. and Torres, H. São Paulo: segregação, pobreza e desigualdade sociais. São Paulo, Ed. Senac: 81-104.

Torres, H.; Bichir, R. and Pavez, T. 2006. Mudanças no padrão de consumo da população de baixa renda. Novos Estudos Cebrap, São Paulo, 74: 17-22.

Torres, H. and Marques, E. 2001. Reflexões sobre a hiperperiferia: novas e velhas faces da pobreza no entorno metropolitano. Revista Brasileira de Estudos Urbanos e Regionais, 4: 49-70.

Torres, H.; Ferreira, M. and Gomes, S. 2005. Educação e segregação social: explorando os efeitos das relações de vizinhança. In: São Paulo: segregação, pobreza urbana e desigualdades sociais, edited by E. Marques and H. Torres. São Paulo, Ed. Senac: 123-148.

Trotter, R. 1999. Friends, relatives and relevant others: conducting ethnographic network studies. In: Schensul, R. Mapping social networks, spatial data and hidden populations. London, Altamira, 1999.

Uehara, E. 1990. Dual Exchange Theory, Social Networks, And Informal Social Support. American Journal of Sociology 96: 521-557.

Valladares, L. and Preteceille, E. 2000. Favela, favelas: unidade ou diversidade da favela carioca. In: Queiroz, L. O futuro das metrópoles: desigualdades e governabilidade. Rio de Janeiro, Observatório/Ed. Revan.

Valle Silva, N. do. 2007. Prefácio. In: Ribeiro, C. Estrutura de classes e mobilidade social no Brasil. São Paulo, Edusc/Anpocs.

Veiga, D. 2009. Social inequalities and socio-spatial changes: the case of Montevideo. ISA/RC21 Conference, São Paulo.

Vetter, D. 1981. A segregação residencial da população economicamente ativa na região metropolitana do Rio de Janeiro, segundo grupos de rendimento mensal. Revista Brasileira de Geografia, 434: 587-603.

Vilela, J. 2001. A dívida e a diferença. Reflexões a respeito da reciprocidade. Revista de Antropologia, Vol. 44 (1): 85-220.

Villaça, F. 1998. Espaço intra-urbano no Brasil. São Paulo, Studio Nobel.

Wacquant, L. 1996. Três premissas perniciosas no estudo do gueto norte-americano. Mana: Estudos de antropologia social, Vol., 2 (2): 145-161.

Wacquant, L. 2001. Os condenados da cidade. Rio de Janeiro, Ed. Revan.

Wacquant, L. 2007. A estigmatização territorial na idade da marginalidade avançada. Berkeley, draft. Available at: http://sociology.berkeley.edu/faculty/wacquant/wacquant_pdf/LW-estigmatizacaoterritorial.pdf.

Wacquant, L. 2008. Urban outcasts: a comparative sociology of advanced marginality. Cambridge: Polity Press.

Wasseman, S. and Faust, K. 1994. Social Network Analysis: Methods and Applications. Cambridge, Cambridge University Press.

Weber, M. 1999 [1922]. Economia e sociedade: fundamentos da sociologia compreensiva. São Paulo, UNB/Imprensa Oficial,

Wellman, B. 1979. The community question: the intimate networks of East Yorkers. American Journal of Sociology, Vol. 84(5): 1201–1231.

Wellman, B. 2001. The persistence and transformation of Community: from neighborhood groups to social networks. Toronto, draft. Available at: http://www.chass.utoronto.ca/~wellman/publications/lawcomm/lawcomm7.PDF.

White, H. 1995. Network switchings and bayesian forks: reconstructing the social and behavioral sciences. Social Research: An international quarterly of the social sciences, Vol. 62, (4): 1035-1063.

Wilson, W. 1987. The truly disadvantage: the inner city, the underclass and public policy. University Chicago Press.

Wilson, W. 2002. Expanding the domain of policy-relevant scholarship in the social sciences. London, Case/LSE, Case paper, 52.

Wirth, L. 1972 [1938]. O urbanismo como modo de vida. In: O fenômeno urbano, edited by O. Velho. Rio de Janeiro, Zahar: 90-118.

Wu, F. 2004. Urban poverty and marginalization under market transition: the case of Chinese cities. International Journal of Urban and Regional Research, Vol, 28 (2): 401-423.

Yip, N. 2008. Changing spatial segregation in Hong Kong, 1991-2001. Isa/Rc 21 Conference, Tokyo.

Yinger, J. 2001. Housing discrimination and residential segregation as causes of poverty. In: Understanding poverty, edited S. Danziger and R. Haverman. New York, Russell Sage: 359-381.

Zaluar, A. 1993. Urban violence, citizenship and public policies. International Journal of Urban and Regional Research, Vol. 17, (1): 56-66.

Zaluar, A. and Ribeiro, A. 2009. Teoria da eficácia coletiva e violência. Novos Estudos Cebrap, 84: 175-196.

Methodological Appendix

In each studied location the interviewees were chosen randomly, but without any prior selection of households nor using a leap-frog approach to choose houses and, from them, individuals. They were approached, instead, directly in the streets and in front of their houses, following an intercept approach. These people were chosen with the aim of covering as wide a variety of situations as possible within the studied location. The set of interviews in each field area, however, was controlled through the attributes of sex, age, occupational and migratory status and the region of the area studied, where these applied (worst or best regions defined in previous studies, for example), so that the set of interviews from each location roughly expressed the variability of the population studied. Interviews were conducted both during the week and at weekends. As we shall see later, the comparison of the indicators chosen of the interviewees and the locations studied suggests that this data collection procedure achieved fairly satisfactory results with no significant deviation observed between the study sample and the population of the locations studied.

Ego-centered interviews were conducted (in which a particular individual was asked about his or her own network) on the whole network of their sociability.[1] The full interviews typically lasted between fifty minutes and an hour and comprised two parts. First a semi-structured questionnaire was completed referring to the general profile of the interviewee, including biographic data, family and household composition, employment status, trajectory in the work market, migratory trajectory, associative ties and practices of sociability of the interviewees.

The second part of the interviews includes the use of a collection tool for relational data with a name generator and questions about attributes of the generated names.[2] The name generator, for its part, involves two stages. The first aimed to construct a 'seed'[3] of names for the second phase based on spheres of sociability. The spheres included at least: family, neighborhood, friendship, associative, recreation/leisure, studying and professional/work. If other spheres emerged during the course of the interview, these were added to the list. For example, if the interview indicated that the activity of playing volleyball organized a section of

---

1 The interviews were conducted between March 2006 and February 2007 by a team that included, aside from myself, Renata Bichir, Miranda Zoppi, Encarnación Moyá, Thais Pavez and Igor Pantoja. I thank all of them for their invaluable work.

2 The described procedures represent a refinement of the tools originally established and submitted to a pre-test with twelve middle class individuals.

3 The seed represents an initial list of names to which the name generator adds new names until the borders of the network are almost reached, based on the chosen procedure.

the individual's sociability, a volleyball sphere was added to the list. Additionally, to conclude the seed, interviewees were asked to think about their relations and cite a group of at most five names for each sphere of sociability.

These names formed the seed of the name generator. Next the interviewees were asked to indicate up to three names associated with each name of the seed, with repetitions freely accepted along with the indication of the own interviewee. The new names were added at the end of the list as a seed for a new round of interviewing with the same person. The procedure was repeated three times or until there were no more new names. The method provided us with a set of dyads (pairs of names connected by ties).

Finally we asked the interviewees to classify the names cited according to three attributes: the context of the entry of the node into the personal network, whether the individual lives from outside or inside the studied area, and the sphere of sociability to which he or she belongs. In each case the pre-established values for the attributes can be altered during the actual interview, recognizing the high specificity of the trajectories, spheres of sociability and the networks themselves.

During the phase of the analysis, I compared the attributes of the interviewees living in poverty and those of the residents of the researched areas using indicators from the IBGE Census produced by geoprocessing suggest the absence of bias, although the information is not directly comparable. The exercise was designed to check for bias in the sample potentially caused by the data collection strategies. The study sample was not intended to be statistically representative (and no type of expansion is performed), but the absence of bias strengthens the results obtained.

The average level of schooling of the household head in the surveyed areas was 5.1 years of study, while among our interviewees the average was 6.1 years. Given that schooling tends to be higher in younger age groups, and the latter do not tend to be household heads, the two schooling levels can still be considered very close. On the other hand, the average income of the household head in the areas covered by the research was R$ 547 and the average family income of the interviewees was R$ 1,125: these figures would match closely if each household had an average of 2.1 people generating income, which is fairly reasonable, especially considering an average of 3.8 individuals per household. Among the interviewees 22 per cent of people were living in households headed by women, while the average in the areas under study was 23 per cent. In terms of age groups, 3 per cent of individuals in the studied areas were aged sixty or over, while our set of interviewees included 6 per cent of individuals in this age band. However since we did not interview anyone under the age of twelve, these individuals aged sixty or more represented 4 per cent of the age groups studied in the research locations. On the other hand, at the other end of the age spectrum 20 per cent of the individuals living in the areas studied were aged between ten and nineteen, while 19 per cent of the people involved in the research were aged between twelve and nineteen.

Hence in terms of the basic social attributes of the interviewees we can conclude that the research sample does not show any significant deviation in relation to the overall population of the studied areas.

Afterwards, having already analyzed the networks, I chose a set of individuals for qualitative interviews in order to explore the dynamic of the networks and their mobilization in their everyday activities.[4] Twenty individuals were chosen with different types of networks, based on the typologies developed in Chapter 4. In these interviews, we first presented the sociogram to the interviewee and then asked them about transformations that had occurred in their networks (relative to the first interview, on average conducted about a year earlier) and about the mobilization of contacts in a range of situations including migration, marriage, emotional support, borrowing utensils and food, borrowing money, searching for and obtaining employment, political information and access to public services. The collected material enables the discussion on how relational structures are mobilized by individuals in their everyday situations. Chapters 6 and 7 analyze this material.

---

4   In this phase of the work I once again had the invaluable help of research assistances, whom I thank. As well as myself, interviews were conducted in January and March 2008 by Renata Bichir, Encarnación Moya, Miranda Zoppi and Igor Pantoja.

Table 4   Average indicators by network type

Indicators	Network types				
	Large	From large to medium	Medium	From medium to small	Small
Number of nodes	131	85	58	42	22
Number of ties	328	182	126	73	32
diameter	7.7	7.6	6.5	6.4	4.7
density	0.038	0.060	0.095	0.094	0.174
Clustering coefficient	0.31	0.41	0.48	0.47	0.50
Centralization Index	18.5	22.2	34.4	36.3	56.1
# 2-clans/ Number of nodes	0.9	0.6	0.4	0.4	0.3
# 3-clans/ Number of nodes	0.5	0.4	0.3	0.3	0.2
Efficient size of the egonet	21.7	18.4	19.6	15.0	11.3
Density of the egonet	4.1	5.1	8.8	8.0	10.8
Average normalized degree	2.8	3.7	6.3	8.3	15.0
Information	1.68	1.23	1.54	1.23	1.24
E_I of contexts	0.218	0.283	0.308	0.324	0.332
E_I of spheres	0.244	0.290	0.296	0.271	0.270

E_I of localism	-0.342	-0.238	-0.188	-0.145	-0.094
Number of contexts	4.7	4.6	4.7	4.5	3.8
Number of spheres	4.5	4.1	4.4	3.6	3.1
% of local nodes	64.8	66.6	63.5	59.1	65.5

Source: Author, based on collected empirical data.

Index